W9-CFU-484

FLORIDA STATE
UNIVERSITY LIBRARIES

NOV 23 2009

TALLAHASSEE, FLORIDA

Library Collections

Their Origin, Selection, and Development

McGRAW-HILL SERIES IN LIBRARY EDUCATION

Jean Key Gates, Consulting Editor
University of South Florida

Library Collections

Their Origin, Selection, and Development

Richard K. Gardner, Ph.D.

Professor of Library and Information Science
University of California, Los Angeles
Founding Editor, CHOICE

McGraw-Hill Book Company
New York   St. Louis   San Francisco   Auckland   Bogotá
Hamburg   Johannesburg   London   Madrid   Mexico   Montreal
New Delhi   Panama   Paris   São Paulo   Singapore   Sydney
Tokyo   Toronto

LSL
PROF
Z
687
.G36

In Memory of
C. E. B.
and
C. M. K.

Library Collections: Their Origin, Selection, and Development

Copyright © 1981 by McGraw-Hill, Inc. All rights reserved. Printed in the United States of America. No part of this publication may be reproduced, stored in a retrieval system, or transmitted, in any form or by any means, electronic, mechanical, photocopying, recording, or otherwise, without the prior written permission of the publisher.

2 3 4 5 6 7 8 9 0 D O D O 8 9 8 7 6 5 4 3 2

This book was set in Palatino by Black Dot, Inc. The editors were Rhona Robbin and James R. Belser; the design was done by Caliber Design Planning; the production supervisor was Donna Piligra. R. R. Donnelley & Sons Company was printer and binder.

Library of Congress Cataloging in Publication Data

Gardner, Richard K
    Library collections, their origin, selection, and development.

    (McGraw-Hill series in library education)
    Includes bibliographies and index.
    1.   Collection development (Libraries)   2.   Book industries and trade.   3.   Publishers and publishing.
    I.   Title.
Z687.G36   025.2   80-23831
ISBN 0-07-022850-7

Contents

PART TWO   Finding Out about Library Materials

Preface

The selection of materials for a collection is one of the essential parts of a librarian's job and also one of the most creative and interesting. The quality of the resulting collection is undoubtedly one of the criteria on which a librarian is most often judged. Users may not consciously always make such judgments, but if the collection fails to supply the information they need, they will certainly make an unconscious judgment and go elsewhere. Public service will fail or succeed as a result of poor or good collection development. It is therefore necessary that all beginning librarians have a good grasp of the principles of materials selection, of the many current and retrospective aids available, and of the many problems which occur and which can hinder or help in good selection.

If good materials are to be selected, the librarian must have some idea of how the product came into being and of the diversity of materials available for collection development. It has been my experience that librarians in general know all too little about the publishing industry and the book trade and often out of ignorance make demands that publishers or booksellers are in no position to satisfy. A better understanding of how books and other library materials come into being and reach the public will, I believe, be of immense value throughout a librarian's entire career, whether in acquisitions, cataloging, reference, management, or collection development.

The basic idea behind this textbook is to take the content of library collections—books, periodicals, microforms, A-V materials, and so on—and to trace them from their origin through the various phases of marketing and distribution to their final resting place in a library. Part One discusses the various types of materials that now form the basic elements of a library collection, how they are created, and how they are distributed and marketed to libraries and the public. Much of this information is new to selection textbooks, but some of it is not. For example, many selection textbooks in the past have devoted a certain amount of space to acquisitions—where libraries obtain materials (from publishers, jobbers, and retailers) and how this is done. They also usually discuss the various formats library materials come in. In this book much of this information on acquisitions will be found in Part One (as well as in Chapter 9 of Part Three, on selection procedures) but from a different perspective.

Part Two gives an overview of how librarians find out about materials to add to their collections—through trade bibliographies, the review media, and various retrospective selection guides. Part Three deals with the theory and principles of selection; selection procedures in various types of libraries; the problem of weeding and storage; collection development policies; the evaluation of collections, and standards for such evaluation; resource sharing and networks; and finally, the problem of censorship.

The order of topics presented in this book is one that I feel to be logical. I have worked out this order over more than a decade of teaching the subject at Case Western Reserve University and the Université de Montréal and found it practiced at UCLA when I joined that faculty. However, the actual parts or chapters are self-contained so that instructors can, with little difficulty, vary the order and start with Part Two or Three should they so desire. Within Part Three a different order is also possible. I am well aware that a lengthy unit on publishing and the book trade has not been part of the traditional selection course in many library schools. Perhaps that is because there has been no satisfactory introduction that presents a concise picture and that is specifically addressed to librarians. I hope that the advent of this text will encourage other schools to add it to their basic course, if only as background reading. Since most students do not benefit from a full course in publishing (in the few schools where such a course is given, it is an elective chosen by relatively few students), this seems the most appropriate place to integrate such basic knowledge into the curriculum.

The "Suggested Readings," occurring at the ends of chapters, are limited in number. In general, full-length books or entire issues of journals have been chosen rather than individual periodical articles in order that the student may be directed to in-depth sources. These, in turn, provide further bibliography. The appendixes reproduce the standards for collection development that have been promulgated by the various divisions of the American Library Association, as well as the important background documents on intellectual freedom. They are included for ready reference by students.

Finally, I should like to express my appreciation to the many colleagues in the profession who over the years have stimulated my thinking on the subject of collection development in libraries—most particularly my colleagues at the three library schools where I have taught and my former co-workers at CHOICE. And last, but definitely not least, I should like to thank my two research assistants at UCLA, Timothy McTague and Dennis Frisch, whose painstaking bibliographic and other checking has eased the burden of writing this text. In particular, I should like to acknowledge Mr. Frisch's help with the Glossary and Index. The final preparation and typing of this manuscript have been in the capable hands of Damiana Chavez, and I should like to express my gratitude for her careful work.

Richard K. Gardner

PART ONE
Types of Library Materials: How They Are Produced and Marketed

CHAPTER ONE
Creating Library Materials

The author, publisher, and bookseller are all partners in turning an idea into a finished product ready to be placed in the hands of its reader or consumer.[1] In the early days of the history of book publishing in the United States and Great Britain (and even today in many developing nations), it was the custom for an author to take a manuscript to the local printer, arrange to have it set in type and bound, and once that was done, take it to a few local bookstores for possible sale. The difficulty with such an arrangement—in modern times anyway—is that an author will probably know very little about printing and binding and will therefore be at the mercy of the printer, who may or may not have printed a book before. But an even more

[1]While modern libraries utilize all types of materials—print and nonprint—in their collections, the book is still paramount. Therefore it will be used as the primary example in these first two chapters on the production and marketing of library materials. Readers should keep in mind that much of what is said about the book also applies to periodicals, microforms, and nonprint materials (which are treated at some length in Chapters Three and Four).

serious problem is the fact that sales will be limited to the very narrow geographic area where the author or the author's friends live. The result will probably be a poor or mediocre printing job and poor or mediocre sales.

In contemporary industrialized Western society, it is the publisher who is the unifying force in bringing author, printer, and bookseller together. It is the publisher who plans and who takes the risks. As we shall see, the publisher, rather than the author, can also be the originating force behind a particular work. After creating an idea, the publisher may search for an author to carry out the work. It is very important to realize that it is the publisher alone who takes the financial risks involved in bringing a creative work to the public. If, for example, a publisher commissions someone to write a book and advances money to aid that person while the work is being written, and if the author fails to complete the assignment or does it in a slipshod fashion, the publisher has little financial recourse and will most likely have lost the money. A printer, on the other hand, always works for cash payment upon delivery of the work and takes no risks in printing it. Booksellers likewise (in the United States at least) take far fewer risks in that they may often return unsold books to the publisher.

The author is the formulator of ideas, the creator of a book or other written work. An author may be an individual or two or three individuals working together; or, in the case of reports or similar works, it may be an institution or a governmental body. The rights of authors are protected by copyright (that is, the right to copy), which prohibits unauthorized persons from publishing or otherwise making use of the author's work. Only the owner of a work or the owner's authorized agents have the right to publish a work—to make it available.

An author who grants a publisher the right to publish a work receives in return *royalties*. Royalties are monetary rewards for the work done and are based on the number of copies sold, less returns. The larger the number of copies sold, the larger will be the payments to the author. It is a sad fact of life today that few authors can live off the royalties they receive from the sale of their works. In granting a publisher the right to publish a work, an author enters into a contract in which the publisher agrees to print the work in a suitable format. The author agrees to perform certain duties, such as editing or reworking the manuscript as needed and proofreading galleys as the work goes through the various production stages. The author is also responsible for preparing an index if one is deemed necessary. The author and publisher enter into a partnership together to get the author's ideas before the reading public in the best manner possible and to the mutual advantage of both parties.

MANUSCRIPT SELECTION

Unsolicited Manuscripts

How do manuscripts reach a publisher? In many ways. First of all, a large number of manuscripts arrive at a publisher's door unsolicited. These are sometimes referred to as "over the transom" manuscripts. Some bear no return address; a few even have no author's name attached to them. Some bear little resemblance to the type of book published by that particular house; others may have been directed to just the right publisher. Although some trade publishers (those dealing in fiction and popular nonfiction of the type usually sold in general bookstores) will still examine manuscripts that arrive in this fashion, the proportion that are eventually selected for publication is very small. This is not true of children's books or scholarly or professional books, where unsolicited manuscripts are still important. The great problem facing a neophyte author is choosing the right publisher to whom to submit the manuscript. It is here that librarians, with their intimate knowledge of publishers and the types of works they issue, can be of help to fledgling authors, who can waste many months, even years, submitting their manuscripts to publishers who will not have the faintest interest in the subject.

Literary Agents

Most trade books come to a publisher through literary agents. It is rare today for a work of fiction to be considered by a major trade publishing house unless it arrives in this fashion. Literary agents represent authors and are paid by them to market their works to publishers. They are expected to be knowledgeable about what types of works will interest a particular firm. In fact, a good agent will even be familiar with the interests of individual editors within a house. Agents can also suggest ways in which a manuscript can be made more attractive to a publisher before it is submitted for examination, thus increasing its chances of being chosen for publication or at least of receiving serious consideration. Literary agents are usually paid 10 percent of all the earnings an author receives from the particular work they have sold, even after an author has moved on to another agent.

Once a work has been sold by a literary agent to a publisher, the agent negotiates the contract terms for the author. In this day and age of complicated legal contracts, a knowledgeable literary agent can be of great help at this point in an author's career. Many agents end up guiding the entire career of a popular author.

Commissioned Works

It also very often happens that a publisher—that is, one of the editorial or sales staff—may have the original idea for a work, in which case the process will be reversed. The publisher will have to go out and look for an author who is capable of writing the book rather than the author seeking someone to publish the work resulting from his or her ideas. This is particularly true in the case of much serious nonfiction and many textbooks. Many scholarly and professional publishers utilize the services of consulting editors, experts in the field—often highly esteemed professors—to come up with ideas for new books and to suggest authors for them. These consulting editors may be designated the editors of publishers' series and are paid a small royalty for each manuscript that is selected and becomes a salable book. Persons known as literary scouts are also used by publishers to locate publishable books. Scouts work for the publisher rather than for the author. One of the most common types of literary scout is the foreign agent who looks for books abroad—works worth translating and making available to the local market.

The publisher who sits in the office all day and waits for manuscripts to come in will probably end up publishing a very undistinguished list of books and also end up with very small profits. The best editor in a publishing house goes out and gets the best manuscripts already written and stimulates, encourages, and guides the writing of new manuscripts that appear to meet current needs and will therefore have marketability. Editors, agents, scouts, and sales staff constantly think about books which authors' interests, talents, or experiences equip them to write. These may include a public figure who retires, a scientist who could do a popular science book, or an up-and-coming short story writer who could produce a fine novel. There are also the vast areas of major projects such as reference works or textbook series, which almost always originate within a publishing house.

To Accept or Reject: Some Considerations

With unsolicited manuscripts, many can be immediately rejected as not being suitable for that particular publishing house, as being either too long or too short, or as not being in a physical condition to be read. Other manuscripts will probably receive a preliminary cursory reading by a low-level member of the editorial staff. If the manuscript seems of some worth, it will usually be passed on up the ladder to a more experienced editor with a written report on its merits or interest. A second and more thorough reading will then take place. In the case of serious nonfiction, expert opinion is usually sought from specialists in the field. These persons are paid a modest reading fee and are asked to evaluate the soundness of the content as well as the interest the work might have for other persons in the field. They may make suggestions for revision or even advise that a second opinion be obtained. If a manuscript has been commissioned by a publishing house or if one comes in under the sponsorship of the editor of a series, outside opinions on the manuscript will still be sought before a final commitment is made to go ahead and publish the work.

A manuscript may be of great interest to a publisher and still be refused. Most publishers, before accepting a manuscript, will wish to ascertain the marketability of the work. If the sales department reports unfavorably, the publisher may have to refuse the manuscript. Likewise, if the production staff reports that the book will cost too much to manufacture—because of costly illustrations, charts, maps, etc.—then again the work may have to be refused. Sales and cost factors weigh as heavily in any publisher's final judgment as does the quality of the manuscript. No publisher who wishes to stay in business for long can neglect such matters. In fact, the most successful publishers are men and women who combine literary acumen with sound business sense. While publishers may accept a manuscript with few hopes for an immediate return on the investment, they undoubtedly hope that future work by that author will be more profitable. Once in a while a manuscript will arrive on a publisher's desk that, while of dubious salability, is of such importance that it cries out to be published. It is hoped that a publisher will have made enough money on other works to permit the publication of this loser. Often this is the distinguishing mark of really fine publishing houses—the realization that they have a duty to others that goes beyond mere economic interests. Perfectly good manuscripts may also have to be refused because the house is already committed to publishing a similar book.

Finally and most importantly, there remain the reputation and personality of a particular house. All publishers choose books according to their own likes and dislikes and according to the success or failure they have had in certain fields in the past. No publishing house can do all things well, and most have wisely chosen to specialize in some fashion or other. Even big general trade houses build up reputations for certain types of materials over the years. An isolated science fiction title on the list of a house that has never done one before usually will not sell as well as that same title brought out by a publisher known by booksellers, librarians, and the general book-buying public as specializing in science fiction. For a literary house to bring out an auto-repair manual would be sheer folly for all concerned.

The Role of the Editor

The selection of manuscripts and the development of publishing projects are the work of an *editor* within the publishing house. In a very small house the head of the firm, the publisher, may combine such duties with others, but in most houses this work is the responsibility of the editorial department. [Originally the term "editor" meant publisher, and this is still true in French (*éditeur*) and Italian (*editore*) today.] As we shall see later, this is not the only task of an editor—his or her work is much broader than this—but it is the first and in many ways the most important step. The selection of fiction differs considerably from the selection of nonfiction. First of all, fiction is rarely selected on the basis of a partial manuscript or outline, as is often the case with nonfiction. Fiction must be judged on its literary qualities and as a whole. Only the most famous novelists can demand contracts for unwritten works. While almost all editors insist that fiction is judged on literary qualities alone, there are very few houses where salability is not also taken into consideration. The respective weights given to the two factors will determine the literary reputation of the house. As was indicated previously, an editor may decide to invest in an author for the long term rather than just the immediate prospects. In selecting fiction, not only the hardback rights but also the possibility of paperback publication need to be taken into account; indeed this may be the determining factor. The possibility of sale to the movies or to TV or the sale of foreign translation rights may also be a determining factor in the final decision.

   With nonfiction the picture is somewhat different. Very often the author will arrive with only an outline and a chapter or two of a projected book, or the publisher will feel the need to publish a book in a certain area and commission an author to write it. In the latter case, a decision to publish is made largely sight unseen. The author, it is hoped, will have written other works, even if only journal articles, and these can be used to help determine whether he or she is capable of producing a satisfactory manuscript. Or the author may have such a reputation that the resulting book will sell anyway, even if the editor has to do a great deal of rewriting or even assign a ghostwriter to work with the author. (This is often true of celebrities who are asked to write their autobiographies.) With nonfiction the editor must be first and foremost an idea person, constantly putting forth ideas for books to fill gaps in our knowledge. Combined with this general knowledge and wide range of ideas, the nonfiction editor must have a great variety of contacts in both academic and journalistic circles in order to "marry" the right author to the right idea. The editor must be able to utilize these contacts to provide expert advice when needed. In summary, while the nonfiction editor is open to much outside advice and suggestion, the fiction editor relies almost entirely on personal judgment in selecting manuscripts for publication.

CONTRACTS AND RIGHTS

Once a manuscript has been selected for publication or has been commissioned, a contract between the author and the publisher must be drawn up. The first element in a book contract is exclusivity. The author must grant the publisher exclusive rights to the written work; in other words, a writer cannot sell the same work to two different publishers. In addition, the author may grant certain other rights, known as *subsidiary rights*, to the publisher. These include reprint rights of many kinds—in paperback, book-club editions, serialization, condensations, translations, and extracts for anthologies—and performing rights—motion pictures, radio, TV, and drama. In a few cases, with literary characters such as Peanuts or Hopalong Cassidy, there may be commercial exploitation rights as well. It is not necessary or even customary for authors to grant all the rights to one publisher, but what they do grant is on an exclusive basis. Translation, TV, and film rights are often reserved and sold separately by the author or the agent. In many contracts there may be a geographic limitation; for example, sales may be limited to the United States and/or Canada. In such cases, the rights to publish the book in other countries will be negotiated separately.

Responsibilities of the Publisher and Author

In the usual publishing contract, each party agrees to do certain things. The author (particularly the author of a textbook) agrees not to write a competing book. In other words, an author who has written a basic first-year textbook in electrical engineering for McGraw-Hill will agree not to write a similar work for Wiley or Prentice-Hall. The publisher, in turn, agrees to publish the work within a certain period of time "in suitable form." Leading authors of best sellers may demand that a certain amount of money be spent on publicizing the work once it is published, but as we shall see when we discuss advertising and publicity, most publishers, with good reason, try to avoid such clauses. In return for the granting of publication rights, an author receives royalty payments. These are often a fixed percentage of the book's retail or wholesale price. The rate may go up as sales increase. Such higher royalty payments can usually be negotiated only by a best-selling, established author. If a book fails to sell and is later "remaindered," then no royalty or only a greatly reduced royalty will be paid on the remaindered copies. Royalty payments are made on a quarterly, semiannual, or annual basis. Publishers sometimes offer advance payments while an author is writing a work. These will always be advances against future royalties, and the author will receive no further payments for the work until royalties have reached the payback point. Authors receive ten copies of their own work; additional copies must be purchased—usually at the wholesale price.

Besides preparing and submitting a satisfactory manuscript to the publisher, the author agrees to read galley proofs promptly and to pay for any excess author's alterations (changes made by the author at the galley or page-proof stage). The author is also required to prepare an index, if one is deemed necessary.

Reprint Rights

It is a hard fact of economic life these days that many books cannot be sold at a profit in the original hardback edition alone. Publishers must therefore look elsewhere for additional income. Paperback and book-club reprints are today the most common sources of such additional income. These rights are usually handled and sold by the publisher, and the proceeds are split fifty-fifty between the author and the publisher. Paperbacks are of two types: mass market and trade. Mass-market paperbacks, as the name implies, are those sold through magazine distributors and found in all types of retail outlets from drugstores to supermarkets. Mass-market paperbacks are limited to the most popular titles that will appeal to a wide range of readers. Trade paperbacks are more specialized in interest and are generally sold only in bookstores or in the book departments of large department stores. They are usually printed on a higher-grade paper and are better bound; their price is likewise higher. Income from the sale of paperback reprint rights varies according to how the book is to be marketed. With a few very popular titles, large advances are sometimes paid for mass-market paperback rights, sometimes as much as $100,000 to $250,000. These advances are sometimes obtained by the publisher by auctioning off the mass-market paperback reprint rights to the highest bidder. Trade paperbacks are a different matter. The number printed will be much smaller, and so will the author's income.

In the case of both types of paperbacks, there is very often a waiting period of one year after the hardback edition is published before the paperback edition can be released, and the contract is usually for a five- to seven-year period. In fact, the life of the average mass-market paperback is only a few months. After this initial sales period, the title will be withdrawn from the racks and replaced with another. This creates great problems for the library wishing to buy copies of a mass-market title once the initial sales period has passed, since mass-market dealers are not usually prepared to fill orders of back titles. The same is not true of most trade paperbacks, which are expected to have a long-term sale. The only point confusing to librarians is that a particular title may pass from one paperback reprint house to another after the initial contract has expired— something that is not true of most hardback books unless the copyright has expired and they are now in the public domain.

There were 130 to 150 book clubs in operation in the United States in the 1970s, selecting 3,000 to 4,000 titles a year for their memberships. These book clubs include the well-known general-interest book clubs such as the Book-of-the-Month Club and the Literary Guild, as well as very specialized clubs such as the Antiques Book Club, Ecological Book Club, Civil Engineers Book Club, Real Estate Book Institute, and Detective Book Club. The range of titles that are salable to such clubs is infinite. Members no longer seem to be satisfied with a single monthly selection but want a variety to choose from. Book clubs often arrange to print their own editions from the publisher's plates, sometimes economizing by the use of cheaper paper and binding and by cutting down on the margins. Income from book-club royalties is usually split fifty-fifty between the author and the publisher. The reason publishers are so anxious to obtain book-club adoptions for one of their titles is that substantial guarantees are paid by the larger clubs, running as high as $100,000 to $200,000 on major titles. A book may also be sold to more than one club; few clubs insist on exclusive rights to a title, and then only for a few months. The paperback reprint rights and book-club rights are often financially more important to the original publisher than are the hardback rights, and they can often make the difference between a deficit and a profit on a particular title.

Other reprint rights are of less importance monetarily to the publisher and the author. While hardback reprints of older titles are often of importance to the librarian, to fill gaps in a collection or to replace worn-out copies, they will not bring any sizable income to the original publisher or to the author. Serial rights used to be more important than they are now. In recent years, only a few very topical books have been sold for serialization in newspapers. Once in a while, a chapter of a book will be sold to a magazine such as *Harper's*, the *Atlantic Monthly*, or *Esquire*, but this will bring only a modest amount—from several hundred to a few thousand dollars. The same is true of condensations. Permission to publish extracts of a book or individual short stories or poems in an anthology brings more prestige than profit to author and publisher. Fees may be as low as $25 for a single poem.

Translations from English into a foreign language are an entirely different matter. Foreign publication rights for an English-language edition are usually for a specific geographic area, as we have already indicated. The same is true for translations, although in this case the area is usually defined in terms of language rather than political boundaries. Translations can often bring in considerable additional income to both the author and the original publisher.

Performing Rights

We now reach what the public considers to be the glamorous area of performing rights. Most authors reserve these rights and attempt to market them personally or through their agent. A publisher who markets them gets only a small percentage of the royalties. The reason publishers do not handle performing rights—or, if they do, collect only modest royalties—is that these are not printing rights but something entirely different. Therefore the publisher is not felt to have as much influence or as much expertise in handling such a sale. Sales of performing rights occur only with a minority of books—and most often with novels that can be turned into movies, TV series, or plays. Contracts are complicated and are handled most successfully by agents or lawyers with experience in the field. Royalties can be large and often include various kinds of profit participation. Since a novel may be optioned for the movies or TV and never produced, an initial sales payment is customary. A time limit is often placed on such options, and the rights revert to the author if work on the film or play does not go forward. Radio and TV rights also have time limits in terms of when the resulting product may be shown and how many times. Plays can prove to be very lucrative, particularly those that involve small casts and only one set. These plays appeal to the great number of amateur drama companies scattered throughout the country, all of which must pay a royalty in order to present the play.

In spite of all this talk of subsidiary rights, it is well to remember that the majority of authors do not enjoy income from any of the

reprint or performing rights that we have mentioned. Most professional books and textbooks appear only in the original hardback
format, and while there may be income from translation into a foreign
language, that income will be small.

EDITING

Once a manuscript has been purchased by a publishing house, the
work of preparing it for publication begins. This work is carried out by
editors. We have already discussed the work of an editor in acquiring
manuscripts, in selecting the best available ones for publication, and
in turning an idea into a publishable manuscript through the selection
and guidance of an author. This is only the first part of the job. The
second is to see the manuscript through the various stages of
production to publication. The first task is largely a matter of taste
and discrimination; the second is one of technique. There is also a
personal component to the job. The editor, as the main point of
contact between the author and the publishing house, must play the
role of sponsor of the book within the house and see that it is
handsomely produced, effectively launched, and well promoted for
sale. Most publishing houses consist of three basic divisions: editorial, production and design, and sales and promotion. It is the editor's
responsibility to serve as liaison between the author and the staffs of
these other departments and to coordinate the entire process of
publishing the work.

Much of the technical side of an editor's job consists of copy
editing a manuscript. Copy editing involves expressing the author's
ideas in the clearest, most orderly, and most effective way. It also
includes marking the manuscript with directions for the compositor
so that, it is hoped, the amount of correction needed on the galley
proofs will be minimal. Copy editing can be done by the acquisitions
editor or it can be passed on to a specialist in grammar and
punctuation, who is usually called a *copy editor* and whose sole job is to
correct manuscripts. Copy editing can also be farmed out to a
free-lancer outside the publishing house. Even a large publishing
house with a considerable number of copy editors on its staff may be
overloaded with work from time to time and find it necessary to call
upon the services of free-lancers. Such persons, often of the highest
caliber, are to be found in all the major publishing centers. Smaller
houses with only an occasional manuscript to edit may find it
preferable to use free-lancers all the time rather than undertake the
task themselves. A specialized manuscript may also call for some
outside help.

No author has ever handed in a manuscript completely ready for production. Many authors are so intent on what they meant to say that they do not realize they haven't said it. The copy editor must be concerned with a multitude of details. First of all, the manuscript must be legible. A clean copy must be available to go to the compositor. Next, there must be consistency in spelling, punctuation, capitalization, the use of abbreviations, the use of italics, word division, etc. Is it to be "a traveler who wore a gray suit" or "a traveller who wore a grey suit"? Is it to be "Virgil" or "Vergil"? There are fashions in these matters, and the dictionary the publishing house uses as a final authority may not have been the one the author used while writing the book—or he or she may have used several. Furthermore, has the author been consistent throughout the manuscript? It is easy to forget what one has done in Chapter 1 and do the opposite in Chapter 8. Consistency applies not only to spelling and punctuation but also to content. Has the author forgotten and changed the name of a character or a place midway through the manuscript?

When it comes to grammar and style, the job becomes much more delicate. Some publishing houses limit the authority of the copy editor in these areas, particularly for fiction, poetry, and drama, and insist that the matter be referred back to the general editor, who will then consult the author about major points at issue. With nonfiction there is likely to be less difficulty: The grammar is correct or it is not. As for style, clarity will usually be striven for at all costs. Nonfiction writers are often experts in their fields but may not be particularly good writers. It is then the job of the copy editor to rewrite considerable portions of the manuscript. In all these cases, the copy editor must be a diplomat as well as a master of the English language. Copy editing is an art, not a science.

Another matter that concerns the editor is the factual accuracy of the manuscript. In recent years there has been considerable criticism of publishing houses for their failure to assure accuracy in the books they publish. While editors cannot be experts in the subject of every book they edit, they should be consistently suspicious and query the author whenever they feel uneasy about a statement. If they are unable to understand the text at any point, they should certainly seek clarification. There is also the problem of legality and propriety. The finished book must not expose the author or the publisher to legal suits for libel, obscenity, or infringement of copyright.

Once the text is in final form for publication, a host of production details remain. First of all, the manuscript must be completed by the addition of a title page, a table of contents, and chapter and running heads. A preface or introduction may have to be written. Footnotes, a bibliography, a glossary, tables, illustrations, and maps may have to be created or put in final form, and after the text is set in page proofs, an index (for a nonfiction book) will have to be prepared. All this is coordinated by the editor. The editor will work with the production and design staff to plan how the book will look in its final printed form and to iron out any difficulties that the manuscript may present.

DESIGNING THE BOOK

The job of the book designer is essentially to carry out visually what the author has tried to convey in words. In order to do this, the designer must have a sense of form, space, color, and texture. He or she must also be knowledgeable about book-manufacturing techniques and the various costs involved in production. The resulting book should look attractive and present the author's and illustrator's ideas in the clearest and most intelligible way. Furthermore the finished product should be suitable to its purpose. A poetry book should look like a poetry book and an engineering book like an engineering book. What is suitable for one type of book is not always suitable for another. The designer must also be aware of the book's sales potential, as more money can be spent on a book that will probably sell well than on one that is only expected to break even.

It is true that any printer can set a simple book in type and print the number of copies desired, just as any home owner can draw up plans for a new house, hire a building contractor, and have the house built according to the amateur plans. The results will rarely be aesthetically pleasing, however, and may not even be very practical. Furthermore the owner and the builder will be involved in all sorts of decisions for which they are ill-prepared. The same would be true of an author and a printer who attempted to publish anything but the simplest book without calling in the services of a professional book designer.

What things must be decided by the book designer? They include the size of the page, the kind and size of the type, the width of the margins and position of the type on the page, the length of each line, the amount of space between the lines, the arrangement and type of chapter and running headings, the placement of page numbers, how illustrations, maps, and tables are to be inserted into the page layout, what kind of paper is to be used, what type of binding is most suitable, and what color paper and binding are to be. A technical book or an elaborate art book presents further problems. A children's picture book in which text and illustrations are closely linked is an even more specialized problem. This shows that good book design is not a simple task.

Like copy editing, book designing can be done either within the publishing house or by a free-lancer. Much depends on the size of the publishing house and whether it has enough work to keep a designer busy all the time. An additional advantage to using an outsider is that the best person can be hired for a particular job. Some designers may specialize in children's books, others in professional or technical books or in adult fiction.

The length of the manuscript basically determines the size of the book, but many variations are possible depending on the typeface and size of the type. The selection of a typeface for a specific book is a painstaking operation. Many typefaces are available, but only a certain number will be suitable for a particular kind of book. Some typefaces are heavy, others are light; some are simple and modern, others are elaborate and ornate. Some are easy to read, others are more suitable for decoration. Some are wide and take up a lot of space, others are narrow and compact. Besides different styles of type, each typeface comes in varying sizes, and the optimal size for a particular manuscript must be specified. A children's book or one intended for readers with diminished eyesight calls for a larger size than that used for a college textbook. In a heavily illustrated book such as an art work, the size of the type must be in proportion to the majority of the illustrations. Very large, full-page illustrations will not marry well with very small type for the main text. A further possible limitation is the availability of the desired typeface and size at a particular compositor. The designer must ascertain what typefaces in what sizes are available.

The next step will be to decide the length of the line. This, together with the typeface and size, determines the amount of space to be left between each line. This is called *leading*.

While technical details may create limits in planning the layout of the main body of a book, the designer has great freedom in arranging the *display* items. These include the title page, the cover, the opening page of each chapter, and finally, the dust jacket. The variety of possibilities in these items is infinite. The only thing the designer must keep in mind is that the cover and title page set the mood for the work and must be in keeping with the character of the work itself. This means that the designer must become familiar with the contents of the book; this should be done before the proper typeface is selected.

The *dust jacket* was originally just that, a piece of paper designed to keep the book clean. Dust jackets today are seen as effective selling devices. A book on display on the counter or shelf of a bookstore is in competition with many other titles and must sell itself. This is largely a matter of presentation—how the book looks. The design of an effective dust jacket is therefore of the utmost importance for all trade books. It is so important that it is often considered a specialized art form, and the designer of the book may or may not be called upon to design the dust jacket. Much of the work is farmed out to free-lancers.

Once all the design elements have been decided upon, the book designer must prepare a layout for the compositor. This will show—in great detail—how the pages are to be laid out, how illustrations, tables, etc. are to be handled, and where page numbers are to be placed. The front matter (title page, table of contents, etc.), a sample chapter opening, and the end matter (appendixes, index, etc.) must also be included. This layout, which is usually done in exact size, is the guide for the compositor and must answer all questions about how the book is to be set. At this stage, it is customary to have sample pages set in type by the compositor to make sure there are no further problems and to show all concerned how the final product will look. The copy editor is then asked to mark up the manuscript for the compositor, indicating where each typeface is to be used and in what size, what the spacing is to be, what indentations are needed, and where charts, tables, and illustrations are to be placed. This is a time-consuming but important task. The clearer the instructions to the compositor, the less likely there will be serious errors in composition. One final decision must still be made: the choice of paper. Papers vary in texture, weight, and color, and, just as with typefaces, what is suitable for one type of book may not be suitable for another.

PRODUCING THE BOOK

Once the design has been completed it is time to move to the production stage. The person supervising this step is the production supervisor. Modern technology is responsible for constant changes in the methods of book production; thus, a production supervisor must be alert to new changes as they occur and to the benefits, technical and financial, that they present. He or she must be aware of the changing market in composition, paper, ink, etc., and must know where good work may be obtained at reasonable prices, for very few publishers today (unlike the nineteenth century) have their own printing plants. Most printers are located outside the big cities since printing presses are heavy and require large amounts of space. Space is also needed for storing paper and the finished product—books or periodicals.

Production supervisors are usually responsible for establishing cost estimates once a manuscript has been accepted for publication. Production costs are of two kinds: plant costs and manufacturing costs. Plant costs occur only once, no matter how many copies are printed. They include the cost of composition—setting the type—the cost of making the plates, and the cost of proofs, mechanicals, and any artwork needed for the book or dust jacket. Since these are one-time, fixed costs, the more copies of a work that are printed, the lower the cost per copy. Manufacturing costs, on the other hand, depend on the number of copies printed and bound. They include paper and ink, binding, and presswork (that is, the cost of running the printing presses). It is true that printing a large number of copies at one time will reduce costs slightly since the presses have to be made ready only once.

One of the main duties of the production supervisor is scheduling the work. Delays are costly. If a book is not ready for press at the scheduled time, another book will be substituted and the originally scheduled work will have to wait for another opportunity. This will undoubtedly cause missed publication dates and disrupt publicity and sales plans. Delays can be very costly for a book of current interest, since the audience may have disappeared by the time the work appears or another publisher may have captured the market with a similar book on the subject.

The designer, it has been noted, is sometimes responsible for choosing the paper for the book. More often it is the production supervisor. What qualities are looked for in a good paper? First of all, color. Even paper which at first appears to be white will upon closer examination prove to be a particular shade of white. Another factor of great importance to readers is opacity—how much show-through there is from one side to the other. Then the finish or smoothness must be considered. Here the greatest contrast can be seen in comparing the rough, or antique, finish used for most novels with the glossy paper used for many art books. Weight and bulk are two other characteristics. At first these may seem to be synonymous, but this is not true. A bulky paper can be very light simply because air has been blown into the fibers during manufacture. On the other hand, glossy papers are apt to be very heavy because of the coating that has been applied to the fibers. In choosing a paper for a particular book, bulk may be important if a publisher wishes to make a book look bigger than it actually is. The width of the margins and the size of the type may also be used to increase the number of pages, but these are more noticeable to the average reader than the use of a lightweight but thick paper. A heavy, glossy paper may be necessary if halftone illustrations are to be widely used. The final element that the production supervisor must consider is price. Most often a compromise must be struck between what the designer would really like to have and what is economically feasible.

COMPOSITION, PRINTING, AND BINDING

Once the production supervisor has made the cost estimate, decided on the paper to be used, and gotten bids from the various suppliers, it is time to move to the actual production stage. Until the end of World War II, there had been few developments in composition and printing technology for well over a century. Since 1945, however, there has been one change after another. It is not the purpose of this book to go into all the technical details of composition, printing, and binding. There are many books on these topics, the best of which are listed in the "Suggested Readings" at the end of this chapter. It will suffice here to give a general overview of the major types of composition and printing currently in use, and their advantages and disadvantages, so that librarians can judge the quality of the final product—the books that they are called upon to purchase every day.

There are three basic processes involved in producing a book: composition—that is, setting the words in type so that they may be reproduced; presswork—applying ink to paper or otherwise producing the printed page (much of this is now done photographically); and binding—gathering the sheets of paper, folding them, cutting the edges, and fastening them together.

First, let us take composition. The oldest method is typesetting by hand, letter by letter, and locking the resulting lines into a frame. The great disadvantage of this method is that the various slugs of type must be kept locked in place and cannot be used for anything else until the page has been printed. Furthermore slugs wear out as time goes by. It is also a great chore to replace all the slugs in their little boxes once a page is broken down. Machine composition was introduced in the late nineteenth century. Linotype and Intertype are the two most widely used machines and are practically identical in operation. With these machines the operator sits before a typewriter-like keyboard, and as the keys are punched, a matrix or mold drops into place from a magazine above. Once all the letters (and spaces) for a line are in place, the entire line is moved into a position where molten metal is forced against or into the molds, thus casting an entire line of type. The original matrixes or molds then return to their places in the magazine. The great advantage of this method is that fewer duplicates of each character can be kept on hand since they are quickly returned for reuse. On the other hand, if it is necessary to correct a letter or word, the whole line must be recast—with the possibility of making a second error. A similar method of typesetting is Monotype. Here the keyboard produces a perforated tape that is then used to call up individual letters; the letters are cast separately in hot metal rather than as a whole line, thus making corrections of one letter possible.

With all of the above methods, once the lines have been set, they are grouped together to form a complete page. Then, instead of being held indefinitely in a frame, they are customarily made into a plate. In the beginning, metal plates were the most common. In recent times, plates made of a rubberized or plastic material have been found to be most useful since they are lighter and can be bent for use on rotary presses, which have huge drums. While the original lines can be melted down and the metal reused once the plates have been made, the plates themselves must be stored if further printings are planned. Storage costs have risen considerably in recent years and must be taken into consideration in calculating the cost of publication.

Phototypesetting is a postwar development that has assumed great importance in recent years. In this form of composition no metal type is used; instead, letters are reproduced optically on film. One of the great advantages of photocomposition is that through the use of different lenses, the size of the type can be varied; furthermore justification of lines can be done optically. By *justification* we mean the filling out of a line with additional space so that the right-hand margins are just as even as those on the left. If you examine a printed page, you will notice that certain lines seem to have less space between words than others. In fact, some lines may seem very crowded. No two lines are likely to have exactly the same number of letters. Thus it is necessary to add extra space between words in order for all lines to come out the same length. In setting type by hand, spacing must be done once the line is finished; this is a laborious and time-consuming process. With Linotype and other machines, wedges are forced down into the spaces between words, more or less deeply as the spacing requires, to fill out the line. How much easier to have all this taken care of by a lens and a photographic camera!

There are many types and makes of photocomposers, but all of them utilize a keyboard much like a typewriter keyboard. The main difference is that some use punched paper tape to activate the composing mechanism, while others use the photographic element directly. Photocomposition is most often used in conjunction with offset printing.

A third type of typesetting is typewriter composition. This is sometimes called *cold-type composition* to differentiate it from the more traditional hot-metal methods. It is a direct-impression method, and copies can be made only with the use of carbon paper or by photographing the resulting page. In recent years, vast improvements made in this method now permit justified right-hand margins and the use of various typefaces. The advantage of cold-type composition is that it may be done by any typist rather than by a highly paid compositor. The disadvantages are serious, however, and most publishers hesitate to use it for book production, except in limited-run scholarly or professional books that could not see publication using a more expensive method. These disadvantages are most serious in the area of quality of impression. It is very difficult to get as sharp an image as with other methods of typesetting, and it is even more difficult to achieve uniformity of impression.

The most interesting developments in recent years have come with the increasing use of computerized composition. From the computerization of parts of the composition process, developments have now reached the stage where not only composition of a text is possible, but page layout as well. Newspapers have been the first to adopt these new methods. *The New York Times* is now produced by computer, with the journalists typing their copy directly into the computer terminal and making corrections themselves. The printing of books should not lag far behind. One of the options now available is that of handling composition in the editorial office, with the advantages of control of the content and the possibility of last-minute changes and corrections. It will be interesting to see how these technological improvements affect the production of books in the years ahead.

At this stage, and before the type is set into page form, galley proofs are pulled and are sent to the editor and the author to be corrected. The compositor may do a preliminary proofreading in order to catch gross errors, but the responsibility for the tedious task of ferreting out the compositor's mistakes lies with the editor and author. More than one reading is essential if most of the errors are to be caught and corrected. Few books are printed that do not contain at least one or two misprints. At this stage an author may also make changes. Sometimes a sentence or paragraph that looked perfectly all right in the manuscript will suddenly loom up as an outrageous or erroneous statement or as very awkward in structure. It is far better to correct such mistakes now than to let them go through unchanged. Some authors have the unfortunate habit of practically rewriting their entire manuscript in the galley proof stage. Since this adds greatly to composition costs, most publishers allow authors only a certain amount of *aa's* (author's alterations), beyond which the author must pay all costs. In correcting one error, it is easy for the compositor to make another, particularly since many composition processes involve the resetting of a whole line. Even if this is not so, unless the correction involves the substitution of the same number of letters in a line, several lines, even whole paragraphs, may have to be reset to accommodate the inserted material. When an author makes wholesale changes in the text, this necessarily complicates the situation.

Once the corrected galleys are made up in page format, another set of proofs, known as *page proofs*, is pulled and sent for correction to the editor and author. Page proofs are the first to include page numbers, and it is only then that an index can be prepared. The responsibility for creating the index lies with the author. There are many types of indexes. Name indexes are the simplest to make, subject indexes the most difficult. A happy medium must be struck between an index that repeats everything in the text and one so sketchy that is has no value. Librarians are more aware than anyone of the value of a good index. Publishers need to be told that nonfiction works without an index are practically useless in libraries and in the long run will lose sales. Naturally the index must also be proofread, and since it cannot be prepared until the rest of the book is in page format, proofreading is sometimes done very hurriedly in order to meet deadlines. All proofs should be corrected with standard proofreader's marks, which can be found in any style manual.

Printing

Following composition comes presswork. The most common for many years was letterpress printing. With this method, ink is applied to the raised type surface, which is then pressed against the paper. In modern times, as has been previously mentioned, a plate made of metal, plastic, or rubberized material is usually substituted for the type. A more usual method of printing books today is *photo offset lithography*, more commonly called simply *offset*. The principle of this type of printing is the antipathy of grease and water. It is known as photo offset since the plates are produced with the use of film. Several different types of plates can be made depending on the quality and durability of the plates desired. In this process, chemicals are used to make sure that the parts of the plate to be inked are water-repellent and the nonprinting areas are ink-repellent. The original film can be stored for future use and new plates (electros) made as needed.

The printing of illustrations and artwork is a more complicated process. It must be understood by librarians so that they may be better able to judge the products of various publishing houses. The most common method of reproducing illustrative matter is the halftone process. A cross-line screen is used to break up the original photograph or drawing into a pattern of little dots. (Put the average newspaper photo under a magnifying glass and you will see clearly how it is done.) Larger dots closer together produce the darker areas, smaller ones farther apart lighter ones. The finer the screen used, the better will be the results of reproduction.

With colored illustrations, additional problems arise. Although multicolor presses do exist, it is not always economical to use them. In this case, the traditional method of running the sheets through the press separately for each color is used. When this is done, the presses must be washed carefully after each run-through so that no trace of the previous color remains on succeeding passes. By using the principle of primary colors in various shades, any color desired can be obtained through the imposition of one color on top of another (blue and yellow making green, for example). The difficulty with such imposition (and with most multicolored illustration work, whatever the method used) is in *registering*. Great care must be taken to assure that each color is imposed exactly where it is needed over the previous one. If this is not accomplished, the result will be fuzzy at best and a muddled mess at worst. Many factors hinder good registering—faulty mounting of the plates, moisture in the paper, or slightly irregular trimming of the sheets. A further problem arises when the printer wishes to reproduce as faithfully as possible the true colors of an artwork or original illustration. *Full-color printing*, as it is called, involves first of all the separation of the original work into its primary colors by means of a camera utilizing various colored filters. Theoretically this should result in an exact copy, but unfortunately, due to variations in paper, film, and filters, corrections must often be made. In recent years, electronic means of correction have been added to the manual or photographic methods previously available. In any case, great time and effort, sometimes involving the presence of the artist, is necessary in order to achieve the finest results. Good color reproduction remains a costly process, and thus no librarian should expect a good art book at a low price.

Each page of a book is not printed separately but rather as part of a large sheet containing eight, sixteen, thirty-two or sixty-four pages of the book (all other multiples of eight are possible but less economical). In planning the book, the designer will seek to have the number of pages in the book come out to one of these multiples; otherwise a few extra pages must be added—a costly process. This factor will influence the designer's choice of size of type and paper. To a novice, arranging the various pages on the large sheets so that they fall in the right order once the sheets are folded and cut will always remain a mystery. Needless to say, it varies with the number of pages on the sheet. It also varies with the type of binding equipment used. Thus the production supervisor must know who is going to bind the work and on what machines before starting the actual printing.

Binding

Binding is the final step in the production of the book. It is necessary in order to hold the pages of the book together in proper order and make them easy to handle. Two basic methods of binding are in use today. First is the traditional method of sewing the sheets together; this is known as *edition binding*. The other method involves gluing the sheets together and is known as *perfect binding*. Satisfactory perfect bindings have been developed only within the last two decades or so through the use of plastic adhesives. The first step in any binding process is to fold the sheets according to the predetermined arrangement of the pages (*imposition*). The group of pages resulting from the folding of one sheet is known as a *signature*. Many printers place a small black mark on the fold of each signature or a number in the margin in order to simplify the gathering of the various signatures together and to make sure that all of them are in place. The signatures are usually assembled on large gathering machines. Once all the signatures have been gathered together, they are ready for sewing or gluing. There are two types of sewing; the most satisfactory is *Smyth sewing*, in which threads are passed through each signature at the fold and then attached to the next signature. The other type is *side sewing*. This is satisfactory only with very thin books, but it is very strong. In this method, threads are passed through the entire book from the side. The results are the same as if several pages had been stapled together at the side. The book cannot be opened wide to the fold, and the pages must be bent back.

With perfect binding no thread is used. After the signatures are gathered together, the back edges are roughed off and an adhesive is applied. Sometimes a coarsely woven fabric is applied to give added reinforcement. In recent years, plastic adhesives, which are flexible and durable, have come into general use. Interestingly enough, gluing is also used with sewn bindings to hold the signatures in place. With sewn bindings it is also necessary to press the signatures together, as they will have acquired added thickness with the use of the thread. This is called *smashing*. At this point, the pages must be trimmed to make them uniform and to open up the various folds.

Next, the back of the book is rounded and prepared for backing by creating the little ridge into which the covers will fit. Finally, it is time to attach the covers. One or more strips of gauze (and sometimes a strip of strong paper) are glued to the back edge of the book extending out on either side. To these strips the boards of the cover are attached. The boards are covered with various types of material, from standard cloth to plastic or paper. Sometimes a cover will be of two different materials—cloth at the back and front edges and paper in the middle. The final step in binding is the printing of the title, and the names of the author and publisher on the back edge and sometimes the cover. Some covers may have designs or colophons embossed into them. This is done with stamping dies. When the separately printed dust jacket is added, we have a finished product that is ready to go to the book reviewer, the sales force, and the bookstore. It is also ready to be copyrighted.

COPYRIGHT

Since January 1, 1978, the works of U.S. authors have been protected by a new copyright law, passed by Congress in 1976 and the first revision since 1909. The new law was needed because of the vast changes in communications technology during the twentieth century. In addition, it was necessary to bring U.S. practice closer to that of other countries. One of the greatest changes made by the new law was to institute a single system of copyright for both unpublished and published works. Under previous U.S. laws, a work was protected by common law before it was published and by federal statute thereafter. Under the 1976 law, a work is protected by federal law from the moment of its creation, rather than from the moment of its publication. Since no other country had anything resembling the earlier U.S. law, this change should contribute to international understanding in an age when works can be published simultaneously in different countries.

Copyright now applies to "original works of authorship which are fixed in a copy" rather than to the "writings" of an author. Literary, musical, dramatic, choreographic, pictorial, graphic, and sculptural works, motion pictures, and sound recordings may all be copyrighted. The works must be original and creative. In other words, a person may not copyright something that has been copied from another work. Ideas, methods, systems, and principles may not be copyrighted; a work must exist in concrete form. Works of the U.S. government are likewise excluded.

The main problem in creating any copyright legislation is to protect the owner's rights, which almost always translate into money, without restricting use of the material unnecessarily. Under the new U.S. legislation the creator of a work has five basic rights: (1) the right to reproduce (that is, print or publish) the work; (2) the right to prepare new versions (revisions, abridgments, condensations, translations, and other art forms such as motion pictures, dramas, etc.); (3) the right to public distribution by sale, gift, or rental; (4) the right to public performance (profit or nonprofit); and (5) the right to public display (TV, film, or stills). When revisions or derivative works are made, only the new material is copyrightable. The older or unchanged portions of the derivative works remain under the original copyright.

As was indicated above, copyright now occurs at the time of creation and is for the life of the author plus fifty years (it used to be for a maximum of fifty-six years). The date of the author's death now determines the length of the copyright rather than the date the copyright was registered. This makes it more difficult to tell when a work has passed into the public domain, although the new law specifies that the Copyright Office is to record the deaths of all authors that become known to them. If no other information is available, death can be presumed seventy-five years after first publication or one hundred years after creation, whichever comes first. Registration is not compulsory—a work retains its protection from the moment of creation even if it is not registered with the Copyright Office—but it is a condition for bringing infringement suits and incurring penalties for infringement.

Copyright is usually in the name of the author or authors (rights being shared equally when a work is coauthored). However, if an employee prepares a work for publication as part of his or her daily employment, then the employer is entitled to hold the copyright. Certain types of works may also be commissioned by a publishing company, the publisher again being entitled to hold the copyright. Such works include contributions to a collective work (such as an encyclopedia), compilations (anthologies), textbooks, tests and answer material, supplements to previously published works which serve to introduce or explain them, translations, atlases, and parts of motion pictures and other audio-visual materials. These are known as *works for hire*, and copyright protection for them is for a term of seventy-five years from first publication or one hundred years from creation, whichever is less.

Works which were copyrighted under the 1909 law and were still under copyright protection when the new law went into effect have had their protection extended from the original fifty-six years to seventy-five years. Anyone may obtain a U.S. copyright for a work published in this country if he or she is either a U.S. citizen or a citizen of a country which adheres to a copyright convention recognized by the United States. Even if only one author of a collective work is eligible for copyright, the work may be copyrighted.

Each copyrighted work must bear a copyright notice in a prominent place (usually on the verso of the title page). This notice has three elements: (1) the letter c in a circle, ©, or the word "Copyright" or its abbreviation, "Copr."; (2) the year of first publication; and (3) the name of the copyright owner.

The United States now has in operation—as part of the copyright law—a system of *dépôt légal* (legal deposit), which requires that two copies of every copyrighted published work be deposited with the Library of Congress. These may be the copies submitted with the copyright registration form; otherwise, two other copies must be submitted directly to the Library. Failure to do so upon demand of the Library can result in fines. This is another revision in the law that brings the United States in line with the practice of other countries and with the recommendations of UNESCO.

One of the problems with the earlier copyright law was the principle of indivisibility of copyright. Under this principle, authors were often pressured into signing away as many of their rights as possible to one person, even when it was not known at the time how valuable they might later become. Because of considerable pressure brought to bear on the framers of the new legislation, authors are now much better protected. The principle of indivisibility has been abolished, and authors can sell or lease rights separately however, whenever, and to whomever they choose. Furthermore any rights not transferred in writing by a legal document are retained by the author. Another gain for authors is the new possibility of terminating certain transfers of rights and licenses—upon due notice—after a certain period of time (usually thirty-five to forty years after the rights have been granted). Thus, if certain rights become very valuable at a later date, authors or their heirs can eventually get them back and sell or lease them again on better terms.

Another annoying problem under the earlier law—the problem of who owned the copyright to works published as contributions to periodicals or other collective works—has been resolved by the 1976 law. Now, while a single copyright notice and registration of the entire periodical issue by the publisher is permitted, the publisher is only allowed to reproduce and distribute the contribution as part of that particular issue. The rights to the individual contribution are held to be distinct from those of the collective work and remain vested in the author. He or she therefore has protection over their further use.

One facet of the new copyright law which affects librarians and should be mentioned here is the extension of copyright protection to unpublished works. Many librarians have large numbers of manuscripts—literary works, autobiographical works, letters—in their collections and from time to time have either published some of them or allowed other persons to do so. The fact that these works were protected by common law was not always a deterrent. The 1976 law is very clear on this matter, however. Librarians need to obtain a written agreement stating who owns what rights for manuscripts deposited with them in the future and, if possible, for those they already own. The new extension of U.S. copyright makes it more difficult to track down owners of manuscripts, especially when the original donor has died and the rights have passed on to his or her heirs.

A clause in the new law deals with a problem peculiar to the United States: the so-called manufacturing clause. In 1891 in an earlier copyright law, this clause was introduced to protect the fledgling American printing industry. It required that for a work to receive U.S. copyright protection, it had to be printed in the United States. Only a limited number of copies of books printed abroad could be imported for sale in this country (most recently 1,500 copies). The manufacturing clause will be done away with entirely on July 1, 1982.

As our discussion of the new copyright law indicates, authors are now much better protected than they were. Whether the balance has swung too far toward protection and away from use of copyrighted works, only time will tell. The new law provides for a review of the law and how it is working every five years, so that changes can be discussed and if necessary adopted.

SUGGESTED READINGS

Several good books on publishing are suitable as background reading for all chapters of Part One. The most important of these are:

Dessauer, John P. *Book Publishing: What It Is, What It Does.* New York: R. R. Bowker Co., 1974.

While Dessauer covers the creation and production of books, he concentrates heavily on the financial aspects of book publishing. This is the most recent general book on the American publishing world.

Grannis, Chandler P. (ed.). *What Happens in Book Publishing.* 2d ed. New York: Columbia University Press, 1967.

This is an older work that still retains its value, particularly for its discussion of various types of publishers. The chapters on production, manufacturing, and sales have suffered most from the passage of time.

These two works, which are devoted exclusively to how books

are created, are highly recommended for readers who wish to gain further knowledge of the various processes involved in editing, production, and design.

Greenfeld, Howard. *Books: From Writer to Reader*. New York: Crown Publishers, Inc., 1976.

While written for young adults, this book serves as a basic primer for all who are interested in book publishing. It does not talk down to its readers and is particularly good at offering clear, simple explanations of the many technical processes involved in printing. There are excellent illustrations.

Lee, Marshall. *Bookmaking: The Illustrated Guide to Design/Production/Editing*. 2d ed. New York: R. R. Bowker Company, 1979.

This has long been considered the best guide to the techniques of design and production, and has recently been expanded to cover editing as well. Because of its wealth of detail and the many clear illustrations and diagrams, Lee's book is the outstanding source of information in the field.

For the subject of copyright, the following are recommended as basic reading:

American Library Association. *Washington Newsletter*, Special Issue . . . on New Copyright Law, 28 (Nov. 15, 1976).

Holley, Edward G. "A Librarian Looks at the New Copyright Law." *American Libraries*, 8 (May 1977), 247–257.

Both of the readings listed above examine the new copyright law from the point of view of the librarian—most particularly the problem of photocopying. For an examination of the law from the point of view of the publisher, see:

Wagner, Susan. "New Copyright Law Primer. Part 1: The Basics. Part 2: The Formalities." *Publishers Weekly*, 212 (Dec. 26, 1977), 37–42; 213 (Jan. 30, 1978), 65–70.

CHAPTER TWO
Distributing Library Materials

FROM PUBLISHER TO BOOKSELLER OR LIBRARY: SELLING THE BOOK

Now that the book has been printed and bound, it is ready for its consumers—retail booksellers, wholesale jobbers, libraries, and, eventually, readers. But before the book can be sent out of the warehouse, it must be priced. A preliminary price may have been established at the time manufacturing was begun, or even as early as when the contract was signed, but unforeseen delays or additional manufacturing costs may have changed the picture. The sales picture may also be different, thus changing the printing quantity. All these factors will necessitate a reexamination of the price.

Pricing the Book

Undoubtedly most librarians—and even some people in the publishing trade—see the pricing of a book as a mysterious and not very rational business. Librarians undoubtedly feel that there is only one constant factor in this last quarter of the twentieth century: Book prices have continually gone up. However, for every book there is a

31

"get out" or "break-even" point that must be carefully calculated. This involves several determining factors of which librarians should be aware in order to understand better why books cost so much and why they may vary so in price. We have spoken (in connection with estimating production costs) of certain manufacturing and editorial costs. Let us examine these again and in greater detail. Costs are of two types: fixed costs and costs per copy. Fixed costs remain the same no matter how many copies are printed or sold; costs per copy will vary with the quantity produced.

Fixed costs include the following: editorial costs (the cost of acquiring the manuscript and preparing it for the printer); certain production costs (designing the book, typesetting, making plates, preparing illustrations, etc.); marketing (advertising, free copies for reviewers, and the cost of maintaining a sales force); and finally, general administrative and overhead costs (rent, heat, light—any of the myriad costs of running a publishing house). The costs that vary with the quantity sold are, first of all, the author's royalty, then manufacturing costs (paper, printing, binding), and finally, the cost of selling each copy (invoicing, packing, shipping).

A further major factor must be considered when calculating the break-even point: the various discounts allowed to retail booksellers, wholesalers, and librarians who buy the book. This discount varies according to the buyer (wholesale jobbers, since they are middlemen, receive a higher discount than most retailers or librarians, who deal directly with the publisher) and according to the type of book (trade books carry the highest discounts, scholarly and professional materials considerably less).

Once all the above costs are calculated, the retail price can be set. It is hoped that the publisher, before signing the contract, will have made sure that the income will cover all expenses. Some books, because of inordinately high manufacturing costs or low projected sales, may require subsidy. This is true of many scholarly and university press books. Some books may not turn a profit in the original hardbound edition but, through the sale of paperback or book-club rights, may eventually become very profitable. There are always a few books on which some publishers will take a risk because they believe that they should be published even though they will never recover their costs. It is hoped that the publisher will produce other books that will return a handsome profit and keep the firm in business. One thing that a publisher hopes for is large sales, as the fixed costs can then be spread over a larger number of copies and thus be minimized. Another determining factor is the axiom that the lower the price, the greater the number of copies that will be sold. Somewhere along the line there is a "best" price, the price that will return the maximum profit to the publisher. While a certain amount of individual decision making based on prior experience always goes into setting a retail price, the publisher can calculate the options fairly closely and make valid decisions. Prior experience will largely tell a publisher what the market will bear—how high the book can be priced without being priced out of the market. It is certainly true that a publisher who makes wrong decisions in this area will not stay long in business.

Wholesalers, Retailers, and Direct Sales

Once the price has been set, the book is ready to be sold. Sold to whom? First of all, it goes to a wholesaler, who sells to bookstores and/or to libraries, or it may go directly to these outlets. With the vast number of titles being published each year, many retail bookstores and libraries prefer to centralize their ordering by dealing with a wholesale jobber. This part of the book industry was much stronger prior to World War II than it is now. Many jobbers have fallen prey to hard times, to bad management, and most of all, to the difficulty of surviving on the narrow margin of discounts between what they receive from a publisher and what bookstores and libraries demand of them. At the present time, trade publishers grant wholesalers a top discount of about 47 percent, while retailers get about 44 percent. While most libraries and certainly some retail booksellers do not expect to get 44 percent when dealing with a wholesaler, they still expect about 30 to 40 percent, which gives the wholesale jobber little to work on. Some wholesalers deal exclusively with libraries, others with retail booksellers, and some with both.

Besides the centralization of orders for many publishers in one source, libraries find wholesalers useful because they are located nearer to their customers, particularly those far away from the Eastern publishing centers; thus, they can supply many titles far faster than can the publisher. Furthermore it is difficult for the publisher to deal with orders for a single copy of one title on a rush basis. The disadvantage comes when the wholesaler does not have the title wanted in stock or does not have enough copies to supply the retailer's or library's needs and has to reorder from the publisher. This will probably take longer than if the retailer or library had ordered directly. However, with the increasing installation of computer linkups between library and wholesaler and between wholesaler and publisher, this disadvantage should largely be overcome.

If the wholesale situation is not entirely satisfactory for book distribution in the United States, the retail situation is even less so. While the R. R. Bowker Company reported in 1973 the existence of some 12,000 "book outlets of all kinds," only 4,000 of these were members of the American Booksellers Association (ABA). Of these, 600 are variety stores in which the selling of books is only a sideline, and a further 2,000 are small bookstores with an annual volume of $100,000 or less. There are only 200 large bookstores with annual sales of over $250,000 in the whole United States. What is even more disturbing are the vast areas of this country that have no retail book outlets at all. The majority of the members of the ABA are concentrated in the Northeast, one or two states in the Midwest, and California. Two recent developments in the retail book trade are of interest. The first is the expansion of many college bookstores to include large stocks of trade books. Today 500 of them are members of the ABA, out of a total of 2,000 that belong to the National Association of College Stores. The other recent development has been the rising importance of the bookstore chain. The largest of these are the Walden Book Company, Pickwick Book Stores, and B. Dalton Booksellers. Most of the chain stores limit their stock to current hardback best sellers, cookbooks, Bibles, and dictionaries, with a smattering of standard titles. Most of the depth in their stock comes from the paperbacks they handle. Most communities do not have a general bookstore in which genuine book addicts can find what they want or need. Even more likely to go unsatisfied are the persons who have specialized or professional needs. Even in a city the size of Los Angeles there is only one scientific and technical bookstore.

Some sales are made directly from the publisher to libraries. While some publishers discourage individual single-copy sales and most do not give very large discounts on such sales, others—usually the more specialized publishing houses—welcome direct orders. Large reference sets, such as encyclopedias, are almost always sold this way rather than through a jobber or retailer. Many direct sales from publishers to libraries are made on approval plans or such all-inclusive sales arrangements as the Greenaway Plan. All of these plans involve the automatic shipment of books as they are published and thus permit maximum discounts. (See Chapter Nine for further information on these plans.)

The Sales Process

Now that we have identified where publishers make their sales, we shall examine how this is done. Most trade publishers maintain sales departments headed by a sales manager, who is often the third-ranking individual in the firm. Under the manager there are numerous salespersons who work on a salary plus a bonus based on how much they sell. Smaller trade publishers that cannot afford a sales staff or at least enough to cover every part of the United States often utilize commission persons who work independently and represent several firms. They are paid a 10 to 12 percent commission on what they sell. Some smaller trade houses may prefer to have their books marketed by a larger publisher to avoid the necessity of maintaining any kind of sales staff. Each salesperson works a certain territory. Big trade publishers may have a sales force as large as 100. Several persons are assigned to one territory, each handling accounts according to his or her experience and abilities.

A sales campaign begins twice a year in each trade publishing house with a ritual *sales conference*. For many years trade publishers had two publishing *seasons* in which they launched the majority of their titles: one in the fall in time to catch the very lucrative Christmas trade and another in the spring. Seasonal catalogs are prepared to announce the books; these form the basis of the sales force's working tools. The situation is now a little more complicated, as some publishers have added winter and summer seasons as well—although these tend to include fewer books. At each sales conference, someone within the publishing house (a member of the editorial staff or perhaps the sales manager) makes a presentation for each book on the list. The purpose is to give the salespeople as complete a picture of that item as possible so that they have all the information they need in order to answer questions once they get out in the field. Besides the seasonal catalog, the sales staff are given book jackets, sample pages, and illustrations to aid them in their work. They are also sometimes given galley proofs or advance copies of books. It is hoped that they will read as many as possible in order to know intimately the titles they are selling.

Following the sales conference, the sales personnel hit the road and begin to call on their customers. These may be wholesale jobbers or retail outlets. Retail bookstores are usually called on four times a year, wholesalers more often. Good salespeople know their customers, what type of material will sell well in a particular area and what will not. They make recommendations not only about the titles a particular store or wholesaler should stock but also in what quantity. As part of their visit, they check the stock on hand to see how previously ordered books have sold. At this time, they arrange for the return of unsold items that are not moving, since one of the privileges granted to any retailer or wholesaler by most U.S. trade publishers is the right to return unsold merchandise (as long as it is undamaged) for full credit after it has been in stock for about three months. These return privileges end after one year, and they involve some expense to the dealer, who must pay return transportation costs.

The terms on which trade books are sold to retail bookstores and wholesalers vary according to the quantities ordered. Quantities may be of one title or they may be assorted. The average discount to a retailer is 40 percent off the list price. Higher discounts—up to 44 percent for retailers and 47 percent to wholesalers—come into play only with very large quantity orders.

Some retail bookstores do not have managers who are knowledgeable enough to decide what to order and in what quantity. Thus many trade publishers offer automatic distribution plans in which the salespeople decide which titles in what quantities will go to an individual store. Small stores are thus assured of getting best sellers promptly at the best discount possible and of having certain popular backlist titles in stock.

The problem of returns is one that constantly plagues publishers. If a title is ordered in great quantity by bookstores and then fails to sell, the publisher may still believe that it is a best seller, only to find a flood of unsold copies coming back some six months to a year later. This makes the planning of reprintings very difficult. Only salespeople, through their calls on stores and wholesalers, will know how a particular title is doing.

The Library and School Markets

Little has been said so far about the library market. Here there is a difference of opinion between some librarians and some publishers on the effectiveness of sales calls. Most librarians feel that this is not the most efficient method, but a few publishers continue to maintain sales staff whose duty it is to call on libraries. Encyclopedias and large reference sets can still be sold effectively this way, as the librarian often has the opportunity to examine the set firsthand, but librarians in general prefer to be served in other ways. The large publishing houses—of all types, not just trade houses—have now established library and school promotion departments. Originally these departments dealt largely with children's books, but they now promote all types of materials. These departments are often staffed by former librarians who have entered the publishing business or salespeople who have had long experience in dealing with libraries and schools. Their duty is not to sell particular titles but rather to get to know people in authority, those who initiate large orders and influence sales. These salespeople are the eyes and ears of the publisher within the library and school worlds, who try to keep ahead of trends and assess needs—a particular reference book, new subject matter for juveniles, a new type of reader for adults just beginning to read, etc. They explain company policies about discounts, standing order, or approval plans. Contacts are made individually with library leaders and large systems, but this is often carried out in conjunction with national and state library and school conferences, where many people will be assembled together. In recent years, the library promotion departments of some large publishers have begun to issue newsletters to keep their library customers informed of developments within the house. These newsletters may feature announcements of books of particular interest to librarians or excerpts from reviews of recently published titles; they may also include news notes of forthcoming books or of what the publisher is planning. The institutional market is important for the publisher. In some areas, it may represent a huge part of the market—75 to 85 percent for certain types of children's books. It is certainly a steady market, in spite of a loss in the libraries' buying power during the last few years.

As for schools, the situation is similar. Library promotion departments may also handle this part of the publisher's business. Textbook houses generally separate it out into a distinct department. Elementary and secondary textbooks were once sold largely on the basis of citywide or statewide adoption; that is, a central committee or supervisor would choose one textbook for use throughout an entire school system for a certain number of years. Competition was fierce, as an adoption by a state such as Texas could mean millions of dollars in revenue. The trend is now toward multiple adoptions—that is, a list of several texts, all of which are approved, from which the individual school or teacher may select the one desired. In colleges and universities, instructors usually have the right to choose their own textbooks. Salespeople call on those persons responsible for making adoptions. In the case of citywide or statewide adoptions, the sales manager from the home office may be asked to make a presentation since so much is at stake. School and library promotion departments work largely to maintain contacts with persons of authority within the school systems and to sense trends which the publisher can follow up, in the hope of producing needed materials before competitors do.

Mail Orders and Book Clubs

Because of the limited number of book outlets in the United States, there has grown up in recent years a large business devoted to supplying individual customers directly. This is done in two ways: through book clubs and through direct mail-order service. Let us examine the direct mail-order business first. Publishers or retail booksellers can choose to market their wares through the mails by preparing catalogs or brochures, sending them to persons on a mailing list, and filling the orders as they come in. Many professional and scholarly titles are currently sold in considerable quantity this way. How else does one reach all the physicians or lawyers scattered in tiny communities across the land? This type of mail-order business is of little interest to libraries. However, there is another type of mail-order publishing of which librarians should be aware—that of designing and publishing books just for marketing by mail. This type of mail-order publishing has been in existence only about twenty years and was developed largely by mass magazine publishers that were seeking to diversify. Much of the material published is derived from the magazine itself, and the works are often compilations or the work of a staff rather than a single author. American Heritage histories are one example, Time-Life books another. All have become familiar items to the average American family, and some have found their way into public or school library collections.

Mail-order publishing is limited to very popular topics, as the publisher aims to market editions of hundreds of thousands of copies. Careful market research must be done before a title is launched. The first step is to develop an elaborate and eye-catching brochure, which is mailed to millions of potential customers. If the publisher receives a 1½ to 2 percent return of orders from the mailings, this is considered good. Thus it can be seen that mail-order publishing requires a very large investment for every title published. A title must also be fairly expensive for the venture to pay off. Finally the availability of good mailing lists is an essential ingredient for success. Mail-order publishing is a risky business, but the financial rewards can be very great; thus more and more publishers are tempted by it. This type of business is bound to grow in the coming years.

The other type of direct marketing—through book clubs—has been discussed previously in connection with royalties and author's rights. It has been with us since the mid-1920s, when the two giants of the industry, the Book-of-the-Month Club and the Literary Guild, were founded. In recent years the field has mushroomed, with the starting up of many specialized book clubs; it is almost impossible to ascertain how many clubs exist at the present time. The best guess is between 130 and 150. The Book-of-the-Month Club now boasts of a membership of 1.25 million, the Literary Guild of 800,000. The more specialized clubs vary from a few thousand members to close to 100,000 in the case of Doubleday's Military Book Club. The subjects covered range from the environment and outdoor life to cooking and embroidery by way of real estate, accounting, and electronics. The customers are there, waiting in their living rooms to buy the books they cannot get in their local stores; or, confused by all that is available in some large stores, they are waiting to have their books chosen for them.

Book clubs were at first resented by publishers and bookstores alike. That attitude seems to have changed as more and more publishers have grown to depend upon the sale of book-club rights to contribute additional income and as more and more bookstore owners have discovered that book clubs give free publicity to many titles and thus increase sales. Librarians need to be aware of which titles have been chosen by book clubs, as, at least in public libraries, selection may mean increased demand for these titles from library patrons. (Some small public libraries maintain subscriptions to one or more of the general-interest book clubs; see Chapter Nine.) All librarians should know that it is now very rare for one book club, even the Book-of-the-Month Club or Literary Guild, to demand and get exclusive rights to a title. Thus one book may appear on several book-club lists either as a main selection or as an alternate.

As has already been indicated, book clubs usually prepare their own editions, often on cheaper paper and with a cheaper binding. Thus they can offer their wares at lower prices, although this is usually done only for the main selection(s), which have large print runs. For alternate selections (and increasingly members are demanding a wider choice of books), the book club may have to get in on a publisher's regular print run and thus offer only a small discount. All book clubs operate on about the same basis. They offer free books or books at very low cost in order to attract members. These members are then required to purchase a certain number of books during the first year or so. After fulfilling this initial obligation, customers then begin receiving bonus books for every so many titles they buy. If people shop wisely, they can build a library at considerable savings, pocketing the discount that usually goes into the hands of the retail bookseller or the wholesale jobber. One essential element of most book-club operations is the *negative option*, a practice that has come under attack by consumer groups and has been threatened with regulation by the Federal Trade Commission. Under this plan, members receive the main selection each time *unless* they send back a card telling the publisher that they do *not* want it. Through oversight or sheer laziness, many customers end up getting—and paying for—many titles they do not want. Book clubs insist they could not operate any other way, although one or two small ones are trying a *positive option* plan. Most book clubs experience considerable turnover in membership, two years being about average. There is also the problem of those who fail to pay their bills but keep the books. Book clubs are certainly here to stay, however, and do play an essential role in the distribution of books in this country.

MAKING THE BOOK KNOWN

Even before trade publishers start to inform their salespeople about the new books on their list, their publicity staffs will be hard at work trying to think up ways of making the book known to potential readers. A book, once it is in the bookstores, has to sell itself. That is why so much trouble is taken to design eye-catching book jackets. In addition, salespeople attempt to get special display space for a book in the store and sometimes provide posters or specially designed display racks. (Cardboard bins are often used to exhibit certain mass paperback titles that a publisher wishes to push.) But before a book reaches the bookstore, other things must have been done to make the book known.

The Publisher's Catalog

The first and most obvious step is to include the book in the publisher's seasonal catalog and in its complete list of titles in print. These catalogs are of prime importance to both book dealers and librarians. Complete catalogs (which are issued by most publishers— trade or otherwise) are usually arranged alphabetically by author and title; if they are to be useful tools, they must include the author's complete name and complete title, year of publication, and price. The International Standard Book Number (ISBN) is now also usually included. Seasonal catalogs, however, vary a great deal in arrangement and presentation. They are usually heavily illustrated in order to catch the reader's attention. Some titles will get feature presentation; others will seem almost afterthoughts. Arrangement within the catalog can be by publication date, subject, or publishing imprint, or in a simple alphabetical arrangement. Sometimes there seems to be no logical arrangement at all. Whatever the order, unless it is strictly alphabetical, an index is needed by librarians (but unfortunately not always provided). In addition to the items mentioned above for the complete title catalog, the seasonal catalog should include the exact publication date (month, as well as year) and some description of the book. If prepublication reviews have already appeared, quotations— with references to the exact source—can be helpful, although librarians should be aware that an isolated sentence can often present a very distorted image of the complete review. The Library of

Congress (LC) card number is a help to librarians, as is any information as to whether the publisher's books carry Cataloging-in-Publication (CIP) data. Finally, information on the book's physical size and its availability in various editions (hardbound, paperback) is necessary. With audio-visual materials, exact details about the format and whether the visuals consist of artwork or photographs should be included.

In addition to catalogs, the publicity or advertising department produces fliers about most of the books on a publisher's forthcoming list. These are much more lengthy descriptions of the book and its author. These fliers will be sent to booksellers, book reviewers, and librarians. The book itself, when ready, or galleys of the book in advance, are important publicity tools. To get these into the hands of influential people, people who will talk about the book, is one of the main tasks of a publisher's publicity department.

Publicity in Print

Publicity about a book is usually divided into two main types: book reviews and book news columns and then everything else "off the book page." Book reviews and book news columns reach only a limited number of people. First of all, most newspapers and magazines in the United States devote very little space to book reviews and news; secondly, even fewer people read what is available. However, should a TV talk show host or hostess mention a book, or should the editor of the gardening or cooking section of a newspaper recommend a gardening book or cookbook, the effect on sales will predictably be much greater, since the message will reach a wider audience. Publicity directors therefore spend a great deal of time trying to think up new ways of getting information about a specific new book to the public.

The standard ways of publicizing a book are always tried first; most important is to get the book reviewed. Even a bad review is better than no review, as at least someone will have been made aware of the book's existence. Regrettably the book-reviewing media can handle only a fraction of the books published each year. The largest of them—*Library Journal* and CHOICE—each review only 6,000 to 6,500 titles a year out of a total of 38,000 new books that the R. R. Bowker Company estimates are published in the United States. Professional books can hope to find review exposure only in professional journals directed to a specialized group of readers. Thus librarians cannot expect to find reviews of all the books they may want to consider for purchase in any one place. Several sources must always be used. The publicist also faces the problem of getting the book reviewed as promptly as possible. For very important general review media, the publishing house will make available galley proofs of certain of its titles some four to six months ahead of the publication date. While authors have the privilege of revising their work in galley proof stage and while galley proofs do not include any illustrations, tables, charts, or maps and certainly no index, they do provide the only really good notice a publisher can give of a book's content far enough in advance of publication for a review medium to prepare a review prior to or at the time of publication. In spite of its shortcomings, reviewing from galley proofs is widely done for novels and for popular nonfiction. It is rarely done for scholarly or professional books or for reference materials.

Since galley proofs are expensive, a publisher sends them out to relatively few review sources. For the majority of reviewers the publicity department dispatches copies of the finished trade book some four to six weeks ahead of the publication date—at about the same time the books are being distributed to wholesalers and retailers. The review copy will contain a slip indicating such essential information for the reviewer as author, title, publication date, and price (for both hardbound and paperback editions if both should be available). In general the review media are asked to respect the publication date and not publish any review for the general public in advance. This avoids putting booksellers in the difficult position of not having copies of books that have been mentioned in the local press or national news magazines. [Book review media addressed to the "trade" (that is, booksellers and librarians) do not have such restrictions; in fact, they strive to get their reviews out as soon as possible.] Along with the book, the publicity department often sends one of its fliers and sometimes photographs of the author or of illustrations from the book that may be of use to the review journal. The review slip requests that two copies of any review be sent to the publisher.

While review copies do not cost as much as galley proofs, the number of copies sent out can mount up considerably; thus, most publishers find it necessary to limit review copies. The total number of review copies of a popular trade title sent out is anywhere from 250 to 500; for specialized titles the number is less, but still 50 to 100. For very expensive sets it may be limited to a very few, and some publishers may even ask for the return of the sets after review. However, this is difficult to control and may even be difficult to justify since reviewers in most professional journals get no pay for their work and expect to be able to keep the book they have reviewed. In order to control the number of review copies, publishers place only a few very important review journals on their "A" list to receive copies automatically of everything published. Most review journals will be sent an advance copy of the seasonal catalog along with a list to check off those titles they wish to see for review. Some publishers may do the choosing themselves, particularly for scholarly professional journals in which the selection is fairly obvious. Review journals may also request certain books if they fail to receive a copy of something they feel is especially important for their readers and should therefore be reviewed. Failure on the part of the publishing house to send out review copies can have a very serious effect on sales. Trade houses realize this and generally make sure that their lines of communication to the important review media remain open. Unfortunately, small presses, many of those representing minority interests, and some scholarly and professional publishers, do not take reviewing as seriously as they should. Thus the inability of librarians to find reviews of certain types of materials is often the fault of the publishers themselves.

Some publications have book news columns in addition to book reviews. Most of this news is derived from the fliers sent out by publishers. Librarians need to learn to differentiate between this publicity-type news and real reviews based on disinterested opinions.

Publicity in Person

When it comes to "off the book page" publicity, publicists have free rein for their imaginations. It is hoped that all efforts will result in special stories or features about the book or its author in a newspaper or magazine or on radio or TV. If a work is a special-interest book, appealing to a particular audience, then attempts are usually made to reach that audience through its regular sources of information. For example, if a publicist can get the financial editor of a magazine or newspaper to take an interest in and mention a new book on the stock market, this will be far better than a review in the general book review section. Since much effective book publicity is by word of mouth, publicists seek to influence certain opinion makers by sending them free copies of the book in the hope that they will talk or write about it.

Every trade publishing house also tries to use its most popular authors to promote their own books. Some authors, of course, do not have the flair for public appearances, but those who do are booked for interviews, lectures, press conferences, and autographing parties, both in New York City and throughout the country. Publishers' cocktail parties are another possibility. Conventions of booksellers, librarians, or members of different professions often provide focal points for such appearances. The most sought-after exposure is on

the TV talk show. *Publishers Weekly* regularly runs a column announcing such appearances. Awards are another source of publicity for
publishers, and publicists must make the necessary submissions to
juries. For a children's book to win the Newbery or Caldecott Award
is a sure sign of increased sales. Exhibits at professional meetings are
also important for book publishers. Very few will consider missing
the annual national library meetings or those of the major professional societies. Even state meetings draw the larger publishers. At library
conventions such exhibits are often in the hands of the firm's library
promotion person.

Publicity through Advertising

One of the most costly ways of promoting a book—and to many
publishers one of the least effective—is to advertise it. The purpose of
advertising is to increase the sales by creating readers. Besides being
directed to the individual consumer, advertising can also be done
merely to influence the trade, that is, to get booksellers to stock a
certain title and to push its sales rather than a competitor's.
Advertising can also be done to influence reviewers so that they will
decide to cover one book rather than another or to give more review
space to a particular title. It is true that review media are very much
aware of what is being promoted simply by the avalanche of publicity
releases that come to their desks. If a book is being heavily promoted,
they may feel that they should have their say, even if only to
denigrate it. Publishers may also advertise a work in order to
influence the sale of subsidiary rights. By keeping a book on the
best-seller list an extra few weeks, they may be able to get a better
price for the paperback rights or in a movie sale. Finally, some books
are advertised, or advertised more than their sales warrant, simply to
keep an author or his or her agent happy.

While advertising can help sell more copies of a book that is
already selling, many people believe that it can do little to push a
book that the public is just not interested in buying. There is always
an optimum point for advertising after which no further investment
will help boost sales. The advertising manager's job in a publishing
house is to ascertain just when that point has been reached.

The greatest difficulty with advertising books (unlike advertising soap products, for example) is that each item is different. Thus the
advertising for each book must be planned separately. Each adver-
tisement is different from the previous one. During a particular two-
or three-month period, it may be possible to use the same ad in two or
three different journals, but that will be the maximum repetition
possible.

Rates for advertising vary largely according to the number of subscribers to the magazine—that is, with the number of potential readers or industry figures who will be reached—and according to the size of the ad. Full-page ads in professional journals will cost far less than a one-eighth-page ad in *The New York Times*.

Publicity budgets in trade houses are often set at 10 percent of the projected net sales of the book. The amount available for advertising a new novel may be no more than $2,000 or $3,000. This must cover advertising to the trade (in *PW* and the library journals), consumer advertising in newspapers and popular magazines, sales promotion to dealers, the cost of review copies and catalogs, and finally, the advertising department's own overhead and general expenses. This is very difficult to accomplish on such a small budget.

Trade ads appear first, often before publication, in order to bring new titles to the attention of booksellers and librarians. These ads often give the exact date of publication (month and year). Consumer ads are placed in newspapers—the book sections of the major metropolitan dailies and, most importantly, *The New York Times Book Review*—and in general-interest magazines. Local advertising, usually in collaboration with a local bookseller who can get more favorable rates, is usually done in the home town of the author or in the locality depicted in the book. Advertising in *The New York Times* is very expensive and so is done only for very popular titles. Most scholarly and special-interest books are more effectively advertised in professional and special-interest journals, where the advertising rates are relatively low and where the publisher is more sure of a good response from readers. Most publishers feel that trade advertising is essential, and even the smallest houses will try and place some ad listing their major new titles in *PW* and in the library journals at least once or twice a year. Librarians will find the advertisements in the spring and fall announcement numbers of *PW*, *LJ*, and CHOICE of particular interest for selection and acquisition purposes.

Finally, what has been said here about distributing trade books can also be applied in general to other types of books and printed materials, as well as nonprint items. Differences with other materials will be brought out in Chapters Three and Four.

SUGGESTED READINGS

Both the Dessauer book and the Grannis book mentioned at the end of Chapter One will provide background reading for this chapter as well. In addition the following articles give added information on the specific topics mentioned in the titles.

Coqui, pseud. "Selecting the Retail Price." *Publishers Weekly*, 193 (Apr. 1, 1968), 15–17.

Dessauer, John P. "Some Hard Facts about the Economics of Fiction." *Publishers Weekly*, 206 (Aug. 5, 1974), 22–25.

Fast, Betty. "Publishers' Catalogs: Puffery or Resource?" *Wilson Library Bulletin*, 51 (Oct. 1976), 178–179.

Kayle, Hilary S. "Booking Authors on the 'Today' Program: An Insider's Account." *Publishers Weekly*, 215 (Feb. 5, 1979), 57–58.

Walker, Greta. "Making the Rounds with Zeb Burgess: A Week in the Life of a Harper Book Salesman. . . ." *Publishers Weekly*, 204 (July 30, 1973), 52–57.

Weyr, Thomas. "The Booming Book Clubs." *Publishers Weekly*, 201 (Mar. 13, 1972), 36–42; 201 (Mar. 20, 1972), 28–36; 201 (Apr. 3, 1972), 26–29.

CHAPTER THREE
Types of Publishers

Most of what has been said about publishing up to this point has been confined to one type of publishing, that of adult *trade books*—those books, fiction and popular nonfiction, found in the average bookstore catering to the general public. Librarians, however, buy many other kinds of materials, and it is now time to say something about these materials—how they are authored, how they are edited and printed, and how they are marketed to their respective audiences. We shall start with those types that form part of the merchandise of most trade bookstores—children's books, paperbacks (both mass market and trade), and religious books. We shall then go on to technical and professional books and to textbooks. Reference and subscription books are very important to librarians and so must be dealt with at some length. Then there are the fine publications of the many university and scholarly presses, as well as those published by the many small presses—as varied a collection of presses as there are ideas in this country. Something must also be said about self-publishing and the so-called "vanity" presses. Finally there are periodicals and micro-forms. Audio-visual materials, computer-based materials, and such specialized materials as those for the handi-capped and government documents, all of which form extensive parts of library collections today, will be discussed in Chapter Four.

CHILDREN'S BOOKS

Most trade book publishers have children's book departments. There are also a few publishing houses that publish nothing but children's books. While the general steps in publishing a children's book are the same as those we have outlined for adult trade books, there are some differences. These are caused mostly by the fact that illustrations are an important element—sometimes the overriding one—in children's books. Thus more attention must be paid to the design element and to the choice of an illustrator and the results of his or her work. Unsolicited manuscripts are still a good source of children's books, in contrast to adult trade books. Literary agents began to work in this field only in the early 1960s.

The work of a children's book editor is often more detailed than that of an adult trade book editor. The text of most children's books is fairly brief and will be gone over word by word many times. The editor, rather than the author, usually decides who will illustrate a particular book. Thus the editor must be aware of the different styles of the leading book illustrators and be able to sense who will do the best job—that is, be most sensitive to the mood of the book. Royalties for illustrated children's books must be split between the author of the text and the illustrator. For a children's picture book the average 10 percent royalty is usually divided fifty-fifty. With other children's books, the split depends on the proportion of text to illustrations. Only popular, best-selling children's authors can command more than 10 percent royalties.

The book designer, not the illustrator, has ultimate control over the book. It is the designer who decides the size of the book, the typeface, and how much and what type of color can be used. The illustrator may want to use a panoply of colors but is usually restricted by financial considerations. The illustrator will usually be limited to a few basic colors—three or four—and their combinations, sometimes to only one or two. The designer works with the illustrator to see that the illustrations can be reproduced as the illustrator wishes. The designer must also work closely with the production staff since children's books come in a multitude of formats and sizes and often require unusual type sizes and sometimes special paper.

The marketing of children's books varies a great deal according to whether the books are aimed at the school and library market or at the mass market. Those aimed at schools and libraries are also sold in quality bookstores, but 75 to 85 percent of them will be bought by schools and libraries. These are the higher-priced children's books, each individually designed. A special library prebinding will often be prepared for those institutions that feel the need for a stronger binding than is found on the regular trade edition.

Children's books aimed at the mass market are usually older titles that are now in the public domain and for which no royalty has to be paid or repackaged titles for which a reduced royalty has been negotiated. Mass-market children's books are planned for sale in all types of outlets, including supermarkets and wherever magazines are sold. They are printed in much larger quantities and are sold at much lower prices than those marketed for schools and libraries. Furthermore they are often sold and publicized as series. Among the best known of these are "Golden Books" and "Wonder Books." A recent development in the children's field has been the launching of children's paperbacks. Like the hardcover mass-market juveniles, these are generally reprints of older titles. Many of them contain color illustrations. Large printings are standard in order to maintain low prices. Both mass-market and trade publishers are bringing out children's paperbacks. Another recent development has been the phenomenal success of student book clubs. Scholastic Book Services and Xerox Education Publications have operated these for a number of years. The book clubs were made possible by the advent of the children's paperback. The student book clubs operate through the classroom rather than through sales to the home.

Little publicity is undertaken for any children's books in consumer magazines. Most of it is concentrated in periodicals aimed at the book trade and libraries. Review copies are sent to large school and library systems as well as to the journals that review children's books (not all do, as we shall see later). The R. R. Bowker Company publishes an annual *Children's Books in Print* as well as a *Subject Guide to Children's Books in Print*. Each spring and fall, *Publishers Weekly* has a special children's book number listing new titles forthcoming over the next few months. *Library Journal* and *Booklist* also have special children's book issues which feature advertising for new titles. All this information enables the librarian to keep up with developments in this specialized field. One of the most knowledgeable persons, and one who is much in evidence at the publishers' exhibits at library conventions, is the school and library promotion person for the publishing house. Unlike promoters of adult books, these people have an intimate knowledge of each title on the publisher's list and can be of great help to an undecided librarian.

PAPERBACKS

Paperbound books are so much a part of the intellectual life of the last part of the twentieth century that it is hard to realize that they have not always been with us, and certainly not as parts of library collections. The truth is that the first paperbacks, as we know them today, were not published in the United States until 1939, when Pocket Books was founded, issuing largely reprint titles at 25 cents each. Pocket Books had been preceded in England by Penguin Books, founded by Sir Allen Lane in 1935. While paperbound dime novels had existed in the second half of the nineteenth century, these were mostly pirated works and were killed off in the United States by the Copyright Act of 1891. Attempts in the 1920s to launch paperbacks failed because of distribution problems. Pocket Books was able to solve this problem by linking its distribution and sales to magazine dealers rather than to traditional book dealers. Thus was born what we today know as *mass-market paperbacks.*

Paperbacks were given a great boost by the introduction of "Armed Forces Editions" during World War II. Returning servicemen and women who had grown accustomed to this new type of book formed a ready market for paperbacks, and the years following World War II saw several other firms enter the field: Bantam, New American Library, Dell, Avon, and Fawcett. From a mere 112 mass-market titles in 1945, the number of works published annually grew to approximately 4,000 by 1977. The number of paperback books sold in 1977 rose by 7.3 percent over the previous year to 531.2 million. While there are signs that business is leveling off, mass-market paperbacks remain an important part of the book trade and reach untold millions who would not otherwise be able to buy a book. This is because paperbacks are sold in all types of magazine outlets, drugstores, supermarkets, airport terminals—wherever a wire rack can be put up and serviced by the local magazine and newspaper distributor.

A second revolution in the paperback industry occurred in 1953, when Jason Epstein of Doubleday launched Anchor Books. Instead of the popular titles that had been (and continue to be) the mainstay of mass-market paperbacks, Epstein chose to reprint serious, scholarly works. These became known as *trade paperbacks,* and while they carried a higher price tag, they were printed on better-quality paper and had more solid bindings. They were aimed particularly at a new type of college course that required collateral reading in a variety of works rather than in one textbook or anthology. Once Anchor Books proved to be a success, various types of publishers jumped into the market. It is rare today to find a publisher of hardbound books that does not also publish paperback editions of its own works or arrange for the reprinting of its titles by other publishers. Trade paperbacks, as the name implies, rely upon the traditional trade channels for distribution and are more often sold in regular bookstores than at magazine distribution points. The latter distinction, however, is becoming somewhat blurred as stores stocking only paperbacks have come into existence and as magazine outlets have sought to increase the variety of their book stock. Between 8,500 and 9,000 trade paperbacks are now issued each year.

While the mainstay of paperback publishing has always been the reprint, original paperbacks have come to assume an important place as well. Penguin Books had been a pioneer in this phase of the industry; many U.S. publishers soon followed suit. Original paperbacks can be found in both the mass-market and trade categories. Many of the light romances, gothic novels, or westerns sold by the mass-market paperback houses are originals and are never published in hardback format. Also certain scholarly or professional books or books for a very limited, special audience are economically feasible only in paperback editions, which can be priced low enough to encourage a wide sale to the particular audience. Reprint editions offer a clear advantage to the paperback publisher for several reasons. First of all, the market has already been tested and the book has been reviewed. (A perennial problem for the publisher of original paperbacks is getting the books reviewed, as many review journals pay little or no attention to paperbacks.) Secondly, there are no editorial costs, no need to maintain an expensive staff. Then, since paperbacks represent a subsidiary right, there are reduced royalty charges (largely made up for the author by much larger editions). Finally, there is the infinite variety of titles from which a reprinter can choose.

Publishers of mass-market paperbacks depend for their success on how quickly and how readily they can respond to the demand of the marketplace for a certain title or for a certain type of work. Every mass-market paperback publisher seeks to have a few blockbusters on the list each year that will sell millions of copies. In recent years, this has led to certain very popular books being auctioned off to the highest bidder. To avoid conflict with sales of the original hardbound edition, the paperback reprinter must usually wait a certain period (usually one year) before putting the new edition on the market. The sales contract then runs for five to seven years, at which time the rights may be sold again to another publisher by the author or the original hardbound publisher. (This causes some confusion for librarians, who find a title reprinted in paperback first by one house and then by another.)

Even though the reprint contract may run for five to seven years, the average life of a mass-market paperback in the retail outlets is only a few weeks or at most a few months; after this, unsold copies are returned to the distributor, and the racks are filled with new titles. One of the main problems facing mass-market publishers and their distributors is that the store's racks will not hold all of the titles published each month. Furthermore, some retailers want to stock and push only the bestsellers, even though statistics show that backlist titles (those published in previous seasons, but still available) often account for the majority of sales and profits.

Mass-market paperbacks are distributed in several ways. More than 50 percent pass through the hands of eleven national paperback distributors, which are generally owned by communications conglomerates. Some are part of the parent publishing house and limit themselves to selling that publisher's books; others are independent and distribute several lines. Publishers also sell directly to bookstores and department store chains and to wholesalers dealing with libraries and schools. They also sell directly to the approximately 450 independent wholesalers of magazines, who operate largely on a regional basis throughout the United States. These wholesalers (often known as IDs—independent distributors) are more often supplied, however, by the eleven national paperback distributors. They, in turn, service the 60,000 to 80,000 retail points of sale, most of them nonbook outlets. One of the great problems of mass-market paperbacks has been the large number of returns (sometimes running to 30 or 35 percent). Mass-market paperback distributors have yet to work out a really satisfactory method of redistributing these books to other points of sale where they might sell better.

Very little advertising or publicity is possible for paperbacks other than to the trade, as the margin of profit on individual titles is very low. Only blockbuster best sellers can be promoted to the general customer. Most paperback publishers rely on self-sale; that is, the cover of the book must do the selling. Therefore they try to arrange for cover-out display as much as possible.

As the foregoing discussion implies, mass-market paperbacks present great problems to libraries that wish to acquire them. First of all, magazine wholesalers, which distribute mass-market paperbacks, are not used to dealing with schools or libraries and cannot be bothered with single-copy or small-order sales. Furthermore they are not equipped to handle orders for backlist titles in an efficient way. As a result, some publishers are attempting to market their titles directly to schools and libraries. A few national distributors have become aware of the potential business to be derived from schools and libraries and are attempting to service them, usually through special staffs. Most libraries wishing to order mass-market paperbacks either depend on a library jobber to handle the order for them or turn directly to the publisher.

Trade paperbacks present no such problems to schools and libraries, since they are marketed through regular book distribution channels. Furthermore their life expectancy is much longer than that of a mass-market paperback, and the backlist is a much more important part of the publisher's and retailer's business. Since trade paperbacks are usually printed on better paper and are better bound than mass-market paperbacks, they have gradually been adopted as essential parts of library collections. While there was clear resistance in the early days to the use of paperbacks in libraries, the development of inexpensive plastic bindings and other means of reinforcing the covers has countered some of this reluctance. The fact that certain out-of-print hardbound titles were available only in paperback forced some libraries to purchase them initially. Once it was shown that they were more durable than they seemed—and furthermore, were extremely popular with readers—the final barriers were broken down. Most recently, paperbacks have begun to look increasingly good to librarians faced with shrinking book budgets. The variety of materials available in paperback makes them essential elements in most libraries. Fortunately the trade and library media now review some paperbacks, particularly if they are originals. Thus librarians have no excuse for omitting from their collections one of the most pervasive elements in contemporary life.

RELIGIOUS BOOKS

It may seem strange to single out books in one subject field for special treatment in a text such as this. However, the publishing of religious books is today increasingly in the hands of specialized religious publishing houses, which operate in a different world than that of trade publishers. Therefore they present certain problems to librarians and need to be examined separately.

Religious books are a big industry but one that lies to a great extent outside the general trade channels. Religious book publishing has followed the changes in religion itself in the United States over the last two decades. The major denominational bodies, almost all of which maintained publishing houses in the past, have experienced declines in membership. Catholic publishing, in particular, has been through a disastrous period which has seen the complete disappearance of such publishers as Bruce, P. J. Kenedy, Benziger Brothers, Herder and Herder, Helicon, and Burns & Oates. Faced with enormous changes within the Catholic Church following Vatican Council II, which outdated most of their backlists, these companies were unable to react swiftly enough, often through lack of capital, but also through lack of vision and foresight, to save their investments and therefore went under. Certain Protestant houses, such as Seabury, underwent difficult periods but, through reorganization, were able to survive. Some of the greatest difficulties have affected the general trade houses which had for many years maintained religious book departments. Because of the great changes in people's attitudes toward religion, they were unable to determine with any success just what a religious book was. The distinction between the books of the religious book department and those of the trade division became increasingly blurred; in a number of cases, the religious department disappeared.

But while this was happening, out in the hinterland, a group of new publishers was springing up in the Bible belt. These houses were publishing books for the huge conservative, evangelical subculture that had never heard of the big New York publishing houses. These people generally bought their books at local "ma and pa" bookstores, often devoted largely to selling religious books, or through the mail directly from the publishers. They were reached through advertising in religious periodicals and literature distributed by their local churches. The result was books that sold in the millions and made more money for their publishers than many titles on the best-seller lists (where they were completely unknown). Most of these books were never reviewed in the general or library book review journals; only denominational periodicals paid any attention to them.

Before proceeding further, let us attempt to define a *religious book*. It is a book published by a religious book specialist, reviewed and advertised largely in religious periodicals, and sold through religious book outlets to persons interested in religion. It is often denomination-oriented. Books published by such houses can be on any topic and can even be novels or poetry, but each title stresses the values espoused by the religious group behind the publishing house. Books about religion itself make up the bulk of such publications. They can be divided into four types: (1) Bibles and other liturgical and service books; (2) inspirational and devotional works for the laity; (3) theological works largely intended for the clergy; and (4) instructional works, including textbooks, intended for religious education.

Such religious works present several problems to publishing houses. First of all, good manuscripts are very hard to find. The average preacher or religious scholar is not a particularly good writer, and often much in-house editorial work needs to be done before manuscripts are ready for publication. Most manuscripts arrive over the transom or are commissioned by a publishing house on the basis of the author's reputation within the field of religion. Very few literary agents work in this field. Furthermore royalties are often less than for trade books, many times based on wholesale rather than retail prices. Lower royalties mean lower retail prices; in general, religious books are priced fifty cents to a dollar less than the average trade book. Religious houses spend far less money on production and design than do trade houses, so that the end product can be rather dull-looking. Advertising budgets are low and are spent largely in religious periodicals. A few of the major houses advertise their forthcoming lists in the semiannual religious book numbers of *PW* or occasionally in CHOICE. Religious publishers depend largely on mail-order sales. Mailing lists are easily obtainable from the parent religious body and offer a carefully targeted audience from which returns should be high. Many denominations publish religious catalogs in which books can also be advertised or listed. Finally some denominations maintain church stores that feature these publications. Some Americans feel safe only when buying books in such stores, as they know that the contents of the books have been approved and will not conflict with their religious beliefs. The same certainty is offered by the religious book clubs, of which there are more than twenty.

For many years, sales of Bibles and other liturgical works were the mainstay of religious publishing houses. Since they sold in the millions, they often subsidized all the other publications of the house. Other religious publishing houses receive subsidies from the parent religious body.

For librarians the selection of religious books has always been difficult. Most public libraries limit themselves to buying Bibles and liturgical works of the major denominations, and to books explaining these works and the history and beliefs of a denomination. Very few, if any, books intended for the indoctrination of the believer are bought. Theological works are left largely to the university library, or more likely to the theological seminary library. But for those religious books that the library does wish to purchase, there remains the problem of finding out about them—who publishes them, where they may be obtained, and what the relative value of their content is. Since the more specialized religious publishing houses, particularly those of the more evangelical faiths, lie outside the mainstream of U.S. trade publishing, the usual information sources will not suffice. It is all too easy for librarians to ignore this material since they see few advertisements or reviews. A conscious attempt must be made to seek out the sources and to ask to be put on mailing lists for catalogs and fliers. If comprehensive collections are to be built up or if the needs of a large body of readers are not to be ignored, then librarians must make the effort to be informed about this type of publishing.

TEXTBOOKS

Textbooks represent a very important part of the book industry in the United States. The Association of American Publishers has estimated that in 1975 textbook sales reached $1.049 billion out of a total of $3.81 billion spent on all types of books. While most of these sales have been to schools and universities and their students, some textbooks find their way into libraries since they are often the only succinct introduction to a field of knowledge. Few libraries can ignore such classic texts as Paul Samuelson's *Economics* or Allan Nevins's and Henry Commager's *Short History of the United States*. Since textbooks are created, manufactured, and sold on a different basis than trade books, it is helpful to examine how this is done.

Since textbook publishing is a lucrative business, many of the big trade publishers, such as Harcourt Brace Jovanovich and Harper & Row, have long had textbook divisions. Other publishers, such as Ginn, D.C. Heath, Allyn & Bacon, and Scott, Foresman, have specialized in textbooks and have done little trade publishing. While there is currently some feeling in the industry that the restrictions now being placed on school budgets and the shrinking school-age population have caused a crisis in textbook publishing, no textbook house has gone bankrupt in the past few decades. Furthermore almost all of the textbook publishers in existence in 1950 are still in operation today, some thirty years later, and seemingly doing well. Also, there seems to be a place in the textbook market for the smaller house that specializes in a certain subject or age group.

The most striking characteristic of the textbook industry is the immense amount of capital needed to launch a series of texts. Over a million dollars can be spent to produce a series of five or six elementary textbooks in a subject over a period of four or five years before any return can be realized on the investment. The process of creation is long and involved, as we shall see. Furthermore textbook editors must always be thinking of the future, of what teachers will want five or six years hence. Textbook publishing is also a highly seasonal business, with most orders coming in between June and October.

Textbook houses usually have two divisions: elementary and secondary (known together in the trade as *el-hi*) and college. A few firms operate only in one area and ignore the other. El-hi books are sold directly to school systems, while college texts are sold in college bookstores to students. Marketing is thus very different for the two divisions. Besides the basic textbook itself, all textbook publishers provide supplementary materials such as teacher's manuals, tests, workbooks, and audio-visual materials. The tendency is more and more toward the instructional package.

How is a textbook package created? Very often, particularly at the el-hi level, the initial idea or impetus comes from the publisher's staff. Textbook houses that publish at all grade levels and in all subject areas must maintain large staffs. Many staff members at the el-hi level have had teaching experience before entering the field of publishing. It is their responsibility to keep up with developments in the world of education and foresee future needs. Textbooks can be written by this in-house staff, but more often an outside author will be chosen— someone actively engaged in teaching the subject. In such cases the editorial staff still remains a dominant force in the creation of the textbook by criticizing, revising, and editing the final manuscript. Textbooks are often written by authors under the copyright provision of "for hire." Textbooks may also be written by teams of authors, or the publisher may engage a series of advisers or consultants to propose ideas and to check the work of individual authors.

In addition to the problems of subject content, elementary and secondary textbooks must be written to a certain grade level. Vocabulary and sentence structure must be carefully controlled. Most textbooks at the el-hi level are also tested in the classroom on a trial run basis using a preliminary edition before the signal is given to commit the publisher to printing vast quantities of the new text. Much reworking may be required after such test runs. It is not unusual for textbooks to be three or four years in the writing and testing stages before printing actually begins. This is why so much investment capital is needed in a textbook house. Fortunately the returns, once the textbook is on the market, can also be very great.

How is a textbook sold? For many years most states had uniform adoptions; that is, schools could buy only the textbooks approved by a state committee. Often only one or two texts per subject and grade level were approved, thus creating great competition within the industry to win such adoptions. Today less than half of the states still have statewide adoption requirements, and even in those states the effect has been diluted by longer and longer lists, permitting considerable freedom of choice at the local level. In some of these states, too, books not on the adoption list can be purchased through the use of local, rather than state, funds. In the other states it is the local school boards, or even the individual teacher or school, that decide which books are to be used. School districts may have districtwide committees of teachers and administrators who make the final decisions, but the decision making is much more spread out than it once was and thus presents marketing problems. It is now necessary for the publisher's sales force to call on many different people before getting a firm order. With states still having statewide adoption plans, since so much is at stake, the marketing director from the main office may make the presentation before the state committee or officials. In the college field it is the individual professor, except for some basic courses with multiple sections, who makes the decision to adopt.

One curious result of the statewide or systemwide adoption of textbooks is that publishers must keep more than one edition of a textbook in print. The reason is that they usually contract to supply a school system with the adopted textbook over a certain period—usually four to six years—at a given price. This arrangement is found nowhere else in the publishing business. Librarians who purchase textbooks need to know that discounts are not as large as for trade books. They are usually 25 percent for el-hi textbooks and 20 percent for college textbooks. The reasons for this are varied, but they include the fact that the retail price is set as low as possible so as to put the textbook within the range of the average student (in the case of college textbooks) and to take into account the large quantities that must be bought by any major school system. Probably the biggest reason for lower discounts is that there is no middleman, most books being sold directly to the consumer. Librarians utilizing the services of book jobbers can therefore expect to receive little or no discount on textbooks.

Finally few textbooks are reviewed in the media used by librarians. CHOICE reviews a few basic college textbooks, mainly in the sciences, as well as some types of supplementary text materials, but the other library and trade review media largely ignore them. In no case will textbooks be available for review before the publication date, a fact librarians need to keep in mind when searching for reviews. The most likely place for a textbook review would be some of the education journals, particularly those addressed to teachers in specific subject areas.

TECHNICAL AND PROFESSIONAL BOOKS

The term *technical books* can include textbooks but, in general, as utilized in the publishing industry, it refers to books aimed at workers in a particular field. Technical books cover the social and natural sciences, technology, medicine, and law. They include how-to-do-it books for the amateur as well as advanced monographs for the researcher. Handbooks, presenting vast compilations of data, are important in this field, but monographs on a single topic are probably the most common form of technical books. One of the greatest problems with technical books in recent years has been the proliferation of new topics, the "twigging" phenomenon, with resulting smaller and smaller audiences.

Producing technical and professional books is a costly process, but not for the same reasons as with textbooks. Technical titles are usually developed in isolation rather than in comprehensive packaged series. Editorial expenses can be quite high, as many researchers are not particularly good writers and their work must be heavily rewritten, but the highest are the production costs when mathematical formulas or charts and graphs are involved. Illustrations are another expensive item. The possibility of selling large numbers of copies of a technical book (other than a handbook or a how-to-do-it book on a popular topic) is remote. Initial printings of a technical book most often range from 2,000 to 5,000 copies. Technical books are also affected by shifts in interest within a field and by the growth or lack of growth within certain professions. Publishers of technical books must constantly be aware of changing requirements within the fields they service.

But if technical publishing is an expensive and risky business, it can also be a very profitable one. First of all, the market for most technical books is very predictable. Advertising and direct-mail marketing (which are used extensively in this type of publishing) can be targeted directly to potential buyers. Advertising is not in the expensive general media but largely in the more modest professional journals. Technical and professional books are fundamentally tools of a trade, and the best of them often become indispensable to workers in a particular field. Consider, for example, how many scientists require the latest edition of the *Handbook of Chemistry and Physics* or how many auto mechanics the latest Chilton auto repair manuals.

Since accuracy is essential in technical publishing, publishers often submit manuscripts to other members of a profession for criticism. Great care is also taken in proofreading, and a technical book without an adequate index is unthinkable.

Librarians in academic and research libraries must purchase vast quantities of technical and professional books. As with textbooks, they will find that discounts are much smaller than with trade books, usually ranging from 10 to 20 percent. Unfortunately, unlike textbooks, prices will usually be very high. This is because of the higher editorial costs and also because of the much smaller market for most of these books. Thus each copy must bear a higher percentage of the total cost. Technical and professional books are reviewed in the professional journals, as well as in CHOICE and *Science Books and Films*. *Technical Book Review Index* provides a handy way to find reviews scattered throughout the professional literature. Librarians should realize that reviews of technical and professional books appear only after the publication date, often several months later. This is partly because technical publishers may not be as prompt in getting out review copies to the journals but more likely because most professional journals work under far less pressure than the general review media. The necessary wait is usually balanced by the high quality of the reviews.

Professionals working in the field are ill served by retail book outlets, very few of which stock technical or professional books. Thus they usually buy technical books through the mail. Librarians are more fortunate in that some library wholesalers stock technical books, at least those of the major publishers. Much library purchasing is also done directly, with some publishers offering approval plans.

REFERENCE AND SUBSCRIPTION BOOKS

After textbooks, the largest segment of the book business is that which is devoted to reference and subscription books. It is estimated that over 20 percent of book sales are in this field. It is, of course, an area of great interest to librarians since so much of their funds are spent on this type of material, much of it very expensive.

The development of reference books, particularly multivolume works, is, like textbooks, a multi-million-dollar affair, with returns coming in long after the original investment has been made. Four companies account for the largest portion of the reference book business in the United States. These are the major encyclopedia publishers: Britannica, Macmillan (*Colliers*), World Book, and Grolier (*Americana*, etc.). Their markets can be divided into three segments: home and office, which accounts for approximately 75 percent of their business; mail order, which takes in about 20 percent; and school and library, which represents the smallest amount, about 5 percent. The home and office sales are direct sales carried out by a large sales staff. Encyclopedia publishers have frequently been criticized, and have even been the subject of investigations and lawsuits by the Federal Trade Commission, because of the alleged high-pressure sales tactics employed by some of their personnel. Certain forms of protection for consumers have now become law, such as a required three-day cooling-off period during which a buyer may revoke without penalty any contract he or she has signed.

Because of the bad reputation subscription book publishers have gained in this area, at least one major publisher has recently announced that it will rely much more on mail-order sales and promotion in the future. Another is preparing to market its encyclopedia through regular book stores. Some cheaper-priced encyclopedias (largely reprints of older works) have been sold in supermarkets. The major encyclopedia houses still send salespeople to call on librarians in order to present their companies' products; they are among the few publishers' representatives that a librarian sees regularly. The great advantage of such visits is that it usually permits personal examination of the reference set and enables the librarian to ask pertinent questions that may not be answered in the brochures and advertisements. For most librarians, however, a major reference set will not be purchased until reviews have appeared in the major library review media, particularly *Reference and Subscription Books Bulletin*.

The term *subscription books* refers to books sold on the installment plan and sometimes before publication. Because of the heavy investment necessary for the production of reference sets, many publishers take orders in advance, offering slight discounts to those who will pay for an entire set all at once. If the publisher is reputable and the initial volumes indicate high quality, libraries may opt for this type of purchase plan. The other possibility is for the library to pay for each volume as it is published. Families who cannot pay for an expensive reference set that has already been published will often purchase on an installment plan. Carrying charges and interest will, of course, increase the price of the set.

While the four publishers mentioned earlier control most of the encyclopedia business, there are many other publishers in the business as well. Between fifteen and twenty subscription books publishers are active today. In addition, many trade and textbook publishers produce an occasional reference work, particularly one-volume works that do not require the investment of such large sums as does an encyclopedia. Charles Scribner's Sons is one trade publisher that has built up a considerable reputation for fine reference works, including such multivolume sets as the *Dictionary of American Biography* and the *Dictionary of the History of Ideas*. McGraw-Hill can be cited for its publication of the *New Catholic Encyclopedia* and the much-praised *Encyclopedia of Science and Technology* and *Encyclopedia of World Art*. Another type of reference book publisher requiring special skills and know-how is the dictionary publisher, most prominent of which remains the G. & C. Merriam Company, publishers of the Merriam-Webster dictionaries.

What characterizes almost all of these reference publishers is the size of their in-house staff. Workers are needed not only for editorial, production, and marketing functions but also most essentially for research and writing. Over time, the putting together of a major reference work has passed from one man writing the entire work to an editor-in-chief who supervises a large editorial staff, which in turn marshals the services of hundreds of scholars and other experts. In addition, there is usually a board of consultants and subject advisers. When reference books are being prepared for children, reading-level consultants must also be employed. Even with adult reference works, the level of reading comprehension must be considered.

The publisher of a reference work must assure that the work is not only authoritative but also accurate in every detail. The two are not necessarily arrived at in the same fashion. Authoritativeness usually results from using the best experts in the field to write the articles. However, even experts may slip up. Most reference book publishers therefore employ large research staffs to check every fact in every article submitted to them against other available reference sources. Many of these research staff members are librarians. Authoritativeness is also the responsibility of the consultant or advisory committees.

Keeping a reference work up to date has always been a major problem. Various methods have been tried, from complete rewriting every few years (as was done with the early editions of the *Encyclopaedia Britannica*, as well as the most recent edition) to loose-leaf binders for the insertion of new material to the issuance of supplementary volumes. Most of the major encyclopedia publishers today employ the principle of "continuous revision." *World Book Encyclopedia* claims that it revises approximately half of the set's 12,000 pages each year. Some of these revisions are mere updatings of isolated facts and figures, but in others, entire articles have been rewritten. This type of revision is always hampered by the amount of space available at a particular place. Often additional pages must be inserted and page numberings such as 119a, 119b, 119c, etc., used. What is to be revised and when is not an easy problem to solve either. Certain events force the revision of some articles, but others may go neglected for years and result in eventual misinformation. No ideal solution has ever been devised; all have their advantages and disadvantages.

All reference book publishers must be concerned with ease of use. This applies not only to reading level and comprehensibility, as we have discussed earlier, but also to the development of elaborate systems of cross references and indexes. Nothing is more frustrating to the librarian than a compilation of facts that are irretrievable. Reference book publishers must therefore have their own staffs of indexers or engage outside experts for each major project.

Reference book publishers are always anxious to know what librarians want. They constantly seek to develop new products in answer to expressed needs. Librarians should not hesitate to make their desires known, particularly if the need can be satisfied with a one-volume work. In recent years a number of smaller publishing houses specializing in reference works have sprung up, most notably Gale Research and Pierian Press. Since these publishers are much more dependent on library sales than the major encyclopedia and dictionary publishers, they attempt to maintain close contact with the library field and welcome suggestions from reference librarians.

While domestic sales of encyclopedias and other large reference works to the general public have fallen off in recent years, the industry has remained healthy by great expansion in the overseas market. It is estimated that 47 percent of sales are now made abroad. In some cases, translations have been made, particularly into Spanish, which also opens up another market within the United States. In other cases, supplementary volumes are written to place more emphasis on the regions in which the work is to be marketed. *World Book* has done this for the British Isles and Australasia. With no end in sight to the information explosion, the reference book segment of the book industry seems to have a healthy future.

SCHOLARLY BOOKS

Scholarly books are published for the most part by nonprofit institutions—learned societies, museums, research institutions, and most widely by university presses. Trade houses have largely abandoned the publishing of scholarly books in the last decade, since they think in terms of a minimum print run of 15,000 and the average scholarly nonfiction title sells 1,300 copies over a period of five years. Since the audiences for most scholarly works are small, some kind of subsidization is usually necessary. This may come in the form of grants from foundations or societies or from the subsidization that university presses enjoy because of their tax-exempt status and their low overhead in occupying university facilities. However funds are obtained, scholarly publishers, particularly university presses, believe that they have a mission to advance the cause of scholarship and to publish works even though they may not be financially profitable. That such publishers succeed as well as they do is a minor miracle. As Chester Kerr, former director of the Yale University Press, phrased it some twenty-five years ago: "We publish the smallest editions at the greatest cost, and on these we place the highest prices, and then we try to market them to people who can least afford them. This is madness."[1]

In spite of all these difficulties, university press publishing was, at least until recently, a growing business. In 1975 there were seventy-five university presses that belonged to the Association of

---

[1]As quoted in Gene R. Hawes, *To Advance Knowledge: A Handbook on American University Press Publishing* (New York: American University Press Services, Inc., 1967), p. 50.

American University Presses, compared with thirty-five in 1948. These presses published 3,338 title in 1975 and now have sales that total nearly $60,000,000 annually. Furthermore, for libraries, this sector of the book industry is of great importance since libraries are the largest consumers of scholarly books. University presses have come of age since World War II and now employ as knowledgeable staffs as any commercial publisher and utilize the most advanced techniques of production and marketing. Some university presses remain very small operations, publishing no more than six to ten titles per year; others, such as Oxford University Press, are among the largest publishers in the world. Several U.S. university presses— Harvard, Yale, Chicago, California—outdistance many of their commercial rivals by publishing more than 100 titles per year.

University press books have traditionally been written by scholars to communicate information and ideas to other scholars, often the results of research. Such works may often be difficult to understand if one is not already working in the same field or a similar field. Increasingly, however, university presses have turned to works that have a wider audience and are of interest to general college-educated readers. Since university presses are scattered throughout the United States and Canada, rather than concentrated in one or two metropolitan areas, they have found a mission in publishing books of value and interest to the region in which they are located. Such works help to increase the visibility of the press locally as well as bring in needed profits. Some university press books become best-sellers quite by chance. The most notable example is David Riesman's *The Lonely Crowd*, originally published by Yale in an edition of only 1,500 copies. There are certain types of books that most university presses avoid. These include such things as cookbooks, self-help books, popularizations of academic subjects, and personal reminiscences. University presses have entered the field of reference book publishing when they have been able to obtain the necessary capital. Interestingly, however, only a few of them have attempted to publish textbooks, and then mostly at an advanced graduate level. This is probably because of the large sums of money needed to develop such works. It would seem to be a logical expansion of their activities—and a most lucrative one—as Oxford has found out with its English-as-a-second-language readers and grammars. Another area that university presses have traditionally avoided, believing it to be the province of the trade publisher, is fiction. Recently, however, at least two university publishers have launched reprint series of neglected early-twentieth-century novels. Also, since trade publishers have tended to ignore the short story, a few university presses have entered the field in this way. Poetry has never been a very profitable venture for any publisher, and here university presses perform important service. If it were not for them, little poetry would see the light of day in the United States.

To be successful, university presses must be assured that the sponsoring university recognizes the need for ongoing subsidy. Most university presses are set up as separate entities, with a controlling board of directors representing the faculty and administration of the university. Internally the press operates much as a commercial trade publishing house under the supervision of a director.

Most university presses find it wise to concentrate in certain subject areas—usually the areas of strength of their own faculty. In fact, one-third to one-half of what a university press publishes is usually the works of its present or former faculty, and much of the rest comes in through their interest and influence. Most manuscripts are submitted directly by their authors; literary agents play very little part in university press publishing. Because of the scholarly nature of the subject matter, almost all manuscripts are submitted to two or three outside readers for their opinions on whether the work is sound and merits publication. After these readers' reports (for which they are paid a nominal sum) are received, the manuscript is submitted to a faculty advisory committee (sometimes, but not always, the same committee that oversees the running of the press). Their vote on whether a manuscript should be published is final.

Authors usually receive the standard royalty of 10 percent of the retail price, but because editions are very small, no writer makes much money from a university press book. Publication is sought for reasons of promotion within the university, since unfortunately "publish or perish" is still a major criterion for survival in the academic world.

In addition to exercising more quality control of manuscript content than most trade publishers, university presses also usually have higher copy editing and design standards. For years university press books have won prize after prize for their design. University presses never have to sacrifice quality for the sake of speed. Thus the average manuscript is more than a year in preparation. All told, the average university press book is a much handsomer and much higher-quality product than the average trade book. It is usually worth the higher price that must be charged.

Academic presses depend for most of their profit on their backlists. They thus tend to keep a book in print much longer than the average trade house. This is, of course, a great help to librarians. In selling their works, they tend to depend a great deal on direct-mail promotion. Advertising is limited largely to trade and library journals and to the professional journals in the book's subject area. University presses also believe in exhibiting as much as possible at library and professional meetings. Some of the smaller presses usually join together to keep down the costs of such exhibits. A few university presses have their own paperback lines; many issue both hardbound and paperback editions at the same time; all welcome the opportunity to sell individual titles to other paperback publishers.

Until the advent of CHOICE, librarians often had a difficult time locating reviews of university press books, as the general review media did not often cover them and both *Booklist* and *LJ* considered them of marginal interest to their readers. All that has now changed, as CHOICE reviews 85 to 90 percent of all university press books issued each year. Only the most esoteric subjects are excluded. Scholarly books are, of course, heavily reviewed in the professional journals, but the disadvantage is that librarians must search in many different places for evaluative judgments. Certainly no academic or research library, and even most public libraries, can neglect the output of America's university presses.

REPRINTS

A part of the book industry closely related to scholarly publishing is the reprint industry. Largely a post-World War II development, it came into being for several reasons but was made possible only by new developments in offset printing, which permitted reproduction of entire books by photographic means rather than by resetting of type. Reproduction of materials in microtext form also occurred at the same time, but the term *reprints* is usually used only when referring to printed books or periodicals and is so used here.

Among the reasons for the sudden burgeoning of the reprint industry was the great increase in the number of new colleges being founded as well as the expansion of already existing ones. All needed books for their libraries—not just new titles but also vast quantities of older standard titles. Copies of certain books on the shelves were also found to be in deteriorating condition and had to be replaced. The publication of *Books for College Libraries* in 1967 pushed many libraries into competing with each other for copies of titles on this standard list, as they all sought to upgrade their collections. In the late 1950s and early 1960s, further impetus to the reprint business came in the form of large infusions of federal funds for the purchase of library materials. Finally new subjects were being introduced into college and university curricula for which most libraries did not have the supporting materials—notably black studies and women's studies.

The first reprinters were for the most part antiquarian book dealers or secondhand periodical dealers, who were unable to meet the demand for certain titles in the original published format and so resorted to reprinting. Often a periodical dealer would offer part of a set in the original format and the rest in reprint. The original publishers were generally not interested in getting into this business since the sizes of the reprint editions were seen as too small to be worth the trouble. Reprinters proved, however, that the business could be financially profitable. Little capital—only a few thousand dollars—was needed to start a business, and if prices were set fairly high, the small editions could be made to pay. Most reprinters opted for hardbound reprints rather than paperbacks since their customers were almost entirely libraries, which stressed durability.

Reprints developed into several different types. The easiest to produce was the completely unaltered reprint. Often, however, a publisher felt that the book would be more useful to modern scholars if it were brought up to date or corrected by the addition of a new preface or a bibliography. Indexes were also added to books that had not had them before. However, correction of individual pages was not usually feasible given the photographic printing process used. Reprints could be sold as isolated titles or could be grouped into series or sets on a particular topic, such as the aforementioned black or women's studies. Although expensive, often totaling thousands of dollars, these sets were a way for libraries to acquire an instant collection, already chosen for them, on a particular topic.

How were books selected for reprinting? Since many of the original reprinters were antiquarian booksellers, they already knew which titles were most in demand. Other reprinters scanned the want lists to be found in the weekly *Antiquarian Bookman* or talked with faculty members about their needs. Consultants were often hired, especially for the longer series.

Once a book was selected, how was it reproduced? First of all, a master copy had to be obtained. If one was not obtainable by purchase on the secondhand book market, then attempts would be made to borrow a copy from a library. Often it was necessary to get hold of several copies if the first, as was often the case, was defective in some way. In return for loan of the copy, the library would usually be paid—often with a copy of the reprint edition. (Unfortunately, in order to be reproduced, the original book had to be taken apart for photographing or bent back so far that the original binding would be destroyed and the pages often damaged. This caused some libraries to refuse to lend many items.) At this stage, it was necessary to decide on and to commission, if necessary, any additions to the book and to arrange for their separate printing. Permission to reprint was often unnecessary, as many of the books were in the public domain, usually because the copyright had not been renewed after the initial twenty-eight-year period or because the book had originally been printed in England and never copyrighted in the United States. Some reprinters obtained permission from the original publishers, if they were still in business, and from the original author or his or her heirs, out of courtesy. The standard royalty of 10 percent was paid on all books still under copyright and sometimes even, again as a courtesy, for those that were not.

The size of most reprint editions is very small, varying from a low of 200 to 300 copies to a high of 1,000. In order to determine whether reprinting of a certain title was worthwhile, many publishers have engaged in "fishing expeditions," announcing titles as being available but not printing them until a sufficient number of orders have come in. As a result, many announced titles have never been published, and libraries have lost funds that had been committed for purchase but were never spent and instead reverted to the central funding source at the end of the fiscal year. This infuriated libraries and caused much hard feeling between them and the reprint industry.

Another problem for libraries was poor workmanship. Many fly-by-night outfits got into the reprinting business and produced very poor merchandise. Typical problems were poor paper and binding and uneven and too faint printing. Libraries sometimes found, too, that secondhand copies could still be obtained—and at less cost than that being charged for the reprinted edition.

The most serious problems, however, were bibliographic. Some publishers—fortunately only a few—failed to identify a reprint as such and tried to hoodwink librarians into thinking it was a new title. More common was a failure to give adequate bibliographic data in the book itself (and in the publisher's catalog and advertisements) as to which edition was being reprinted. Sometimes the information given was erroneous or so incomplete as to be totally confusing. Most of these problems occurred because the reprinter replaced the original title page and its verso with new pages. Finally, although additions and corrections to the original books were usually strong selling points to libraries, publishers sometimes failed to say what they had actually done in altering the reprint edition.

Selection problems were often compounded by the fact that the same book would be reprinted by several different publishers, and because most reprints were not reviewed anywhere (since most review media felt the reviews the book had received when it was first published were sufficient), it was difficult to ascertain which reprint edition was best. Gradually libraries became aware of which reprint-ers did the best job, but decisions usually had to be based on general reputations, not on the specific title. Most serious of all for libraries was the fact that much outdated and superseded scholarship was being reprinted, some of it against the wishes of the authors themselves. Since many British books had never been copyrighted in the United States, some authors could do little about it.

At the height of the reprint boom in 1970, Carol Nemeyer identified 269 publishers as being active in the reprint business and estimated that at least 85,000 titles had been reprinted up to that date—possibly as many as 100,000 or more.[2] Most of the reprints have been English-language titles, although in the past decade a few Europeans, mostly Germans, have gotten into the reprint business. In the United States, however, the bottom dropped out of the market in recent years as the saturation point was reached in many subject areas. Reprinters who had limited themselves to very narrow fields found that they were reprinting more and more esoteric titles for which there was less and less of a market. Many of them went out of business. Other reprinters began to diversify and to publish original scholarly books. The main reason for the decline in sales was the shrinking of most library budgets in the late 1970s. Libraries were having a hard time keeping up with new publications and had little money to spend on retrospective titles.

The reprint industry has probably now settled down to a healthy period in which much needed titles will be brought back into print while the more esoteric ones will be allowed to drift into oblivion. For these, the type of on-demand reprinting of individual titles offered by Xerox University Microfilms will largely fill the bill.

SMALL PRESSES AND SELF-PUBLISHING

Besides the commercial publishers, there exists in the United States and Canada another type of publisher, variously called the *small press*, *alternative publisher*, or *independent publisher*. It publishes what the commercial presses are not interested in, generally works that will not make any money. Furthermore, instead of trying to publish a large variety of works, most small presses specialize, with the intention of serving particular minorities that are not fully integrated into the commercial mainstream. While small presses have existed since the beginning of printing in the United States, they became very visible in the social upheavals of the 1960s. They concentrate on such areas as feminist books, social revolution, poetry, and experimental fiction. These are the publishers that, as Richard Kostelanetz has said, "issue

[2]Carol Nemeyer, *Scholarly Reprint Publishing in the United States* (New York: R. R. Bowker Company, 1972), p. 67.

manuscripts that commercial publishers would reject as 'too incoherent,' 'too esoteric,' 'too provincial,' 'too peculiar-looking,' 'too personal,' and 'too idiosyncratic.' "[3]

Small presses exist on very little capital, most of it contributed by the owner or his or her friends. These people are in the business in order to publish something, not to make money. Much of the labor will be volunteered or will be paid for at very low rates. Small presses operate out of owners' basements and garages or out of tiny apartments. Most of the owners must have other jobs to support themselves. They perform an important function in today's society in seeing that worthwhile works, even though they may have a limited audience, get published.

Self-publishing is much the same as the small press, with the added criterion that the author puts up the money to get the work published rather than another person or group. The United States has a long tradition of self-publishing. From Thomas Paine to Walt Whitman to Carl Sandburg, many writers were forced to publish their own works initially. How many librarians know that the first editions of Robert's *Rules of Order* and Bartlett's *Familiar Quotations* were self-published? Small-press authors or self-published authors are sometimes picked up later by commercial publishers, but the majority are not. They remain largely unknown to the general public.

Small publishers often own their own printing presses and do the work themselves. Otherwise the work is usually farmed out to a local job printer. Distribution always remains a problem. Again, the owners of most small presses wrap their own packages, carry them to the post office, and write their own invoices. Publicity is another problem. Fortunately the library review media do make some attempt to keep abreast of what small presses are publishing, although much hinges on the initiative of the presses themselves in getting review copies to the review journals. *LJ* runs a regular annual survey of small-press output written by the ubiquitous Bill Katz. CHOICE and *Booklist* review a certain number of titles, particularly poetry. Of course, most small presses have very little money for advertising or exhibits. Increasingly, however, they have been participating in special book fairs in some of the larger cities, and most library organizations have made exhibit space available to them—usually just tables—on the fringes of the commercial exhibit areas at annual conferences. Most major U.S. cities have a few bookstores that stock small-press publications, usually specializing, as do the publishers, in one or two subjects.

---

[3]Richard Kostelanetz, "Alternative Publishing: New York Fair Highlights Growing Interest in Books by Specialized Publishers," *Publishers Weekly*, 212 (Nov. 14, 1977), p. 28.

The number of small presses has grown tremendously since the 1960s and with it the need for information on these presses and their publications. Fortunately Len Fulton, himself a small-press publisher in Paradise, California, now issues an annual *International Directory of Little Magazines and Small Presses* and a monthly *Small Press Review*. In *Small Press Record of Books in Print*, Fulton attempts to compile annually as complete a listing as possible of small-press books, many of which fail to get listed in the regular trade bibliographies. There is an organization of small publishers—COSMEP (Committee of Small Magazine Editors and Publishers), founded in 1968—that issues a valuable newsletter for those wishing to keep up with developments in this ever-changing field. Librarians have found in recent years that they could not ignore the work of the small presses, even though they presented unusual selection problems and were often hard to locate. The future seems to hold more, rather than less, small-press publishing or self-publishing as commercial houses face increasingly high costs.

VANITY PUBLISHERS

Vanity publishers differ from self-publishers in that they are commercial operations that will publish any work for an author if the author puts up the necessary cash. They often like to be called *subsidy* or *cooperative* publishers rather than by the pejorative term *vanity presses*. In return for the subsidy from the author, vanity publishers offer their editorial, production, and marketing expertise. Actually it is mostly production expertise that comes into play, as little editorial work is done on the manuscripts submitted and there is little a vanity publisher can do to help sell the books. Since there is no control over the quality of the manuscripts published by vanity presses, the review media cannot be bothered trying to find the one or two good books among the hundreds published each year; thus any vanity press book is automatically rejected. Even the Library of Congress rejects vanity press books as being unsuitable for its collections. Sometimes the publisher can arrange for review of a book in the author's hometown newspaper and for the local bookstore to stock a few copies for sale to the author's friends, but that is about all. In reality, whatever books are sold will probably result from the author's hard work.

Vanity publishers have frequently been investigated by the Federal Trade Commission and Better Business Bureaus. Many of them have operated as confidence games, charging the author everything they thought the traffic would bear, rather than basing their charges on actual costs. Furthermore they tended to promise much more in the way of promotion than they could ever deliver. Royalty payments are often very high—40 or 50 percent—but one must remember that authors are only getting their own money back. Only the manner in which vanity publishing is sometimes conducted, and not vanity publishing itself, is in any way a crime.

The leading vanity publishers get their business by advertising in local and national magazines and newspapers to solicit manuscripts. Costs by the more reputable vanity houses are based on both the number of pages in the book and the number of copies to be printed. Many times a vanity publisher refrains from binding many of the copies printed, knowing that only a few will ever be sold. Eventually the author is asked to take over the storage of the unsold copies.

Who takes advantage of the services of a vanity publisher? Authors of novels and poems rejected by commercial publishers; authors of personal reminiscences and of local history and genealogy; and frustrated professors who cannot get a university press to accept their doctoral dissertation or esoteric research report. Many of these people would be better off resorting to self-publishing. At least they would not suffer the opprobrium of being published by a vanity press. About all that can be said to librarians is that they may have a responsibility to collect the works of local authors and books on local subjects published by vanity presses. Most of these will probably be offered as gifts by their authors anyway, so most libraries will have few dealings with the presses themselves, although their reference departments may often be asked questions about vanity publishers and how they operate. For that reason alone, librarians should be knowledgeable about this segment of the book industry.

PERIODICALS

The twentieth century has seen a phenomenal growth in periodical publishing. It is currently estimated that 3,000 new periodicals are launched each year. *Folio: The Magazine for Magazine Management* has counted 488 new titles in the field of consumer magazines alone in the period 1975–1977. In the scholarly field the number of new journals being launched each year is staggering as smaller and smaller subject fields require their own means of communication (the twigging pheonomenon, mentioned earlier). Most of these new magazines do not survive long, but every one that dies seems to be replaced by two or three new ones. One interesting development of the past few years is the almost total dependence of some scholarly journals on library subscriptions, with little attempt made to woo the individual scholar.

Subscription prices for these journals are usually set very high. Even popular magazines are commanding prices unheard of just a few years ago. Subscription prices for many periodicals have increased far more quickly than the cost of living, and libraries are finding it more and more difficult to continue to subscribe to periodicals in the great numbers that they once did. This is most unfortunate, as the scholarly journal is the main means of communication in most scientific fields; most original research appears here long before it is included in monographs. Even in literary and humanistic fields, much important critical work, as well as poetry, short stories, and essays, appears first in periodicals. It can be said, however, that some journals seem to exist mainly as a vehicle for author recognition, a necessary stepping stone on the road to academic promotion, rather than as a means of communicating knowledge.

How do periodicals function? In general, manuscripts of articles are obtained much as in book publishing, with the same differences between scholarly and popular magazines as between scholarly and trade books. Some are commissioned by publishers; others are submitted "over the transom" by authors or are sent in by agents. Scholarly articles are almost always submitted by their authors directly to the journals most likely to be interested in the subject. There is no such thing as royalty payments for magazine articles. All authors are paid a one-time fee for publication rights. In the case of scholarly journals, authors are only too glad to see their articles in print and never think of making money. They consider themselves lucky to escape having to pay certain publication expenses (the so-called page charges). Who owns the copyright has been clarified by the new U.S. law, as was explained in Chapter Two.

The internal organization of a periodical publishing house (or the periodical division of a book-publishing house) is much the same as for book publishing, except for the addition of an advertising and subscription fulfillment department. All periodicals have editorial, production, and marketing departments whose work is similar to that of book publishers. However there are differences, major and minor. First of all, editorial standards may not be as high as with books. Many more periodical than book publishers have volunteer rather than professional editorial staffs. Furthermore all periodicals are faced with tremendous deadline problems. An issue is scheduled to reach subscribers and newsstand dealers on a certain date, and all the necessary work must be finished by that date. Therefore less attention can be given to correcting typographical errors, bad grammar, and other problems. This is especially noticeable with daily newspapers, in which errors abound. The more prestigious and scholarly journals, of course, try to achieve high editorial standards, but deadline pressures are always there. On the other hand, the more frequently a periodical is issued, the more up-to-date the contents can be—a problem that a monograph writer can never hope to solve in a completely satisfactory manner.

How are periodicals financed? Mainly through two sources: advertising revenue and subscription income. Journals cannot exist without the solicitation and publication of advertisements unless the sponsoring organization is willing to subsidize them. Subscriptions are an interesting phenomenon in that individuals and libraries are being asked to pay in advance for something that does not yet exist. The advantage to publishers is that they receive large sums of money in advance which they can use to pay their bills; the disadvantage is that as costs go up with inflation, subscription prices are difficult to adjust fast enough. The publisher always has a commitment to supply a certain number of issues at the old price. Nothing can be done to get more money from a subscriber until the subscription comes up for renewal. Another source of revenue may be the selling of the list of subscribers to individuals and companies wishing to market a product through direct mail. This may annoy subscribers, but publishers usually consider it an important and relatively easy source of income that they are unwilling to forego. Members of scholarly and professional societies usually receive a journal as one of their membership perquisites. In this case, the money to finance the journal comes out of the membership fees, and it will be up to the society to decide how much, if any, advertising they will accept to supplement their other income. Nonprofit institutions and associations also receive subsidy in the form of special reduced postal rates, although these have been going up steadily in recent years.

While professional journals are sold almost entirely through subscriptions, magazines for the general public, both of the specialized and more general types, are sold heavily through newsstands in all types of retail outlets. The distribution of such periodicals is in the hands of wholesale distributors, as we have previously mentioned in connection with mass-market paperbacks. The problems of magazine distribution are much the same as with paperbacks, particularly those of adequate display and the large proportion of unsold copies returned for credit.

While newsstand sales create problems for the magazine publisher, so do sales through subscriptions. First and foremost these days are the increasing postal rates and the very poor service being offered by the U.S. Postal Service, with the resulting loss or mutilation of copies. Also, the accurate recording of subscriber information, from correct address to expiration date, requires careful work by the subscription department staff.

Subscribers may deal directly with the publisher or, as with most libraries, they may employ a middleman, a magazine agent or jobber. These wholesalers are generally given a discount from the magazine's list price—usually 10 percent—and this is their source of revenue. Increasingly in recent years, professional organizations have been unwilling to grant such discounts; the jobber then resorts to tacking on a service charge in order to stay in business. The library must then decide whether the convenience of having all periodical subscriptions handled by one dealer outweighs the additional costs involved. Some publishers, particularly in the science field, charge libraries a higher rate than individual subscribers. Some librarians feel that this is unfair and try various methods to circumvent the price differential.

While magazine publishers work mainly to supply current issues to all customers, there remains the problem of back issues. All publishers maintain stocks for a limited period (up to one year) to supply replacements for issues that are lost or mutilated in the mails. Whether they maintain—or even print enough copies to maintain—stocks to supply extra copies beyond that date usually depends on what type of publisher they are. Publishers of professional and scholarly journals usually overprint all issues in order to have a stock of extra copies on hand for several years after publication. The stock of certain issues will be used up first, creating gaps in what can be supplied. Whether a publisher orders the printer to keep the original plates or reprints copies by photo offset depends on the cost of such a run and the demand. Most publishers eventually refer requests for back issues that they cannot fill to secondhand periodical dealers or to the microprint publishers with whom they may have a contract. Publishers of popular magazines, distributed through the vast network of magazine wholesalers, find it most difficult to supply back issues; most of their stock is out in the field, and the unsold numbers may be pulped rather than returned to them. These publishers do not feel the responsibility to maintain stocks of back issues, as do the professional journals. Secondhand dealers then become the librarian's major sources of supply.

MICROFORMS

Microform is a generic term referring to any information storage or communication medium that is made up of images too small to be read by the naked eye. Micropublishers are the persons or companies that issue microforms in multiple copies for sale or distribution to the public. The essential element here is "multiple copies." It is this that differentiates micropublishers from any person or institution that makes one microform copy of a work for the use of an individual for research purposes.

Microforms have existed for more than a century but were not used by scholars or libraries to any great extent until the 1920s and 1930s. Then U.S. libraries began to use microfilm as a means of obtaining unique research materials (primarily manuscripts and rare books) from foreign archives and libraries. The impetus and funds for some of these microfilming projects often came from the learned societies, which were concerned that U.S. scholars (particularly in the humanities) were at a disadvantage compared with their European colleagues since they had to travel great distances to use many of the materials needed for their research.

Micropublishing began in the 1930s, when the retrospective and current files of *The New York Times* were made available on microfilm. This was followed by such projects as the publishing in microform of the books listed in Pollard and Redgrave's *Short-Title Catalogue* and the nineteenth-century British Parliamentary Papers. The micropublishing business had its ups and downs in succeeding years, due largely to changes in technology. Currently, however, it is prospering and offers much needed materials to libraries, often at prices lower than would be possible with conventionally printed copies. Micropublishers can be either commercial or institutional (nonprofit) in nature. The institutional micropublishers are libraries, archives, government agencies, universities, and professional associations. All are characterized by a desire to make available research materials, often of a highly esoteric nature, which have a limited market and are therefore produced in very small quantities. Commercial micropublishers are in the business for profit. Therefore they avoid research materials in favor of titles that have more marketability. Their markets are almost exclusively libraries, so they must produce materials that libraries need and at attractive prices. Commercial micropublishers can be branches of diversified corporations (such as Bell & Howell or Xerox University Microfilms), or they can be microfilm service bureaus (such as General Microfilm Company). Regular book or periodical publishers can also offer their publications in microform in addition to or in place of regular print production. A few small micropublishers have been created to produce one or two major microform projects; once these are terminated, they may go out of business. Since little capital is needed to produce microforms, the small publisher can enter the field quite easily, just as with the reprint business. In fact, much micropublishing is really a branch of the reprint industry.

Microforms come in various shapes and sizes but are mainly of three types. The oldest and best known is microfilm, now more specifically called *reel microfilm*, as there are now also microfilm cartridges and microfilm cassettes. The term *roll microform* is also used. Reel microfilm is 16 mm or 35 mm wide. The 16 mm type is standard in offices, banks, and other commercial applications; the 35 mm type is standard in libraries because of its ability to display whole pages of newspapers at a satisfactory reduction ratio. Smaller film sometimes requires too great a reduction and subsequent loss of legibility. *Micro-opaques*, utilizing paper rather than film supports, were the next to come into wide use in the United States. There were three types: microcards, microlex, and microprint. Although widely sold for some twenty years, the first two types are no longer produced; only microprint continues to be produced by the Readex Microprint Corporation. Microcards were 3 × 5 inches, whereas microprint utilizes a 6 × 9 inch card with ten rows and ten columns. Reduction ratios for both microfilm and microprint range from twelve times (expressed usually as 12X) to twenty-four times, the latter being considered the upper limit for library materials. The third type of microform, *microfiche*, has come into widespread use in the United States only since the early 1970s, although it has been widely used in Europe since the 1950s. (The Europeans never had much use for micro-opaques.) The European standard size is gradually being adopted in the United States. This is a fiche 105 × 148 mm (approximately 4 × 6 inches). It can hold a maximum of ninety-eight pages (seven rows and fourteen columns) at a 24X reduction. Both microfilm and microfiche have the advantage of being easily duplicated on demand, one copy at a time if needed, at about the same cost as a copy made by Xerography. Microprint cannot be easily duplicated and is produced only in sizable editions. Since the flexibility of on-demand publication is highly desirable in the micropublication business, microprint has lost out over the years to the two other types. Another version of the microfiche is *ultrafiche* or *ultrastrips*. This form uses much greater reduction ratios—as high as 210X—in order to get long documents or whole books on one fiche. Unfortunately a master is very expensive to produce, and it cannot be duplicated on demand for purchasers. Like microprint, therefore, ultrafiche is used only for multiple-copy editions.

All microforms require special equipment for reading. While 35 mm microfilm readers were the first to be developed, the current trend in business is to use 16 mm. Thus in recent years there have been few technical improvements in 35 mm readers, and the price has not come down. The advantage of microfiche is in the sophisticated yet inexpensive equipment that has come on the market; it is now possible for scholars to have their own readers for less than $100. (This is not true of ultrafiche readers, which are few and expensive.)

Most micropublishing is retrospective, being merely the reprinting in microform of previously existing materials. However, it can also be simultaneous with publication in hard-copy form or even original. Retrospective materials in microform are of several kinds. The first to appear was newspapers. Libraries needed to preserve crumbling files of original wood-pulp editions and to conserve space. They also had to fill in incomplete files or to acquire other, and often rare, newspapers. Periodicals came next. In addition to the need to preserve deteriorating files and to save space, there was the advantage of not having to replace missing issues prior to binding and of avoiding the cost of binding altogether. Individual issues would be kept for two to three years (until their use had declined substantially) and would then be discarded, leaving the microform edition as the permanent library copy. Other types of reprinted materials available in microform came to include out-of-print books (the best-known example has been Xerox University Microfilms' "Books on Demand" program, which will provide a single copy of any work that can be located and filmed.) In the 1960s micropublishers began to offer large microform sets to libraries seeking to develop their collections in certain subject areas or for larger institutions wishing to acquire rare research materials. Finally, most recently, government documents have become available. Of particular interest are the hard-to-obtain items of a nondepository nature.

Simultaneous publication in both hard copy and microprint has not yet achieved much success. It has been offered largely by scientific journal publishers. The advantages are quicker service (air mail delivery from Europe, for example) and sometimes better cumulations of indexes. The price factor will probably determine whether libraries will switch to the microform edition over the long run. Only by offering substantial savings are publishers likely to attract more customers away from the hard-copy to the microform editions.

Original materials offered solely in microform are becoming increasingly important in the micropublishing business. They make possible the publication of material for which there is a limited or unpredictable demand or which contains a great deal of illustrative or graphic material. For many years, the most common materials published in microform were doctoral dissertations. Technical reports are now widely disseminated in this form, as are papers presented at professional meetings. ERIC and NTIS are major publishers by any standards, with their vast number of reports being made available to a wide audience. A few highly specialized journals are available only in microform. University presses are experimenting with microform publication, some of it simultaneous publication (as with the University of Toronto) but much of it unique material not otherwise available. One of the most interesting developments in recent years has been the University of Chicago's Text/Fiche editions, wherein large numbers of art, architectural, or archaeological illustrations are published in microfiche along with a brief text in pamphlet form. Included in this series have been such projects as more than 1,000 photographs of the 1905–1907 Breasted expeditions to Egypt and the Sudan and 419 paintings from the private collection of Duncan Phillips. The complete papers of some historical figures have sometimes been made available in microform to supplement biographical studies in hard copy or very abridged hard-copy editions of the papers. Finally, another type of original publication of increasing importance to libraries are the bibliographies and catalogs produced by the (computer-output-microfilm) COM method, in which computerized data is reproduced on microfilm or microfiche without first being produced in hard copy. This method was first developed in the business world, with Lockheed producing a catalog in this fashion for its Technical Information Center in 1967. COM products, such as the British Library's *Books in English*, are now being produced for mass sale.

As can be seen from the preceding outline of micropublications—their various types and uses—editorial work on such publications is very limited. Even the original publications are often large masses of material reproduced in toto rather than edited down to a manageable size or for popular consumption. Instead of big printing presses and concern over design, paper, and choice of typefaces, the production problems in micropublishing are very few. Only a camera, some film, and some processing and reproduction equipment are necessary. A micropublisher can easily purchase all the equipment and do all the printing personally. Since the business is largely done on demand, there is little need for large outlays of capital for stock or storage. Marketing is largely a matter of contacting the few institutions interested in purchasing the work, through either direct mail or advertisements in scholarly and library journals. Sales are usually made directly to the customer, so there are no middlemen or wholesalers. Discounts are rare, except as part of prepublication offers.

Libraries do have problems with micropublications, however. Sometimes publishers do not supply the material as advertised, or they fail to complete a long set. Ascertaining the quality of a product is often difficult since most libraries have neither the time to examine each frame or fiche individually nor the equipment to do so adequately. They must therefore rely on outside evaluating sources, which until recently have been few. They must also acquire equipment for the use of each type of microform. Furthermore, some companies go out of business and entire forms (such as microcards) are dropped by the industry. Finally there has been great user resistance to microforms. Recent research has shown that if microforms are used for reference purposes and for a relatively brief period, resistance is soon overcome. This has been the case with catalogs and bibliographies. If, however, the microform is for study, then long-established study habits have to be modified—from posture to the placement of documents in front of the user to the fact that in general the readers are available only in a few fixed locations. It has been proven that there is added eyestrain involved in the use of microforms, but whether this is due to the type of materials reproduced in microform or to the form itself has not been determined. Most users also perceive microforms as benefiting the institution more than the user, even when unique materials are involved that would not have been available otherwise. Nevertheless it appears that because of both the uniqueness of many of the materials available only in microform and the savings involved, libraries will continue to acquire microforms in ever-increasing numbers.

SUGGESTED READINGS

Grannis, Chandler P. (ed.). *What Happens in Book Publishing*. 2d ed. New York: Columbia University Press, 1967.

This work, cited in Chapters One and Two, offers much background material for this chapter as well.

Children's Books

Karl, Jean. *From Childhood to Childhood: Children's Books and Their Creators*. New York: The John Day Company, Inc., 1970.

A fascinating glimpse of how children's books are created by a leading expert in the field.

Paperbacks

Dystel, Oscar. "The Paperback Revolution: Where Has It Gone?" *Publishers Weekly*, 212 (Nov. 14, 1977), 31–33.

An examination of problems currently affecting the paperback book trade.

Religious Books

Every February and September, *Publishers Weekly* devotes an issue to religious books. A perusal of several recent issues is recommended to get a feel of what is going on in this field. Recent issues have included articles on religious book clubs, best sellers, and alternative religious publishers.

Reference and Subscription Books

McCabe, Edward A. "Subscription Books," *Publishers Weekly*, 191 (May 29, 1967), 36–40.

Although more than a decade old, this article still gives the best overall background information on subscription book publishing.

Scholarly Books

The literature about scholarly publishing is very extensive. The field has its own journal, *Scholarly Publishing*, published by the University of Toronto Press. The basic book on the subject remains:

Hawes, Gene R. *To Advance Knowledge: A Handbook on American University Press Publishing*. New York: American University Press Services, Inc., 1967.

A good recent survey of university press publishers is:

Goellner, J. G. "The Future of University Presses," *Library Journal*, 103 (Sept. 15, 1978), 1695–1699.

Reprints

Nemeyer, Carol A. *Scholarly Reprint Publishing in the United States*. New York: R. R. Bowker Company, 1972.

The principal source of information on the reprint industry remains Nemeyer's doctoral dissertation, written just as reprint publishing reached its height.

Small Presses and Self-publishing

Henderson, Bill, (ed.). *The Publish-It-Yourself Handbook: Literary Tradition and How-To*. Yonkers, N.Y.: Pushcart Book Press, 1973.

An anthology of articles on small presses and self-publishing.

Vanity Publishers

Morris, Roger. "Vanity Publishing," *American Libraries*, 5 (Sept. 1974), 420–422.

A good survey of vanity presses—how they operate, their motives, etc.

Microforms

Saffady, William. *Micrographics*. Littleton, Colo.: Libraries Unlimited, 1978.

Everything anyone wants to know about microforms, micropublishing, and so on is included in this basic manual.

CHAPTER FOUR
Nonprint and Other Specialized Materials

Following our discussion of various types of printed materials—how they are produced, what problems they present to libraries, etc.—let us now turn to nonprint and other specialized materials: computer-based materials, materials for the handicapped, and government publications.

NONPRINT MATERIALS

Few libraries today can build satisfactory collections unless they also include nonprint materials, particularly audio-visual materials. Nonprint materials can be recreational—as with many 16 mm films—or they can be strictly educational. All these materials need equipment in order for their contents to be read or used. Many publishers are now offering multimedia kits that include several different kinds of materials—both print and nonprint—centering on one topic. Many of the so-called "new media" are not new at all; they have been around for years. They have just not been seriously considered for inclusion in library collections up to now.

Nonprint materials entered the mainstream of school and library use beginning in the 1950s and early 1960s but reached maturity only in the 1970s. The impetus came from two directions. First of all, the traditional textbook and reference book publishers began to hear from educational researchers that materials other than the traditional textbook could be used to much greater advantage. Working with these researchers and teachers in the field, publishers began to explore the possibility of the use of films, filmstrips, slides, audiotapes and records, and other nonprint materials in conjunction with the traditional textbook package (which already included tests, workbooks, and teacher's manuals) that they were publishing. Secondly, developments in the field of information science showed that there were better ways of storing and retrieving information, largely through the use of computers, microforms, and other mechanical and electronic filing and sorting devices. The result was the movement of many traditional publishers into these new fields, and, more importantly, the launching of many new firms specializing in the new media. The traditional publishers were often unsuccessful in trying to integrate production and sales of the new media into their traditional work patterns. As a result, only a few of them have developed substantial business in the field. This has left the area open to many enterprising new businesses, which have largely chosen to concentrate on one aspect of the field and to develop and refine it. Let us now consider the main types of nonprint materials, beginning with audiotapes and recordings.

Audio Materials

Audio materials presently come in two forms—tapes and discs (often called *phonorecords* or, simply, *records*). Tapes may be in open reel-to-reel or cassette forms, the latter increasingly popular with the general public and liked by libraries because of the greater ease of handling and the fact that they are less subject to damage while being used. Records are manufactured in various sizes to be played at various speeds. Most libraries limit themselves to collecting 12-inch 33 ⅓ rpm long-playing microgroove recordings in either stereophonic or monaural sound. Stereophonic recordings have two channels, which attempt to reproduce sound as it would be heard originally in the concert hall by a pair of ears rather than just one (monaural sound). Stereophonic recordings were first marketed in the mid-1950s, shortly after the introduction of the long-playing record in

1948. All current recordings are made only in stereophonic sound, but many monaural recordings of historic interest are still being marketed. The 12-inch long-playing record can accommodate approximately thirty minutes of top-quality music on a side. Speech recordings, or recordings of music at lesser fidelity, can run as long as forty-five minutes at 33 ⅓ rpm. Broadcasting stations sometimes use larger discs turning at 16 ⅔ rpm to record for in-house purposes. The 7-inch 45 rpm recording was very popular at one time for single recordings of popular songs (that is why it is commonly referred to as a "pop single"). As of 1975, however, its share of the market dropped below 8 percent, and most libraries make no effort to include such recordings in their collections since most pop singles are also available as part of long-playing records. Reel-to-reel tape has been popular only with serious record collectors for the preservation of programs taken off the air from radio broadcasts or made from live performances. The commercial sale of recordings in this format has never been a big business. This has changed, however, with the development of tape cassettes. The early cassettes did not have the same high fidelity as reel-to-reel tape or discs, largely because they were played at a slower speed. Recent technical developments have largely erased the major differences in quality. Where there is a choice of the same work in different formats, libraries still usually prefer the disc record. It is easier to find an individual selection or part of a work on a disc than it is on a tape, which must be wound and rewound.

Recordings are usually made today by using reel-to-reel tape. A different tape will be used for each channel. Both classical and popular recordings use many channels in the original recording process (as many as sixteen). These channels are then combined by highly experienced recording engineers to provide a satisfactory two-channel disc or tape recording for mass marketing. An attempt to launch four-channel ("quad") sound on the market in the mid-1970s seems not to have taken hold. Once the master tape is prepared, copies of it can be transported to various countries where the commercial discs or tape cassettes are manufactured. Sometimes sound on a tape will be altered ("remastered"), producing an inferior or superior recording of the original performance. Records can also be manufactured in one country for sale in others, as the record business is today completely international. The largest producers are multinational corporations operating in all the developed nations under the same or different trade names. Thus the company known as Columbia in the U.S. markets its products in England under the CBS label. Decca in Great Britain is known as London in this country. RCA Victor was long known abroad as His Master's Voice (HMV) or its foreign equivalent. And so it goes. A recording of the Boston

Symphony will be sold as widely in Europe as in the United States, and few classical companies—or popular ones, for that matter—will undertake a recording unless there is hope of worldwide sale. Even recordings made in the Soviet Union are regularly sold in Western Europe and the United States under the Melodiya label. One of the things a librarian buying recordings should learn are the various company names under which the same product is marketed in different countries. Oné might think that it is necessary to know only the American brand names. Unfortunately, however, some of the best selection aids, as we shall see in Chapter Six, are issued in foreign countries, particularly Great Britain. A library is all the poorer for not taking advantage of these aids by learning a few facts about the organization of the recording industry. It is also true that manufacturing quality standards are higher in Western Europe and Japan than they are in the United States; therefore, better-quality recordings can be obtained by purchasing foreign pressings. Such pressings are now widely available, thanks to numerous import firms, in the larger record outlets in major U.S. cities. It should be emphasized that recordings are only as good as the equipment they are played on. Poor equipment can make the best recordings sound terrible.

A word also should be said about the "directly cut" discs that began to appear on the market in the late 1970s. They are a reaction to the multiple splicing and tampering, by recording engineers using electronic equipment, with the original performance. Most recordings are made in sections, with each section being recorded several times. The best "takes" are then spliced together to form a whole—a performance that never existed in reality. With directly cut discs, the performance is recorded directly onto the disc master. The work is recorded in its entirety, and there is no possibility of change or substitution. Certain audiophiles prefer this, claiming that it is closer to reality and therefore more spontaneous. They are thus willing to pay the premium prices charged by the direct-cut manufacturers. These higher prices are largely due to the fact that only a certain number of discs can be manufactured by this process from the original master; thus, all directly cut discs are in reality limited editions.

How do recordings originate? With pop artists and famous classical artists, the performer has the greatest say about what is to be recorded. Usually there is some compromise when a record manufacturer sees little commercial possibility in an obscure work that a performer may wish to record, but in general it is the artist who commands. With lesser-known performers it is the manufacturer that decides what is to be recorded and when. The market is often the prime factor. Record producers seek out compositions that have never been recorded before, or they may decide that a new recording by a particular artist of a very popular composition is needed.

Recordings are marketed through completely different channels than print materials. Little can be bought directly from the record companies themselves; most business is transacted through record dealers. A library has the choice of using a national or regional wholesaler, who gives discounts similar to book materials (20 to 30 percent), or a local retailer, who gives a smaller discount but probably more personal service. Local retailers who carry stocks large enough to satisfy the needs of most libraries exist only in the larger U.S. cities. Elsewhere the library is forced to use a nationally known firm, such as Sam Goody or Chesterfield. Record manufacturers advertise their products only in record journals. Records are not generally available for previewing or "on approval." They may be returned only when they are mechanically defective. Thus librarians buying records must rely substantially on reviews or the reputations of individual performers.

Recordings exist at various price levels. These price differentials are due to the reputation of the recording artists—the most famous commanding the highest prices—and to the age of the recordings; just as with books, there exist reprints of older materials which, like paperbacks, are sold at reduced prices. The latest recordings will naturally benefit from the latest developments in recording techniques, but older ones may not be that sonically outdated, and the performances themselves may be artistically superior. After a number of years, a few performances will have achieved the status of classics and will be more or less constantly available on one label or another. These are usually referred to as "historic" recordings. They include the recordings of such classical artists as Arturo Toscanini or Maria Callas or such jazz musicians as Billie Holliday or Glenn Miller. With such recordings, the quality of the sound is secondary in interest to the style of the performance itself. Much can be learned about the history of the performance of music from listening to recordings from the past.

Visual Materials

Visual materials come in a great variety of formats, each requiring different equipment to enable a viewer to look at the contents. Those most commonly found in library collections are films, filmstrips, slides and transparencies, and video recordings. Films come in various sizes: 8 mm, 16 mm, 35 mm, and 70 mm. These sizes refer to the width of the film in millimeters. The 35 mm and 70 mm sizes are generally used for commercial films, while the smaller sizes are used for educational purposes and are most likely to be found in libraries. Entertainment films originally issued in the larger sizes are usually reduced to 16 mm for marketing to schools and libraries. The 8 mm size is that of the home movie and was long thought not to be of good enough quality for school and library use. However, the introduction of Super 8 mm film by Eastman Kodak some years ago has brought about a great improvement in the image projected, due to the 50 percent larger size of the individual frame. This was achieved through a reduction in the size of the sprocket holes, thus permitting more of the width to be used for the film frame. A magnetic sound track was also added to the Super 8 mm films. This is one way of adding sound to films; the other is an optical sound track, in which the sound track is photographed and converted into bands of light and dark that are then reconverted to sound by a photoelectric cell. The use of films has long been complicated by the troublesome process of having to thread the film into the film projector for showing. This has recently been eliminated in many cases by the use of cartridges that automatically thread themselves, just as with audiotape cassettes.

For many of today's television and movie-oriented public, films present a more satisfactory way of conveying information than do the traditional print media. They convey the greatest sense of reality and can easily transport an audience to another country or back in time to another age. Films are also able, through such techniques as time-lapse photography, to reproduce images that could not be seen by the naked eye in a short time, such as the opening of a flower bud. While a few major textbook and reference book publishers such as McGraw-Hill and Encyclopaedia Britannica have long produced educational films, most are created by specialized educational film producers. Commercial entertainment films are also used in libraries, particularly public libraries, and these too are marketed by film companies.

Just as with audio materials, film producers advertise their products largely in audio-visual publications and professional magazines. There is also a great deal of direct-mail solicitation through fliers and catalogs. In contrast to recordings, most films are still bought directly from the producer. Most library wholesalers do not stock enough of a variety of films to satisfy most libraries' needs. Also, in contrast to recordings, films are available for previewing or for purchase "on approval." With both systems, films are looked at by the prospective buyer before a purchase is made. The difference is that with previewing the film must be returned and another copy ordered from the producer. With an "on approval" order, the film may be kept and paid for or returned and the bill canceled. Previewing may be done at the producer's, if such facilities are available, at library meetings, or in the individual library. One great difference in the marketing of films is that purchasers are usually required to sign acquisitions agreements that are in effect contracts governing the use of the material bought. Often the making of another copy of the film will be prohibited. Where and when a film may be shown may also be limited.

Most 16 mm films cost several hundred dollars. They are thus purchased only by school systems or large libraries or by libraries that have organized a film circuit in which films are shared. Many films are never bought but are rented from producers as needed. All films, other than entertainment classics, become dated—in content, attitude, or visual images (the clothes or automobiles of an earlier period)—over time. Renting films is one way of avoiding obsolescence.

So far, we have concentrated on films; however, other types of visual materials also deserve consideration. One of the most popular types, and the one most often found in individual school media centers, is the filmstrip. A filmstrip is a piece of 35 mm film on which a series of pictures has been placed in a fixed order. In order to create a sound track to go along with a filmstrip, it is necessary to produce a separate record or cassette keyed to the filmstrip but played separately. Filmstrips are widely used for several reasons. First of all, they are inexpensive, particularly when compared with films. Further, a wide variety of material is available on filmstrips. They are also easy to use and can be run at any speed desired. They are very compact and can be easily stored. They cannot, of course, show motion. While some filmstrips are produced by regular book publishers as adjuncts to printed materials, many are the work of special educational film companies. More filmstrips than films can be obtained through wholesale library jobbers, but again, dealing directly with the producer may be the most satisfactory method.

Another type of still picture is the slide. The most common size now in use is the 2 × 2-inch size used by amateur photographers, although the slides are usually mounted in a heavier and more substantial mounting than for home use. Many slides are produced locally by the individual school or library, but sets can be purchased from educational publishers. Art museums are a fine source of reproductions of art works in their collections. Travelers can often buy excellent sets or individual slides at historic sites. Slides have the advantage over filmstrips of being able to be arranged in any order desired. Otherwise their uses are much the same.

Transparencies—large acetate sheets, usually 8½ × 11 inches—

are also marketed by educational publishers, most often as adjuncts to printed books. Transparencies can be made quite elaborate by the use of overlays to portray increasingly complex relationships or progressive stages of development. Like slides, many transparencies are produced locally.

Video recording is still changing rapidly, but it promises to be of widespread use in the future—if only manufacturers could agree on standard formats! Videotape looks much like audiotape, but images and sound are both recorded on the tape. Video discs have been talked about for years, but there is as yet no standardization; one manufacturer's products can be played only on its own equipment. The most common form in use to date is the video cassette. Video cassettes can be played back on a regular television set through the addition of a special attachment. With the increasing availability of videotape recorders at affordable prices, it has become possible to record programs off the air for later playing or for preservation. Video cassettes may also be purchased commercially. Their use, while still a rarity in most libraries, would seem to be a definite factor to be taken into consideration for developing library collections in the near future.

As has been mentioned before, many publishers are packaging various types of print and nonprint materials together and marketing them as multimedia kits. Many libraries have also assembled their own kits around a particular topic. Another type of material that is often included in such kits, but usually marketed separately, is instructional and simulation games. Some of these are produced by educational publishers; others are the products of game companies or of an individual who has the flair for creating such educational tools. The sources of supply for these games are varied. Most must be ordered directly from the producer.

Computer-based materials

Computer-based materials are a recent development but have quickly become extremely important to libraries of all sizes. We are referring specifically to *computerized data bases* of a bibliographic nature. Included are cataloging data bases such as OCLC and BALLOTS, which supplement or replace the national and trade bibliographies. Most, however, are subject data bases indexing quantities of specialized information. These data bases have been developed almost entirely outside the traditional book industry by both private and nonprofit organizations. Most of the data bases are available, at least in part, in printed form, and the computerized data banks often grew out of automation of the printing of these indexes. Once the data were computerized in order to activate new methods of printing, it was an easy step to make this machine-readable data available on a subscription or other basis to the consumer.

Machine-readable data bases have several advantages over their printed counterparts. These include greater speed in searching, particularly when multiple weekly or monthly issues have not been cumulated; greater currency (the printing of most indexes takes a minimum of six weeks); and the possibility of printouts of the information found, thus eliminating tedious recording of citations. Most important of all, many of these data bases offer more in-depth access than do the printed versions. It is more feasible to use multiple subject headings or other points of access than in the traditional methods. Furthermore the information sought can often be printed out in the form desired by the searcher. There is no need to reorder the material manually. Since many of the computer-based materials duplicate and improve on printed versions of the same material, it is possible in some cases—if the publisher permits this and if the data bases contain all the printed material—for the library to replace the printed indexes or catalogs with the computer version, thus saving some money. Unfortunately the computerized versions of all these indexes have proven to be, initially at least, much more expensive. Ease and depth of access do have their price.

It was mentioned earlier that most of the computerized data bases were developed outside the regular book industry by both nonprofit and private bodies. This has given rise to what is now widely known as the "information industry." The American Institute of Physics and the American Chemical Society are two of the nonprofit organizations engaged in producing computerized data bases. The U.S. government, through such agencies as the Library of Congress, the National Library of Medicine, and the National Technical Information Service, is a large, if not the largest, producer of such data bases. *The New York Times* Infobank is an example of a private producer. The producers of these data bases can and often do market their wares directly to library consumers. Other data base producers reach their markets through regional library information networks, such as the Midwest Region Library Network (MIDLNET), or through commercial distributors. The two commercial distributors that currently dominate the market are Lockheed Information Service, with its DIALOG system, and the Systems Development Corporation, with ORBIT. Since each system has exclusive rights to some data bases, most libraries that wish to acquire such data bases must deal with both corporations. It is highly probable that additional distributors will become active in the field in the next few years.

Marketing of these products to libraries is accomplished largely by advertising in the library and information industry periodicals and by exhibiting these wares at library and information science meetings. This is an expanding industry, of increasing importance to libraries, and one that needs to be watched carefully.[1]

MATERIALS FOR THE HANDICAPPED

The provision of materials for the blind was long a responsibility of the federal government and a number of private social agencies. In recent years, commercial publishers have also entered the field. Until 1966, the federal program was limited to the legally blind. It is now available to any physically handicapped person who is unable to read conventional printed materials. Materials for the blind and physically handicapped include braille books, magazines, and music, as well as talking books and magazines on disc and tape. These materials are all produced by the government or private agencies serving the blind and handicapped. Commercial publishers have entered the field with large-type books. Work in this area was pioneered in this country by Keith Jennison in 1965 and at about the same time in England by Frederick A. Thorpe, who founded Ulverscroft Large Print Books. Ulverscroft markets its books in the United States, and Thorpe and Jennison have since been joined by a number of other U.S. publishers, the largest of which are G. K. Hall and Large Print, Ltd. All the houses offer the works of many different publishers, whereas such companies as Harper & Row and Macmillan confine their large-type publications to their own backlists.

It is strange that publishers failed to go into the production of large-print books until the mid-1960s; private agencies, after all, had been producing textbooks in this format since the 1940s. Undoubtedly it was felt that production costs would be too high for the limited market. As it has turned out, the market has proven to be much larger than anyone hoped or anticipated. To be successful in this specialized field, however, a publisher must produce a large number of titles and maintain them in print for a long period. Keith Jennison has stated that he will not add any book to his list unless he believes that it is worth keeping in print for twenty years. As of 1978, Bowker listed some 3,000 books, plus magazines and newspapers, in the latest edition of its *Large Type Books in Print*. These are published by some seventy publishers and associations. Materials are of all types—both scholarly and recreational. They also include children's books and even some in foreign languages. Some reference tools have been produced in this format, and a few magazines, such as the *Reader's*

---

[1]For further information on computerized data bases, see William A. Katz, *Introduction to Reference Work*, Vol. 2: *Reference Services and Reference Processes* (3d ed., New York: McGraw-Hill Book Company, 1978), Part III, pp. 123ff.

Digest, and at least one newspaper, the weekly edition of *The New York Times,* are available.

The revolution in large-type books was made financially possible by developments in photo-offset printing in the 1960s. Many large-type books are simply photographically enlarged copies of the original edition. Unhappily not all typefaces enlarge satisfactorily, and so several publishers reset their editions in the best type for this format. Some works become so bulky that they must be issued in multiple volumes. Most sales of large-type books are to libraries, although occasionally bookstores will get orders for individual buyers. It is possible for any book to be enlarged; a few publishers carry out such orders, naturally on a no-return basis.

Large-type books are the only type of material for the handicapped that are produced commercially. Braille materials and the various talking books are the work of the Library of Congress—the federal agency responsible by law for service to this group—or of private associations and social service agencies. While originally talking books were available only on 16 rpm discs, several changes have come about in recent years. Increasingly 8 rpm is becoming the standard speed for discs. A thin, flexible plastic disc that plays only a limited number of times has been adopted for magazines and newspapers, while books are recorded on more durable microgroove records. Reel-to-reel tape has been used for some time to produce limited numbers of copies of textbooks and more scholarly materials needed by a few persons, but recently tape cassettes have supplanted that form and only the master copy is preserved in reel-to-reel form. All the talking books and those in braille format are supplied free of charge to certified users. For discs, playback machines are also supplied free, but for cassettes the borrower must purchase a machine. Talking books and braille books are all reprints. Talking books wear out faster than braille books, and the Library of Congress must allocate some money each year for the rerecording or retranscribing of older popular titles. In 1978, 1,562 titles were recorded as talking books and 385 were issued in braille form by the Library of Congress. Many other titles are recorded by volunteers throughout the country for specific needs, particularly for students and professionals, so in actuality many times these numbers are available for blind and handicapped users.

Libraries are increasingly including materials for the handicapped in their collections. Indeed the ALA *Standards for Library Services for the Blind and Physically Handicapped* state: "Every kind of library should make a special effort to include blind . . . and handicapped people in all the services provided for sighted patrons." Since most of these materials are produced and marketed outside regular book channels, it is necessary to become aware of sources of supply. The brochure, periodically revised, by Howard Haycraft, *Books for the Blind and Physically Handicapped*, is a good place to begin. Above all, librarians have a responsibility in this area and should not neglect these materials just because they fall outside the traditional areas of publishing and of library collections.

GOVERNMENT PUBLICATIONS

Almost every type of publication we have discussed so far is the product of a commercial company or a private organization. Little has been said of the publications of the various government agencies, except for materials for the handicapped. Discussion of these publications has purposely been left to the end since government publications include every type of publication issued by the private sector. Thus it is appropriate to end with this all-encompassing type of publishing activity.

There are many definitions of a *government document*. Title 44 of the U.S. Code defines it as "informational matter published as an individual document at government expense or as required by law." ("Document" is now interpreted to include any form of publication.) Government agencies can be international, foreign, or domestic and can exist at the federal, regional (state in this country), or local (county or city/town) level. Government documents seem to come forth in a never-ceasing flow. Wherever there is a government agency that has access to a printing plant or to a duplicating or mimeograph machine, there you will find government publications. Because they are issued by such a variety of offices, they are extremely difficult to find out about or to track down. Since much government agency material is for internal use only, no attempt is made to inform outsiders about it. Furthermore governments, by their very nature, are secretive about their operations, even in as open a society as the United States. Thus they do not publicize many of the results of their work or research. In spite of these difficulties, a large research library may acquire as many as 150,000 items published by government bodies in the course of one year. Many of these are in pamphlet or leaflet form or may be single sheets, but some are large-scale monographs and reference works. They include microprint and all types of nonprint materials, as well as books and periodicals. In some areas of publishing, the government may be the major source, as with books for the blind or technical reports. In other areas, the government's activity may be peripheral to the general commercial industry, as with audio-visual materials.

It is impossible, within the confines of this book, to go into great detail about how documents are published and marketed by international or foreign agencies or by state and local government bodies in this country. Instead we shall take as an example the publications of the U.S. federal government. In all government bodies, documents are the work of government employees or of persons contracted with by the government to pursue certain research. Many of these authors remain anonymous. In any case, they are not remunerated through royalties and there is no question of selling subsidiary rights. Payment comes one time only in the form of a regular pay check or a contract payment. The author cannot even copyright the work, as government documents generally must remain in the public domain.

Production of documents may be in-house. This is a favorite device often used by government agencies to limit knowledge and distribution of a publication. It may also speed up publication of an item. In any case, with the widespread use of photo-offset and other duplicating equipment, vast numbers of government documents are issued in this "near-print" format. The standard procedure is for U.S. federal documents to be handed over to the Government Printing Office (GPO) for design and printing. The GPO formerly did all of its printing at its own printing plant in Washington, D.C. In recent years it has outgrown that facility and established field printing plants in various parts of the country to take care of certain regional needs. Also, since 1968 it has turned increasingly to private commercial printers by contracting the printing of individual items through regional procurement offices. This utilization of commercial printers will undoubtedly continue to grow. It is already well over 50 percent of all printing done.

The marketing of government documents differs greatly from that of commercial publications. The U.S. Superintendent of Documents is charged with issuing catalogs and publication lists. Various federal agencies also issue their own bibliographies. This remains the principal method of making known what the GPO has for sale, as little advertising is done and few if any review copies are sent to library or professional journals. Direct-mail solicitation is the main way of reaching the potential buyer. Government bodies in general have never viewed their publishing programs as anything more than a public service and have rarely seen the need to launch an aggressive sales program. It is up to the customer to seek them out. The federal government sales program is required by law to be self-sustaining. Prices are set at cost plus 50 percent. For many years, prices were set at a much lower level than in the commercial sector (cost plus 10 percent). This resulted in prices drastically lower than for commercial publications of the same quality. In 1973 this was changed and some publications were repriced at two or three times their previous cost, shocking librarians throughout the country. The new pricing program is currently producing a profit of about $1 million a year.

Traditionally government documents have been sold through the mail, with payment being demanded in advance. Beginning in 1967 the GPO began to set up branch bookstores outside of Washington, D.C., in federally owned buildings in major cities throughout the country. These stores were planned to stock about 1,000 of the most popular government documents. They were also set up to provide a special-order service for items that they did not have in stock. Their success has exceeded all expectations, proving that the government could realize larger revenues from the sale of its own publications if it attempted a more aggressive sales program. Other government agencies, such as the Internal Revenue Service or the Small Business Administration, are also permitted to sell certain federal publications. Most retail booksellers will not stock government documents, as the profit is so small. The federal government has set 25 percent as the trade discount it will give to retailers. This is not sufficient to attract most retailers. Finally the federal government is very conservative in its print orders. It does not want to be left with unsold copies, and therefore many GPO publications quickly go out of print. While the Superintendent of Documents is authorized to reprint anything in demand, the demand must actually be overwhelming before this is done.

The sales program of the GPO comes in conflict with two types of programs under which the recipients pay nothing for government documents. (Naturally they pay acquisition and cataloging costs and later storage costs, but there is no initial payment for the material itself.) The first type of program is due to the policy of authorizing the GPO to supply a certain number of free copies of most of its publications to members of Congress and senators, who, in turn, give them away to constituents who request them. These constituents may include libraries as well as individuals. The second type of giveaway program is the document depository program, in which selected libraries in a particular region are designated to receive free of charge certain government publications—not everything issued by the federal government but large quantities of materials. The reasoning behind such a program is to make information available to all citizens. Since only a limited number of libraries may be designated depository libraries, most libraries are forced to satisfy their needs through purchase or the occasional gift from a member of Congress or senator. Agencies that issue their own publications may or may not charge for them. In any case, requests for many of these must go directly to the issuing agency.

The pattern for the U.S. federal government is generally repeated with state and local governments, and with the governments of foreign governments, as well as with international agencies. Little of the vast array of publications issued by governmental bodies is handled through regular book trade channels except for some specialized library wholesalers or retailers that will act as the library's agent in procuring such works. It is a confusing and frustrating part of the book trade, but it must be mastered by any librarian who hopes to tap this vast reservoir of information.

SUGGESTED READINGS

Nonprint Materials

There is a vast literature on nonprint materials, most of it dealing with evaluation of materials, use of equipment, or developing audio-visual collections. There is little on the industry itself. The following items are highly recommended:

Expanding Media, ed. by Deirdre Boyle. Phoenix, Ariz.: Oryx Press, 1977.

An anthology of articles on selection, evaluation, programming, production, equipment, etc.

Gelatt, Roland. *The Fabulous Phonograph, 1877–1977*. 2d rev. ed. New York: The Macmillan Company, 1977.

An entertaining popular history of the record industry.

Halsey, Richard Sweeney. *Classical Music Recordings for Home and Library*. Chicago: American Library Association, 1976.

Includes information on selecting classical recordings, organizing the collection, and care and equipment necessary, as well as a recommended basic collection.

Hicks, Warren B. *Developing Multimedia Libraries*. New York: R. R. Bowker Company, 1970.

A basic manual covering all aspects of utilizing audio-visual materials in a library: selection, processing, and use.

Teo, Elizabeth. "Audiovisual Materials in the College and Community College Library: the Basics of Collection Building," CHOICE, 14 (June 1977), 487–501; 14 (July/Aug. 1977), 633–645.

Although aimed at academic libraries, this article forms a good basic introduction for any type of library.

Materials for the Handicapped

Haycraft, Howard. *Books for the Blind and Physically Handicapped.* 4th ed. rev. New York: H. W. Wilson Company, n.d. [1972?]

Includes a selected bibliography of additional readings on the subject.

Government Documents

Morehead, Joe. *Introduction to United States Public Documents.* 2d ed. Littleton, Colo.: Libraries Unlimited, 1978.

The current basic text on U.S. Government documents. Topics of interest to collection builders include distribution and sales of documents, sources of documents, and bibliographic aids and catalogs.

PART TWO
Finding Out about Library Materials

CHAPTER FIVE
Trade Bibliography

Now that we have discussed how library materials are created and marketed, principally from the publisher's point of view, let us examine how libraries find out about such materials. We indicated in Part One that publishers issue seasonal catalogs, as well as many types of announcements and fliers about forthcoming books and books that have already been published. They also, usually annually, issue a complete catalog of all of their books that are "in print." Finally every publishing house advertises in various types of periodicals and newspapers—general newspapers and periodicals, trade journals (for libraries and the book trade), and in specialized and professional journals. Looking at the situation from the consumer's point of view, how does the librarian react?

BOOKS

Fliers, which usually arrive through the mail (although they may be picked up by the librarian at conventions and other library meetings where there are book exhibits), and advertisements alert librarians to the existence of a particular work. Seasonal catalogs do likewise. With some materials, orders can be placed immediately from these fliers and advertisements; for a great deal of material, however, the librarian will wish to wait for reviews (see Chapter Six). Fliers eventually end up in the wastepaper basket, but most librarians file seasonal catalogs by publisher for future reference until the materials listed in them appear in the publisher's complete "in-print" catalog. Even then, some libraries find it helpful to keep the seasonal catalogs for a number of years since they include much descriptive information that never appears in the abbreviated listings in the complete catalogs. As for advertisements, notations of books for possible purchase may be made from them, or they may be clipped. Most likely, however, the only ones that will be preserved for any length of time and referred to for information are those appearing in the semiannual "announcement" numbers of *Publishers Weekly* and *Library Journal*, both of which index the books advertised and organize the ads alphabetically for easier consultation.

Much of this filing of catalogs for future reference is now obviated by the R. R. Bowker Company's publication *Forthcoming Books* and its companion volume, *Subject Guide to Forthcoming Books*. A word should be said here about Bowker. In existence for over a century, this company produces a multitude of bibliographic publications, which together form a fairly comprehensive bibliography of the U.S. book trade. Unfortunately its publications are confined largely to the listing of books and periodicals. As we shall see later, for information about other types of library materials, it is necessary to turn elsewhere. The Bowker Company has refined its gathering procedures over the years so that today it catches most of the printed publications appearing in the United States. The items most likely to slip through its net are works published by the small and private presses. Certain types of printed materials, such as pamphlets under fifty pages, are automatically excluded. Once a work has been announced for publication, it is entered into Bowker's computerized data base and eventually winds its way through the various components of Bowker's bibliographic tools, provided, of course, that it is eventually published. (Some announced books fall by the wayside.) Bowker's bibliographic tools were once based primarily on the publishers' annual catalogs of books in print. This is no longer so. Some publishers are slow about getting such catalogs out; some no longer list everything in these catalogs (because of cost factors); and some may never issue such catalogs. Thus Bowker gathers its information from many sources. Since it is looked upon by the U.S. publishing industry as rendering an important service, it has the cooperation of most publishers.

Much of Bowker's input to its data bases comes from the Library of Congress's Cataloging-in-Publication (CIP) program. Most trade publishers, as well as many scholarly and professional publishers, supply information on future publications to the Library of Congress so that their publications may be cataloged in advance of publication and this information printed on the reverse side of the title page. The publisher fills out a basic information sheet for each book and submits this, along with a photocopy of the title page, if available, and, if possible, with galley proofs. From this the Library of Congress supplies the publisher with author and title entries, subject headings, and classification numbers. It also supplies this data to Bowker and places it in the MARC tapes, so that very early in the publishing process there is a minimum record (usually limited to the basic items listed above) that begins to appear in the Bowker publications and in the various cataloging data bases in this country. (From MARC, the record will be transmitted to OCLC, RLIN, and others.) The principal difficulty with recording information about books prior to their publication has always been that they may never be published. Or they may change their titles once or even several times during the course of publication. They may even change authors. Or the information given the Library of Congress and Bowker may have been so incomplete that a wrong entry was made and must be corrected once the book has been published. All these possibilities present daily problems to the librarian and bibliographer.

To return to *Forthcoming Books*, this is a brief listing by author and title issued bimonthly. The *Subject Guide to Forthcoming Books* provides yet another form of access to this information. Each issue updates the preceding one, and the listings are carried until the book has been published and is listed permanently in *Books in Print* (see below). As each semiannual portion of *Books in Print* is published, large numbers of titles can be dropped from *Forthcoming Books*—in fact, most of the books that have actually been published.

Once a book has been published, the publisher is required by the new Copyright Act to submit two copies of the finished book to the Library of Congress, which catalogs the work and places this cataloging information in its MARC records data base and in its printed catalogs. It then passes this full cataloging data on to Bowker. Bowker is also aware (from information supplied directly by the publishers) of additional publications that the Library of Congress has not yet acquired or is slow to catalog, and it too does a certain amount of cataloging. All these cataloged books form the basis of the *Weekly Record*, which attempts to record the entire production of the U. S. publishing industry. Prior to September 1974, the *Weekly Record* formed the final section of *Publishers Weekly*. Since that date, it has been published and sold separately. The *Weekly Record* differs from

Forthcoming Books in that complete catalog entries are given, with full title, imprint, collation, LC and Dewey Decimal Classification number, LC card number, ISBN, and subject headings. There are also usually some descriptive notes. Certain categories of publications are omitted, however. These include pamphlets under fifty pages, government documents, subscription books, dissertations, and periodicals. The *Weekly Record* is arranged alphabetically by main entry. Since it is the first concrete evidence of the actual publication of a book, it is of primary importance to book selectors.

Every month since January 1960, the entries from the *Weekly Record* have been cumulated and rearranged by Dewey Decimal Classification number and published as the *American Book Publishing Record* (usually abbreviated as *BPR*, not *ABPR*). There is an index by author and title. Further cumulations occur annually and then quinquennially. In 1978 Bowker cumulated twenty-eight years of *BPR* and the *Weekly Record* in the *American Book Publishing Record Cumulative: 1950–1977.* This cumulation also includes additional entries derived from the National Union Catalog and the LC MARC tapes so as to make it more complete than the original published lists.

Meanwhile, another private publishing company has long been at work compiling a different bibliography, this one "a world list of books in the English language." This is the *Cumulative Book Index (CBI),* published since 1898 by the H. W. Wilson Company. *CBI* is now published monthly except for August, with frequent cumulations. The final cumulations used to be at five-year intervals, but the sheer size of the cumulations has made this no longer feasible and annual cumulations are now the maximum. The set as it now appears on most library shelves consists of a base volume, the *United States Catalog: Books in Print, Jan. 1, 1928,* six big volumes covering the years 1928 to 1956, and smaller cumulations since that date. *CBI* attempts to be a comprehensive list of books and pamphlets issued in the United States and Canada and a selective list of books in English published in other countries. It has long enjoyed a reputation for greater accuracy than the Bowker-produced trade bibliographies, although Bowker has narrowed the quality gap in recent years. *CBI* has also had the advantage of being a combined author, title, and subject listing in one alphabet. The fact that it casts its net much more widely than does Bowker also adds a point in its favor, although there is naturally some lag in the compiling of information from foreign sources. In any case, most libraries find that they cannot do without either the Bowker publications or *CBI.* Having two competing firms involved in the bibliographic field keeps each on its toes.

Once a book has been published and listed in the *Weekly Record* and *CBI,* a record of its existence will also be included in other bibliographic tools serving other purposes. The first of these is the *Publishers Trade List Annual (PTLA)*, which appears each year in September. *PTLA* is merely a collection of the catalogs of individual publishers, those that list all the materials currently available. It thus takes the place of a file of publishers' catalogs that the library itself might assemble. Unfortunately it is not as useful as it might be, and most libraries must maintain their own files of catalogs since an increasing number of publishers do not choose to participate in this venture. Whether it is because of the cost involved or simply because the catalogs must be of a uniform size in order to be bound together, certain major publishers and many smaller ones do not appear in *PTLA*. Textbook publishers are notable by their absence, and other publishers exclude certain types of materials. Catalogs of the small presses can rarely be found in *PTLA*.

Books in Print (BIP) was once an index to the catalogs in *PTLA*. Prior to 1973, this index was produced manually—a long and tedious process. This is now no longer the case, as Bowker produces the list from a computerized data base. *BIP* comes out each October and is followed some six months later by a *Supplement*. The fact that *BIP* is no longer tied to *PTLA*, but is based instead on a multitude of sources, makes it much more comprehensive. With a computerized data base, it is also possible to make corrections, additions, and deletions up to the last minute. *BIP* is now linked to *Forthcoming Books*, as we mentioned previously, in that a title continues to be listed in *Forthcoming Books*, even after its publication, until it is picked up in *BIP* or its *Supplement*. Thus there is now no longer any possibility— theoretically at least—of a title disappearing for a few months, a considerable problem in past years, when librarians had to rely on publishers' announcements and the *Weekly Record* for a long period before the permanent entry appeared in the annual *BIP*. Like *Forthcoming Books*, *BIP* has its *Subject Guide to Books in Print* based on Library of Congress subject headings. Since the Library of Congress does not assign subject headings to fiction, poetry, drama, or Bibles, these are omitted from the *Subject Guide*. For a subject approach to this type of material, *CBI* provides good coverage, however.

Since Bowker is now using a computerized data base, more specialized listings of books in print and subject guides to them can be easily produced. Some of these listings are of different types of books; others are arranged by subject area. The listing most frequently found in libraries is undoubtedly *Paperbound Books in Print*. Unlike its parent publications, it combines in one source author, title, and subject approaches. It has appeared with varying frequency since 1955. Currently it appears in two hardbound cumulative volumes each year, in March and November. Certain paperbacks are listed in

Books in Print, but there is much fuller coverage in *Paperbound Books in Print*, particularly of mass market paperbacks. Other types of publications which have their own listings are *Children's Books in Print* (with a separate *Subject Guide to Children's Books in Print*), *El-hi Textbooks in Print*, and most recently *Large-Type Books in Print*. *Business Books and Serials in Print*, *Religious Books and Serials in Print*, *Medical Books and Serials in Print*, and *Scientific and Technical Books and Serials in Print* are examples of the subject approaches to trade bibliography.

The greatest problem with all these lists of books in print is currency. The information found in any of them may already be out of date. This is because it takes six months for some of them to be compiled and published, and during that time publishers will have added new titles to their lists and deleted others. For this reason, a *Supplement* to *BIP* has been found necessary. Bowker also attempts to space the specialized type or subject listings in the intervals between publishing the parent *BIP* and its *Supplement*, so that in some areas the information will be more up to date for the librarian. Not everything will be six months to a year old.

Another problem with the Bowker and H. W. Wilson publications is that they automatically exclude certain types of printed publications and all types of nonprint materials. Therefore the library must rely on other sources of information. For pamphlets the best source of information is *Vertical File Index*, published by H. W. Wilson. It includes vast amounts of free and inexpensive material, much of it listed nowhere else. The more important items eventually appear in *CBI*, although probably not in the Bowker data base, which excludes all publications under fifty pages. The type of published work most likely to slip through the H. W. Wilson and Bowker nets is the output of the small presses. These are traditionally suspicious of the establishment, particularly the East Coast world of publishing, from which most of them have sought to escape. It is only a sympathetic fellow traveler who can enlist their support and issue a regular list of their work. Len Fulton in Paradise, California, is such a person, and every year or so he issues a *Small Press Record of Books in Print*. It is indispensable to the collector of the products of small, independent presses. Reprints are another type of material about which information has often been difficult to obtain; for this the annual *Guide to Reprints* is helpful.

PERIODICALS

For information about new periodicals, it is necessary to turn to a publication of the Library of Congress: *New Serial Titles: A Union List of*

Serials Commencing Publication after Dec. 31, 1949. This is an author (or main entry) listing issued monthly, with quarterly and annual cumulations. Various multiyear cumulations have also been issued. Not only does it list new periodicals, when they began and when they ceased publication, but it also gives changes for all serials regardless of when they started publication. Since periodicals are notorious for changing their names, for cessations and resumptions, and for changes in the sponsoring body, this is a very helpful feature. Unfortunately not every type of serial publication is listed. Newspapers are one serious omission, as are municipal government serials. *New Serial Titles* also serves as a union list of serial holdings by indicating a number of libraries that possess a particular title. New holdings are listed in the cumulative volumes. Bowker has published a twenty-year cumulation which includes many revisions—*New Serial Titles: 1950–1970 Cumulative* (4 vols., 1973). The Library of Congress also issues a "classified subject arrangement" for *New Serial Titles* on a monthly basis, but this does not cumulate. For such a cumulation it is necessary to turn to the *Subject Index to New Serial Titles, 1950–1965*, published by Pierian Press (1968).

If one is seeking a list of serials that are currently available, there are several guides to choose from. The most widely used is *Ulrich's International Periodicals Directory: A Classified Guide to Current Periodicals, Foreign and Domestic*, which Bowker has published every other year since 1932. There is a helpful companion guide, *Irregular Serials and Annuals*, issued in alternate years. *Ulrich's Quarterly* now updates both of these. The *Standard Periodical Directory*, now in its sixth edition (1979–1980), claims to be the most complete guide to U.S. and Canadian periodicals, with 68,000 entries. For newspapers the *Ayer Directory of Publications*, published annually since 1880, is the best source. It includes both newspapers and magazines, but the newspaper listings are the essential element in this directory. Arrangement is geographical. The magazines are grouped under such headings as "Agricultural publications," "College publications," "Black publications," "Fraternal publications," etc. Some of these more specialized listings may include publications not listed in *Ulrich's*. Listings of other directories may be found in the latest edition of Sheehy's *Guide to Reference Books*.

GOVERNMENT DOCUMENTS

The U.S. Government Printing Office issues the *Monthly Catalog of United States Government Publications*. While far from exhaustive in its coverage (technical report literature is one category largely omitted), the *U.S. Monthly Catalog* includes all publications available for sale by the Superintendent of Documents, as well as many other documents available from the issuing offices. In recent years, the quality of the information has improved radically, and full LC cataloging data is now provided for most items. While arrangement is basically by issuing office, there are now personal author, title, and subject indexes. Various cumulative indexes have been published over the years. The Library of Congress issues the best guide to current state publications: *Monthly Checklist of State Publications*. For technical report literature, the various lists of the National Technical Information Service (NTIS) must be consulted.

MICROFORMS

In the area of microforms, a series of publications paralleling those for printed books has grown up over the years. *Guide to Microforms in Print* has been published annually since 1961, and an annual *Subject Guide to Microforms in Print* was begun the following year. *Microform Review* began to publish a *Micropublishers Trade List Annual* in 1976. Thus this increasingly important field is now very well covered bibliographically.

AUDIO-VISUAL MATERIALS

With audio-visual materials, there are two primary sources of information about new publications and what is available generally. The more satisfactory one is for recordings: the *Schwann Record & Tape Guide*. Published monthly since 1949, the guide attempts to list all recordings currently available from manufacturers in the United States, as well as many imports. The monthly issues, now known as *Schwann 1*, contain information on domestic stereo LP records, eight-track cartridge tapes, and cassettes. Especially valuable each month is a section of "New Listings" that includes detailed analysis of the contents of many anthologies, information that is not repeated in later issues. It is also a good way for the record collector to find out about all new recordings as they come on the market. The largest portion of *Schwann 1* is devoted to classical recordings, but other sections cover current popular recordings (including rock, blues, country and western, folk, etc.) and jazz. After two years these are transferred to *Schwann 2*, which appears only semiannually and which covers, in addition to noncurrent pop and jazz music, religious and spoken recordings, as well as historic monophonic classical records and imported records. While it is still possible to find fault with the way certain recordings are listed in *Schwann*, the cataloging has improved tremendously over the past decade as the publisher began to realize its importance not only to record stores but to libraries and record collectors as well.

With visual materials the situation is not nearly as satisfactory. The best current bibliographies are the *NICEM Media Indexes*, published by the National Information Center for Educational Media at the University of Southern California. These indexes cover a wide variety of materials in volumes arranged by both subject and type of material. Among those most widely used by libraries are the guides to 16 mm educational films, 35 mm educational filmstrips, 8 mm film cartridges, educational overhead transparencies, videotapes, and audiotapes. Subjects covered include black history, health and safety education, vocational and technical education, and psychology. Access is by subject headings, and it is here that the problems begin for the searcher. The indexes are computer-produced, and entries for the same subject can appear in various places. There is little consistency in the assigning of headings from one index to another and even within one index. Within a subject heading, entry is usually by title. A search for materials on Charles Dickens reveals, for example, that there is no specific heading for Dickens. Works are found under "Literature—Authors and Their Works," "Literature— Novels," and "Literature—Short Story." Under these headings, further confusion is caused by the fact that the listing is under the first word of the title. Thus few entries for Dickens fall under "D"; most come under "C" for "Charles." Individual works must be searched for under their own titles. Each NICEM index is revised about every three years. In the interval, periodic supplements are issued. Because of the difficulties in using the NICEM indexes and also because they are less comprehensive in their coverage than Schwann, libraries must usually maintain an extensive file of producers' catalogs if they are to have the necessary information for selection and acquisition of visual materials.

LIBRARY CATALOGS

So far, we have concentrated largely on bibliographies issued within the book and A-V trade itself rather than those coming from official government sources. The United States does not have an official national bibliography, as does Great Britain (*British National Bibliogra-*

phy, 1950–). The nearest thing we have are the publications of the Library of Congress, notably the *National Union Catalog,* and the *Catalog of Copyright Entries,* issued by the U.S. Copyright Office. The *Catalog of Copyright Entries* is of little use to the book selector or acquisitions librarian since it appears only semiannually and about a year late. It does include all types of material (anything that can be copyrighted), including periodicals, music, motion pictures, and filmstrips.

The *National Union Catalog (NUC),* as its name implies, is a record not only of what the Library of Congress catalogs for its collections but also of what is cataloged by several hundred other libraries as well. The word "cataloged" needs to be stressed here, as no attempt is made to be completely comprehensive. Certain materials are rejected as not being suitable for the Library of Congress collections, and they may or may not be picked up and cataloged by other libraries. A second feature of the *NUC* that must always be kept in mind is that inclusion is by date of cataloging, not by date of publication. While most publications are cataloged soon after their publication, this does not have to be done, and some materials may appear in the *NUC* months or even years after their first issue. Thus it is not always as much help to book selectors and acquisitions librarians as it might be. Nevertheless the majority of domestic publications do appear fairly quickly in the *NUC.* The *NUC* is published monthly, with quarterly and annual cumulations. The Library of Congress has also entered into contracts with private publishers, notably Edwards Brothers and Rowman and Littlefield, for the publication of five-year and even more extensive cumulations. Besides publication in the *NUC,* catalog entries from the Library of Congress and many of the major American libraries are appearing in various automated, computerized data bases, notably OCLC and RLIN. Information in these data bases appears several weeks, if not months, before the printed catalogs and is very helpful in supplying prompt information about new publications. This is particularly true since CIP entries are also included in the Library of Congress MARC tapes, giving at least abbreviated information about many books some weeks or months prior to publication. Entries in the *NUC* are arranged alphabetically by author or main entry but there is also a subject listing, albeit one limited to Library of Congress printed cards. This is issued quarterly and cumulated annually and quinquennially under the title *Library of Congress Catalog. Books: Subjects.* One further remark needs to be made about the *NUC:* It is not confined to books. Supplementary volumes cover music, recordings, and motion pictures. Coverage is very selective in these fields, however, and far from satisfactory for selection purposes.

RETROSPECTIVE AND OTHER SOURCES

No library, of course, confines its selection to current materials. Library catalogs, while useful for current searching, are especially suited to the identification and verification of older works. It is here that they really prove their worth. In this connection, we should mention the continuing publication of the *National Union Catalog, Pre-1956 Imprints*. Begun in 1968, the work is now nearing the end of the alphabet and will include some 10 million entries by the time it is completed. Through size alone, this still incomplete publication has become a primary source of information on older publications.

Just as the *NUC* and other library catalogs are useful sources of information for older publications, so too are the various historical segments of U.S. bibliography consulted from time to time. These include Evans, Shaw, Shoemaker, Cooper, Roorbach, Kelly, and the *American Catalogue*. Sheehy's *Guide to Reference Books* gives full details for those not familiar with these works from their reference and bibliography courses.

Until now, we have spoken of the ways librarians may learn of the existence of new publications and identify or verify older ones. The emphasis has been on the works themselves. However, there is another problem connected with this work: to identify publishers and locate their addresses. Most of the bibliographic tools discussed in this chapter include lists of publishers' names and addresses. Those in *CBI* and *Books in Print* are probably the most frequently consulted. The older volumes of *CBI* provide a useful retrospective record through which mergers and deaths of publishing firms can be traced. Other useful sources of information on publishers can be found in the various directories. The most important of these are *Literary Market Place* (*LMP*), published annually by Bowker since 1940, and a more recent addition to the Bowker list: *Audiovisual Market Place* (*AMP*), published every two years since 1969. Both of these give considerably more information about publishers than the names and addresses to be found in *CBI* or *BIP*. They include the names of the principal officers of the company and members of the staffs, an indication of the types of publications and of the number issued each year. Subsidiary and parent organizations can also easily be traced through the information given. Another type of question that can be answered concerns the various imprints used by the publishing houses, often a confusing thing to the beginner in the field. *LMP* and *AMP* also offer information on advertising agencies, printers, review media, and others serving the book industry—a gold mine of information on the book and audiovisual trades.

We have limited our discussion of trade bibliography to the

United States, but all nations, at least the developed ones, have their trade and national bibliographies. While these may not contain all the elements to be found in the United States, they usually include adequate listings for books and periodicals. In some countries of Europe, notably Great Britain, France, and Germany, there exists a true national bibliography which has as its principal task the recording of every publication issued within that country. Again, a comprehensive listing of such publications can be found in Sheehy's *Guide to Reference Books.*

BIBLIOGRAPHY

American Book Publishing Record (BPR). New York: R. R. Bowker Company, 1960– . (Monthly.)

American Book Publishing Record Cumulative: 1950–1977. New York: R. R. Bowker Company, 1978.

American Catalogue . . . , 1876–1910. New York: Publishers Weekly, 1880–1911. 8 vols. in 13. (Reprint: New York: Peter Smith, 1941.)

Audiovisual Market Place: A Multimedia Guide. New York: R. R. Bowker Company, 1969– . (Biennial.)

Ayer Directory of Publications. Philadelphia: N. W. Ayer and Son, Inc., 1880– . (Annual.)

Books in Print (BIP). New York: R. R. Bowker Company, 1948– . (Annual with semiannual supplement.)

British National Bibliography. London: Council of the British National Bibliography, British Museum, 1950– .

Business Books in Print. New York: R. R. Bowker Company, 1973– . (Annual.)

Children's Books in Print. New York: R. R. Bowker Company, 1969– . (Annual.)

Cooper, Gayle. *A Checklist of American Imprints for 1830– .* Metuchen, N. J.: Scarecrow Press, 1972– .

Cumulative Book Index (CBI). New York: H. W. Wilson Company, 1898– . (Monthly with cumulations.)

El-Hi Textbooks in Print. New York: R. R. Bowker Company, 1970– . (Annual.)

Evans, Charles. *American Bibliography: A Chronological Dictionary of all Books, Pamphlets and Periodical Publications Printed in the United States of America from the Genesis of Printing in 1639 down to and including the Year 1800; with Bibliographical and Biographical Notes.* Chicago: Printed for the Author, 1903–1959. 14 vols. (Reprint: New York: Peter Smith, 1941–1967.)

Forthcoming Books. New York: R. R. Bowker Company, 1965– . (Bimonthly.)

Guide to Microforms in Print. Weston, Conn.: Microform Review, 1961– .

Guide to Reprints. Washington, D.C.: Microcard Editions, 1967– . (Annual.)

Irregular Serials and Annuals: An International Directory. New York: R. R. Bowker Company, 1967– . (Biennial beginning in 1972.)

Kelly, James. *The American Catalogue of Books (Original and Reprint) Published in the United States from January, 1861 to January, 1871, with Date of Publication, Size, Price and Publisher's Name.* New York: John Wiley, 1866–1971. 2 vols. (Reprint: New York: Peter Smith, 1938.)

Large-Type Books in Print. New York: R. R. Bowker Company, 1970– . (Irregular.)

Library of Congress. Catalogs: Subject Catalog, 1950– . Washington, D.C.: Library of Congress, 1955– .

Literary Market Place: The Business Directory of American Book Publishing. New York: R. R. Bowker Company, 1940– . (Annual.)

Medical Books in Print. New York: R. R. Bowker Company, 1972– . (Annual.)

Micropublishers' Trade List Annual. Weston, Conn.: Microform Review, 1978– . (Annual.)

National Union Catalog: A Cumulative Author List. Washington, D.C.: Library of Congress, Card Division, 1953– . (Monthly with quarterly and annual cumulations.)

National Union Catalog. Pre-1956 Imprints. London: Mansell Information/ Publishing, Ltd., 1968– . (In progress).

New Serials Titles: A Union List of Serials Commencing Publication after December 31, 1949. Washington, D.C.: Library of Congress, January, 1953– . (Monthly with annual cumulations.)

New Serials Titles, 1950–1970. Cumulative. Washington, D.C.: Library of Congress; New York: R. R. Bowker Company, 1973. 4 vols.

NICEM *Media Index.* Los Angeles: National Information Center for Educational Media, University of Southern California.
Index to 8 mm Cartridges.
Index to 16 mm Educational Films.
Index to 35 mm Educational Filmstrips.
Index to Educational Audio Tapes.
Index to Educational Video Tapes.
Index to Educational Overhead Transparencies.

Paperbound Books in Print. New York: R. R. Bowker Company, 1955– . (Semi-annual.)

Publishers' Trade List Annual (PTLA). R. R. Bowker Company, 1873– . (Annual.)

Publisher's Weekly. New York: R. R. Bowker Company, 1872– . (Weekly.)

Religious Books and Serials in Print. New York: R. R. Bowker Company, 1978– . (Annual.)

Roorbach, Orville A. *Bibliotheca Americana . . . 1820–1861.* New York: O. A. Roorbach, 1852–1861. 4 vols. (Reprint: New York: Peter Smith, 1939.)

Schwann Record & Tape Guide. Boston: W. Schwann, Inc., 1949– .
    Schwann 1 (Monthly.)
    Schwann 2 (Biennial.)

Scientific and Technical Books in Print. New York: R. R. Bowker Company, 1972– . (Annual.)

Shaw, Ralph R., and Richard H. Shoemaker. *American Bibliography: A Preliminary Checklist for 1801–1819.* New York: Scarecrow Press, 1958–1966. 22 vols.

Sheehy, Eugene P. *Guide to Reference Books.* 9th ed. Chicago: American Library Association, 1976. *Supplement.* 1980.

Shoemaker, Richard H. *Checklist of American Imprints for 1820–1829.* New York: Scarecrow Press, 1964–1971. 10 vols.

Small Press Record of Books in Print. Paradise, Calif.: Dustbooks, 1971– . (Annual.)

Standard Periodical Directory. 6th ed. New York: Oxbridge Communications, Inc., 1979.

Subject Guide to Books in Print. New York: R. R. Bowker Company, 1957– . (Annual.)

Subject Guide to Children's Books in Print. New York: R. R. Bowker Company, 1970– . (Annual.)

Subject Guide to Forthcoming Books. New York: R. R. Bowker Company, 1967– . (Bimonthly.)

Subject Guide to Microforms in Print. Weston, Conn.: Microform Review, 1962– . (Annual.)

Subject Index to New Serials Titles, 1950–1965. Ann Arbor, Mich.: Pierian Press, 1968.

Ulrich's International Periodicals Directory: A Classified Guide to Current Periodicals. New York: R. R. Bowker Company, 1931– . (Biennial.)

United States Catalog: Books in Print, January 1, 1928. 4th ed. New York: The H. W. Wilson Company, 1928.

United States. Copyright Office. *Catalog of Copyright Entries.* Washington, D.C.: Government Printing Office, 1891– . (Semiannual.)

United States. Library of Congress. Exchange and Gift Division. *Monthly Checklist of State Publications.* Washington, D.C.: Government Printing Office, 1910– . (Monthly.)

United States. Superintendent of Documents. *Monthly Catalog of United States Government Publications.* Washington, D.C.: Government Printing Office, 1895– . (Monthly.)

Vertical File Index. New York: The H. W. Wilson Company, 1935– . (Monthly.)

Weekly Record. New York: R. R. Bowker Company, 1974– . (Weekly. Before 1974, appeared as the last section of *Publishers Weekly.*)

CHAPTER SIX
Reviews and Reviewing

Since most librarians cannot examine each new book, film, or record that they would like to add to their collection, the next best thing is to have someone whom they trust examine that material for them. This trusted individual can be either an outsider (the book reviewer in one of the printed media) or (within a large library system) a coworker—perhaps someone with more subject expertise, as when librarians from subject departments of a main library review books for possible purchase by branch libraries. In this chapter we will examine largely the printed sources available to librarians, but the principles of good reviewing are universal and can also be applied in an internal situation.

If one compares the book reviews published today with those of the nineteenth century, one is startled to discover that the nineteenth-century reviews were generally much more vitriolic. The often anonymous reviewers were not afraid to state their opinion of a book's worth; furthermore they took it for granted that their readers had the leisure time to digest the lengthy essays inspired by the reading of a new book. Today the average review is fairly brief and often gives little more than a summary of the contents of a work. Reviewers often seem afraid to give their opinion of the worth of a particular book. Only in a few literary or political journals does one find the lengthy essay and the opinionated review. The *New York Review of Books* is the major contemporary example of a periodical carrying on this nineteenth-century tradition. Most readers today are interested primarily in information about a book that might have some claim to their attention. We therefore have far too many reviews that sound more like the book publisher's advertising or catalog copy than true reviews. Unfortunately description can never take the place of evaluation.

What should a reader expect to find in a good review? First of all, a description of the contents of a work—what it is about; secondly, an indication of the essence and quality of the work (this, in the case of fiction, poetry, and some nonfiction, will involve a discussion of the style the author has employed); thirdly, an estimate of the work's value; and finally a comparison with other works on the same topic. In nonfiction (more than in fiction) a reviewer must draw on a reservoir of accumulated information and knowledge of the subject. In fiction, poetry, and drama, the question of the reviewer's taste will come into play—a most difficult area since it is so subjective. Still, a reader should expect a reviewer of fiction to be acquainted with the major novels of the past and able to make judicious comparisons and judgments based on a knowledge of previous accomplishments of a particular author or of other writers.

The first three qualities of a book review enumerated above are traditionally given[1] and may well satisfy the general public. For librarians the fourth criterion seems essential since a librarian is not selecting books or other materials in a vacuum but is adding to an already existing collection. The failure to compare a new book, recording, or film with others already in existence denies the librarian an essential element needed for judicious selection.

While the above are the desired contents of a review, all too often the reader encounters other types of reviews, all of them unsatisfactory. The first might be called the "blurb" review since it merely copies the contents of the book jacket or a publicity release sent to the reviewer by the publisher along with the review copy. The clue is the repetition of key phrases in several reviews—phrases that can only have come from a single source. Blurb reviews tend to be paeans of praise. The next type of review might be called the "unfolding the tale" review. It contents itself with a lengthy recounting of the plot so that the reader of the review has little need to read the book itself. Such reviews are particularly prevalent in fiction and

[1]J. Donald Adams et al., "What the Experts Say," in John E. Drewry (ed.), *Writing Book Reviews* (Westport, Conn.: Greenwood Press, 1974), pp. 121ff. (Reprint of 2d ed., 1966.)

biography. Travel books also often suffer the same fate. Finally, for this writer, one of the most obnoxious types of reviews is the "review of a reviewer," which uses the book merely as an excuse for an essay on the subject of the book or maybe even a totally unrelated subject. The book under review will be mentioned only in passing, if at all. The *New York Review of Books* is often guilty of such reviewing.

Just as one searches for certain essential qualities in a book review, book reviewers themselves need to demonstrate certain qualities if they are to gain the confidence of their readers. First of all, they must write well and have a good sense of literary form. Information should be given succinctly without sacrificing literary style. Secondly, reviewers must demonstrate a knowledge of their subject. No reviewer is more suspect than the generalist who reviews anything and everything, all in a most superficial manner. The knowledge of a subject is best demonstrated to librarians by the reviewer's ability to compare new works with ones previously published. The whole bibliography of a field should be at the reviewer's fingertips. Needless to say, the reader has every right to expect that the reviewer has thoroughly read, and not merely skimmed, the book being reviewed. It is also hoped that the reviewer will try to ascertain what the author set out to do and not criticize him or her for not doing what was never intended. Finally, a reviewer should seek to be as unbiased as possible. In certain controversial areas (notably politics and religion) this may be asking too much, but at least the bias of the reviewer should be clear. Of course, the bias of a particular periodical or newspaper may be the reader's real clue, and certain prejudices are expected from all who write for that publication. However, bias may often creep in unintentionally when someone reviews a work by an author he or she knows, has worked with, or has studied under. This is hard for the reader to ascertain; only the scrupulousness of the editor who assigns the book for review can be relied on.

Let us take a moment to clarify the difference between book reviewing and literary criticism. The two are related but are not the same. The distinction may be a fine one, but it is there. The first difference is that book reviewers always work under the pressure of time, whereas critics write in comparative leisure. In contrast, to literary critics, book reviewers must often make a hasty judgment, one that may be revised or rejected in time. Critics, on the other hand, are dealing with works whose value or lack of value has already been established by time or at least is beginning to crystallize. Critics can take for granted that readers have probably read the work being criticized. They are under no obligation to recount the plot or provide a digest of the contents. They will most often choose books with a particular aim in mind. They are more interested in literary ideas and discussions of them than in a particular work. Finally, literary criticism, as the term implies, is limited largely to the field of literature, with similar criticism also being written in a few other areas of the arts and humanities.

Reviewing for an intellectual elite—the worthy few—does partake of elements of both book reviewing and literary criticism. Examples of such reviewing can be found in the previously mentioned *New York Review of Books* and in such political and literary journals as *Nation*, *New Republic*, and *Commentary*. There is a wide gap between this type of reviewing and reviewing for the general public and for the book trade or library profession. The latter types of reviewing shall be the main concern in this chapter.

HOW BOOKS ARE REVIEWED

Most review media review only what they get from the publisher. But since the purpose of a book review, from the standpoint of the publisher, is to get the book before the public, publishers make a considerable effort to channel books to the right review media. The difficulty for all concerned is that currently an estimated 38,000 to 40,000 books are being published each year in the United States. Since the largest of the review media review only some 6,800 of them, many new books are not reviewed anywhere. Naturally more than 6,800 individual titles are reviewed each year since each review journal selects its own titles according to the needs of its readers, but probably not more than a third to a half of all books published get reviewed anywhere.[2] Publishers often state that they prefer a bad review of a book to no review, since then at least someone will have heard about the book, albeit unfavorably.

Most publishing houses have someone in charge of review copies. Review copies can come in various formats, all available at different times in the production process. This accounts for the difference in publication dates of reviews among the different journals. First available are galley proofs. As we mentioned in Chapter One, these are loose sheets, unpaged, and lacking illustrations, maps, tables, charts, or an index. They contain many typographical errors, and the author may make slight or considerable changes in the text at this stage of the printing process, unbeknownst

[2]For an annual survey of the number of books reviewed by each of the principal review media in the United States, see the section "Book Review-Media" in the *Bowker Annual of Library and Book Trade Information* (New York: R. R. Bowker Company, 1956–).

to the reviewer. Galleys are made available to certain review media about six months ahead of publication date simply because these media are in the business of reviewing books *in advance of* publication date, largely for the book trade or libraries. A few of the general review media, such as *The New York Times Book Review*, also use a certain number of galleys in their reviewing. Any review written from galleys should be checked against the final copy of the bound book before being published, but there is not always time, and errors sometimes creep in. The advantage of timeliness has to be weighed against the disadvantages of possible errors or omissions in this type of reviewing.

At a somewhat later point in the production process—say, three months prior to publication date—unbound, gathered sheets become available. By this time, the book is in final page format and usually has the accompanying illustrations and index. Sending out galleys or gathered sheets is an expensive process, and publishers have only a very few such copies available and limit them to the major review media. For most books, publishers wait until the book is available in bound form and then send review copies to the media. For a trade book, this is usually six weeks to a month prior to publication date. Thus these review copies hit the mails at the same time copies are being delivered to bookstores. There is almost no way that reviews prepared from bound copies of the book can be ready at the same time or even shortly after the books appear in the stores. The time lag can be anywhere from a few weeks to a few months (and sometimes, unfortunately, to a year or more) and is usually determined by the importance of the book to a journal's readers.

Since supplying review copies, in whatever form, clearly costs money, how does the publisher decide which review media are to receive copies of which books? The major review media—*Publishers Weekly*, *Library Journal*, *Booklist*, CHOICE, *New York Times Book Review*—are supplied automatically. Some publishers send these review media everything they publish; others request that the review media check off in advance of the publication date those books they wish from a list of forthcoming titles. Some publishers decide what will go to a particular journal without consulting the journal (not a good idea); a few (very few) wait for the review media to request specific titles. Once the general and trade media are covered, the more difficult work for the publisher begins. Other copies must now be distributed on a much more selective basis, usually according to subject matter or age level. Other books may have a regional or local tie-in with the author or with the subject matter, and newspapers and magazines are selected accordingly. A small publisher may send out 50 review copies of a specialized book; it is not uncommon for a major publisher to send out as many as 500 copies of a title that is being promoted heavily. In this day and age, TV and radio must not be neglected either. A mention on the *Today* show is worth thousands of dollars in extra sales to a lucky publisher. Besides being sent to book review editors, books often go to special feature editors of newspapers and magazines. This is particularly true in the areas of cooking, gardening, and sports. Business or financial editors may mention books from time to time and are another likely source of publicity.

Once a book has been received by a book review journal, what happens? This is when the crucial selection process occurs, when someone decides what will be reviewed or consigned to oblivion—at least as far as that journal is concerned. The major library review journals currently receive 16,000 to 18,000 titles a year out of the 38,000 to 40,000 being published. Since *Booklist*, CHOICE, and *LJ* review no more than 6,800 titles from among the total received, it is clear that a book sent for review has only one chance in three of getting reviewed by any of these journals and considerably less at *PW*. When one realizes that a certain amount of preselection has already been done by the publisher or the review journal prior to shipment, the chances for each title are seen to be even slimmer. Each review journal has its own way of handling incoming books. All complain of being overwhelmed from time to time with worthy contenders, but all take their job of selection very seriously. In almost all cases with the trade or library review media, at least two persons look at each book before a final decision is made to review or to reject. At the various library review journals, selection is made by the staff in consideration of the type of library that the journal has been set up to serve. Mistakes are made from time to time and titles are rejected that should have been covered, but a worthwhile book is rarely ignored by all of the major journals. Librarians should not expect great overlapping in coverage of any but the most popular books from the different review media. Each serves its own purpose and reviews a different mix of books. The review media should be looked upon as complementary rather than as competitive.

Once a book has been selected for review, the difficult task of choosing a reviewer for it must begin. This is one of the most important if not *the* most important link in the reviewing chain; if a poor choice is made, only a poor review can result. An editor must have a good knowledge of reviewers—their strengths, weaknesses, and biases—in order to accomplish this vital task. There are ways of remedying a poor choice of reviewer. The most obvious one is to obtain a second copy of a book and get a second review. However, this inevitably delays the appearance of the review, and every book review editor is constantly struggling with the problem of currency and so hates to do anything that will cause delay. A poor review can also be ditched and not published. Readers will then learn nothing about that particular title, which becomes one with all those titles that were not selected for review. Usually the importance of a particular work will determine whether an editor seeks a second opinion or just lets the review fall by the wayside.

Certain types of books traditionally get less than fair treatment from the review media. Paperbacks (many of them, of course, reprints) have often been neglected, even when the book was available in no other format. Happily, at least among the library review media, this barrier is crumbling. Reprints, however, whether in paperback or hardbound, get very little reviewer attention. Review editors argue that these books have already had their day in court and that reviews of the original edition can often be found. This answer is only partly satisfactory, since a book's value to today's readers or libraries may be quite different from the value of the original edition. Other books may have come along to supersede it; the material may now be way out of date and of more harm than good to the novice reader. On the other hand, a preface or index that never existed before may make the reprint of greater value than the original edition. It is regrettable, therefore, that the library review journals do not have more space to review reprints and generally leave it to the largely unknown *Reprint Bulletin—Book Reviews*.

When it comes to fiction, first novels by unknown authors are often neglected by the review media. This is in spite of the fact that fiction in general receives twice as much attention as the total number of books published in this category would warrant on a percentage basis. Poetry and drama are reviewed on a seemingly hit-or-miss basis, with much worthy material falling by the wayside. As for nonfiction, the great emphasis in the general review media is still on history, biography, and travel. Religious books, except for a few popular titles, are largely neglected, perhaps because much of the material published in this field is of interest primarily to the adherents of one denomination or belief. Libraries must look to professional journals for reviews of most of the books in highly specialized subjects—at least those that fall outside the general college curriculum. How-to-do-it books are also only sparsely reviewed, even though they are popular best sellers and remain staple items in public libraries.

REVIEW JOURNALS

In judging any review journal, several factors should be kept in mind: the scope of coverage; editorial bias; authority of the sponsoring body and editorial staff; style and presentation; how often published; and currency of the reviews. There are different kinds of review journals: popular newspapers and magazines aimed at the general public; intellectual periodicals of a literary or political nature aimed largely at the more sophisticated reader; book trade or library review journals; and professional or scholarly journals for the members of a particular subject field or fields. Each of these different types will now be taken up, with outstanding examples discussed in some detail. Since periodicals and newspapers are born and die with some frequency, those cited here should be considered primarily as types. While it is easy to pick out the media offering the largest number of reviews, there remains a middle ground where personal preference will always play a role. The selection presented here is just one person's personal preference. Publications not cited should not be automatically considered to be worthless for library materials selection. Only long-term use can prove whether a particular journal is useful for selection purposes in a specific library.

The Popular Review Media

Newspapers and popular news weeklies such as *Time* and *Newsweek* are the principal conveyors of information about books to the general public. The great fault with such publications is that they review very few books. *Time* and *Newsweek* average 5 or 6 reviews weekly, which add up to only 250 to 300 books reviewed per year. Therefore their use to a library is limited to quick perusal to see what patrons may be aware of and will request. Many large metropolitan daily newspapers review a book or two every day and publish a special book review supplement on Sundays. *The Los Angeles Times* is a good example; it averages some 25 to 30 reviews each Sunday in addition to the daily ones, bringing the total to some 1,300 to 1,500 a year. The Boston *Globe*, which publishes some 2,000 reviews a year, is another example. The granddaddy of the newspaper reviewing media, with the greatest national reputation and the one most widely read by both the general public and librarians, is *The New York Times Book Review*. Some 1.5 million copies are sold with the Sunday *New York Times*. How many of these are actually read is unknown, but in addition, some 30,000 are sold by subscription and 25,000 in bookstores. Recently *The New York Times* has been reviewing between 40 and 50 new titles in each weekly issue, in addition to the one or two reviews (sometimes of the same books) published in the daily editions. This brings its yearly total to about 2,300. (The daily reviews are now being cumulated in a monthly periodical, *Books of the Times*.)

In assessing the newspaper review sources, one must always keep in mind that the primary job of a newspaper is to inform its readers. Books are treated as news. Therefore only if a book is thought to be of interest to a wide spectrum of readers will it be reviewed. Thus the newspapers all tend to review the same books and to emphasize the same types of materials—largely fiction (including science fiction, mysteries, and to a lesser extent westerns), biography, history, and current events. A few works of literary criticism, as well as art books, will be reviewed from time to time, as will some craft, gardening, cooking, and other hobby books. Children's book reviews are limited to a few popular titles, except for perhaps one special children's supplement annually. As for professional or special-subject books, few if any of these will ever be considered newsworthy enough to be reviewed. Furthermore it is the products of the major trade publishers that get the primary attention. Only a few university press books are deemed newsworthy and certainly not most textbooks. Paperback publishers usually have to be content with a short weekly column enumerating in brief fashion a dozen or so new paperbacks. As for the small presses, they will get only token attention. The exception to all this is the book of regional or local interest—a history, biography, or travel book or the work of a local poet or novelist. This is considered news, and good coverage in one or two local newspapers will result.

While some newspapers have a book review editor and one or two staff reviewers (who almost always handle the daily book reviewing), most of the reviewing is done by outsiders. Again the question as to what is most newsworthy usually determines who will be asked to review a particular book. A well-known person will often be asked to review in preference to an unknown just for the news value involved. The ability to write in an attention-getting manner will also weigh heavily. Reporters and free-lance writers are definitely preferred to academics. Sometimes a newspaper editor will select a reviewer knowing that this person will write a controversial or even biased review, but in a manner that will make the sparks fly and therefore be newsworthy. All of this leads to reviews that are sometimes less than knowledgeable and sometimes to reviews that are more style than substance. Particularly lacking in newspaper reviewing is any reference to similar books on the same subject. The reviewing is almost always limited to the book in hand.

One point in favor of newspapers is that, in their attempt to be newsworthy, they are very current, usually attempting to publish a review close to publication date. They are aided by the rapid printing schedules maintained by daily newspapers and by the fact that newspapers generally own their own printing plants. The political orientation of most newspapers is a matter of record, and thus any bias in their book reviewing can be ascertained fairly easily. The daily and weekly publication schedules also aid greatly in keeping the reviews current, especially in comparison with the monthly or even quarterly schedules of many trade and professional journals.

Also important is a group of journals aimed at a more sophisticated public of middle- and upper-class intellectuals, many of them involved in the field of education and likely to be library patrons. Therefore the librarian should be aware of what these journals are reviewing even if a particular publication is not used for book selection. *The New York Review of Books* (*NYRB*) was born during a newspaper strike some years ago which had left New York and the nation bereft of *The New York Times Book Review*. Intended as a replacement or substitute for that august newspaper, it has instead become much more of an elitist and coterie journal, with its book reviews often only excuses for extended literary essays on related or even unrelated topics. Currency is not of prime importance to the *NYRB*. Books are often held until a number have appeared on a given topic, thus providing the basis for an essay by a prominent critic. The *NYRB* probably fits the definition of literary criticism given earlier better than it does that of book reviewing even though it appears on a frequent (twice a month) schedule, more often associated with reviewing than criticism. Its value as a selection tool for libraries is marginal since it is distinctly biased. It has also been frequently accused of cronyism, notably by Richard Kostelanetz in his *The End of Intelligent Writing: Literary Politics in America*,[3] because of the ties between its editors and several prominent big New York publishing houses. These charges are difficult to substantiate. In any case, the small number of books reviewed by the *NYRB* (450 in 1977) makes its usefulness in libraries decidedly limited.

Of much greater importance to all libraries, but especially academic and large public libraries, and some would say of the highest importance, is the London *Times Literary Supplement*. Now in its seventh decade of existence, *TLS* (as it is familiarly called) has maintained the highest reputation for literary excellence of any reviewing medium published today. For many years all its reviews were published anonymously, but with the advent of a new editor, John Gross, in 1974 that policy was changed, and reviews are now signed. It was long known that some of the leading scholars of England (and in recent years the United States) were the authors of many of *TLS*'s brilliant reviews; now the evidence is out in the open. *TLS* attempts to review three types of works: general popular books (as do other newspapers), learned scholarly works (as in any

[3]Richard Kostelanetz, *The End of Intelligent Writing: Literary Politics in America* (Mission, Kans.: Sheed, Andrews and McMeel, Inc., 1974).

scholarly journal), and most particularly, learned works that would appeal to a more general audience if only they knew of them. It is also one of the few English-language review journals (at least those aimed at a general audience) that reviews books written in foreign languages (usually the common European ones). It publishes more than 3,000 reviews a year. While it naturally concentrates on books published in England, the number of books having nearly simultaneous publication in the United States and the United Kingdom is such that any U.S. library can make good use of *TLS* as a selection tool. In recent years, the enormous increase in the number of U.S. university press books being released in England through branches of the U.S. press has brought about very fine coverage of such books in *TLS*, to the benefit of the whole scholarly and library world. The other recent development in the book trade—English publishers setting up U.S. branches or subsidiaries—also means that many other books reviewed in *TLS* are readily available to U.S. libraries from their original publishers. Because of its weekly publishing schedule *TLS* is very current in its reviewing, even though that currency may have less effect in this country due to differences in English and U.S. publication dates. In some cases, however, it gives U.S. librarians advance notice of important books that are due out here at a date some six months hence. In any case, the coverage of *TLS* is much broader than U.S. newspaper reviewing, and the reviews are generally of much higher literary and scholarly quality. *TLS* should be considered a high-priority item in book selection in any medium-sized or large public or academic library.

Many periodicals aimed at an intellectual audience provide a limited number of book reviews each week, month, or quarter. Stress needs to be placed on the word "limited," however, as most offer no more than a dozen reviews per issue. Most librarians do not have enough time to more than glance at these magazines. For many years *Saturday Review*, in its initial guise as the *Saturday Review of Literature*, was one of the mainstays of library book selection. Its exceedingly checkered history in recent years has caused it to lose most of its former favor with all but a few die-hard librarians who still remember its previous incarnations. For most, it is just another periodical to be considered, along with *Atlantic, Harper's, Nation, Commentary, New Republic*, and a host of others, all reviewing largely the same books. Each librarian has his or her favorite; no one can be expected to read them all. Some librarians prefer to ignore them all, feeling that *TLS, The New York Times Book Review*, and the professional and trade journals give them adequate coverage. This writer tends to agree with the latter group. The difference between these opinion journals and the newspapers is that the former are in the business of providing commentary, not news. Therefore they can wait to see trends. They use major literary critics and political analysts as reviewers and believe that the opinions of these people are worth waiting for. Currency is not considered a major goal and lessens their effective use by library book selectors. They may be more useful in retrospective than in current selection (of which more later).

General Book Trade and Library Review Media

For the majority of librarians, the most important review media are those aimed at the book trade and the library profession. These publish the largest number of reviews. The reviews tend to be brief and succinct, and often they contain that comparative element so helpful to librarians who are adding to already established collections. There is little need to wade through discursive essays to find the kernel of judgment needed by the book selector hard pressed for time. Reviews published for the book trade and the library profession often appear in advance of the book's publication date, being prepared from galley proofs. If not ahead of publication, then every library review journal strives to be as current as possible—with, of course, varying degrees of success. Unlike most newspaper and magazine book reviews, which are signed, reviews written for the book trade and for libraries are often anonymous. Only *Library Journal* reviews are regularly signed. Much of this type of reviewing also tends to be done by staff (only CHOICE and *Library Journal* use outside reviewers for all books; the others do so only occasionally).

Two sources of prepublication reviews prepared for the book trade are heavily used by librarians. They are the "Forecasts" appearing each week in *Publishers Weekly* and *Kirkus Reviews*. Since these two services are aimed at the average bookstore, they review primarily popular trade books, although *PW* does review an occasional university press or other scholarly book. The *PW* "Forecasts," under the able editorship in recent years of Barbara Bannon, have built up a fine reputation for fearless and knowledgeable reviews. Bannon and her staff have a fine sense of what is going to be popular. Even when they do not feel a book is very good, they can usually predict its sales potential. The reviews are succinct and very readable. The style is surprisingly varied (a difficult thing to do in brief reviews of 150 to 175 words), and the reviews appear several weeks prior to publication date. Good coverage is given of paperbacks and children's books in sections with their own editors. A total of 4,470 reviews were published in 1977, making this a major source for reviews. For popular trade books, this is where most librarians will see their first review of a particular title. Fortunately it is a very reliable source of information and opinion.

The other prepublication source, written largely for bookstore managers but used widely by librarians, is *Kirkus Reviews*. Like *PW* "Forecasts," the semimonthly *Kirkus Reviews* is the work of a paid staff, with the help of a few outside reviewers for special subjects, all of whom remain anonymous. *Kirkus Reviews* are prepared largely from galley proofs (as are the *PW* "Forecast" reviews) and appear some weeks or even months prior to publication. Thus bookstore owners can decide what books to stock and in what quantity. Here the resemblance of the two review sources ceases. First of all, *Kirkus Reviews* are written in a unique style that many term "Kirk-ese." It is a hyperbolic, smart-alecky, supersalesperson approach that turns off more than a few librarians. More importantly, it is sometimes also a needlessly confusing style, making it difficult to discern just what the reviewer actually thought of a particular book. Most library book selectors would agree that *Kirkus* is not for beginners. Only an experienced selector can make good use of the service. Furthermore *Kirkus* is expensive, far more so than any other review medium currently in widespread library use. Because it reviews only popular trade books (children's and adult), its use is also limited largely to public libraries. Its great strength remains its reviewing of many titles far in advance of publication date. Like *PW*, it publishes more than 4,000 reviews a year.

Like the book trade, the library profession has its own book review media. It is served by three general review periodicals as well as by many specialized ones. Two of the three general review journals, *Booklist* and CHOICE, are published by the American Library Association, the third, *Library Journal*, by the R. R. Bowker Company. The *Booklist* reviews have been in existence the longest, beginning in 1905. The purpose of *Booklist* is to select and review books for the small and medium-sized public library and the school library/media center. It appears twice a month. Like *PW* "Forecasts" and *Kirkus Reviews*, *Booklist* is essentially staff-produced, although it does use a number of outside reviewers for its special columns. All of its reviewers are experienced librarians. In addition to its own staff, it solicits the opinions of a group of cooperating librarians throughout the country on what should be reviewed. It is unique in one important aspect: It publishes reviews only of materials that it can recommend.

These various factors have their advantages and disadvantages. The use of experienced librarians ensures sound opinions on the suitability of particular books for smaller libraries. In the past, however, this often led to overly conservative reviewing aimed at the lowest common denominator. Controversial material was shunned. Happily this has changed in recent years under the editorship of Paul Brawley, although not without making some subscribers unhappy, particularly with the reviews of nontraditional children's books. Most of the librarians on the *Booklist* staff are generalists, and sometimes this shows in a lack of familiarity with certain subjects and a less than critical acceptance of the contents of some books. Furthermore working in the corporate offices of ALA means that the staff is cut off from any library collection. Thus reviewers cannot make judicious comparisons with previously published works unless they are very familiar with a particular work and can find a previous *Booklist* review of it. The fact that only favorable reviews are published leads to a certain blandness of style, which is probably unavoidable. It also leaves the reader wondering why a book not reviewed, though seemingly popular, was rejected.

The greatest asset of the *Booklist* is its coverage of a wide variety of material. In spite of its name, it no longer limits itself to reviewing books. Its coverage is exceedingly wide, including films, filmstrips, multimedia kits, and spoken-word recordings. Within the realm of the printed word, it covers special types of material, such as government documents and foreign-language books. It has many special columns covering such subjects as cookbooks, plants and gardening, arts and crafts, first novels, science fiction, westerns, mysteries, and espionage. Its coverage of children's books has long been considered outstanding. In fact, almost everything that would be of interest to the smaller public or school library is included. Nowhere else is this diversified coverage available in one journal and for a relatively modest price. In 1977 *Booklist* reviewed 4,635 adult books, 1,423 juveniles, and 337 young adult books, for a total of 6,790. In addition, it reviewed 1,756 nonprint items.

In 1964 CHOICE was started by the Association of College and Research Libraries, a division of the American Library Association, to make available a different type of expertise in book reviewing to librarians. This was the subject expertise of college and university faculty members. The original aim was to serve undergraduate and community college libraries, but the monthly journal has since come to be a principal source of reviews for medium and large-sized public libraries as well. A number of special libraries and many foreign libraries also find it helpful. College libraries had long been ill-served by the general and book-trade review media, since they concentrated largely on popular trade books and neglected the more scholarly works that were the stock in trade of the academic library. Unlike large universites, college libraries often lacked subject experts in all fields on their own staffs. There were, of course, the professional and scholarly journals, but their reviews were often so late and so many of them had to be checked individually in order to obtain adequate coverage of the entire curriculum that they were hardly a satisfactory substitute.

The outstanding quality these teaching faculty are able to bring to their reviewing is extensive knowledge of their subject and of the bibliography of that subject. They are therefore often able to make judicious comparisons with books already on library shelves and thus save libraries considerable money when they point out the inferiority of a new book to something that most libraries already own. For librarians building newer collections, the recommendation of older titles has been an incentive to stronger retrospective collection building. It is interesting to note that the inauguration of this type of comparative reviewing has had an influence beyond CHOICE itself in recent years and has led to changes in the reviewing styles of other publications.

The mix of books reviewed in CHOICE is quite different from that found in *Booklist*. First of all, only a few popular trade books are covered. Instead the emphasis is on scholarly material, with university press books receiving especially strong coverage. CHOICE also reviews many imported books, especially those from Great Britain. Its coverage of fiction is limited to well-known authors of established literary reputation or to new talent that would be of interest to writing courses. Originally limited to the traditional liberal arts curriculum, CHOICE has increased its coverage in recent years to include a wide variety of paraprofessional subjects found in community college curriculums. Since it does not use galley proofs in its reviewing, believing them to be incomplete and subject to modification (in fact, galleys are not readily available for most scholarly books), CHOICE reviews appear later than those of *PW* and *Kirkus* and in many, although not all, cases, later than those of *Booklist* and *Library Journal*. Some of this delay is caused by the use of outside reviewers, with the resultant necessity of getting the book to the reviewer and the review back to the CHOICE offices from someone who receives no monetary reward for his or her services. The academic profession must be complimented for the great altruism it displays; some 2,300 professors are willing to work for nothing for a library service such as CHOICE. Unlike *Booklist*, CHOICE does not review A-V materials on a regular basis. It does, however, offer the largest number of reviews of adult books of any review medium in the United States—an average of 6,500 a year (6,735 in 1977). It publishes both favorable and negative reviews, and its high standards have earned it an enviable reputation in the library, academic, and publishing worlds.

One controversial point about CHOICE reviews has been their anonymity. A list of the contributors to a particular issue is included at the back, but individual reviews are not signed. The reasons for this are twofold. First of all, the reviews, unlike *Library Journal* reviews, are often heavily edited or condensed after submission. To resubmit them to the original reviewer would only delay publication, but to print these edited versions over a person's name would not be acceptable to most faculty members. The second reason is that many of the CHOICE reviewers are younger faculty members who find themselves reviewing the work of their elders, persons to whom they are beholden for advancement in their fields. It has been felt that more frank reviewing would result if the reviewer could be anonymous. This naturally places a tremendous burden on the editorial staff of CHOICE to see that the reviewing done for them is responsible. Fortunately the integrity of the magazine has been maintained over the years.

Reviews of books first appeared in the *Library Journal* in 1940 in a "New Books Surveyed" column. The *Journal* itself, the profession's leading news and opinion magazine, had been founded in 1876 by the ubiquitous Melvil Dewey. The book reviews are today a separate section of the magazine, with their own editor who reports to the general editor of the magazine. Issues currently appear twice a month and contain approximately 6,000 reviews of adult books a year. Until a few years ago, *Library Journal*, like *Booklist*, reviewed a wide variety of materials. However, first the children's book reviews were moved to a separate part of the magazine entitled *School Library Journal*, and then *School Library Journal* was broken away entirely and published as a separate magazine. Likewise, A-V reviews were pulled out and are currently published as a separate magazine, *Previews*. This has left *Library Journal* with only adult books; thus it is similar in coverage to CHOICE. However, *Library Journal* is unlike CHOICE in that, while concentrating on the public library, it also attempts to serve a wide variety of other types of libraries. Its coverage tends to be more trade-book oriented than CHOICE.

In the beginning, like *Booklist*, *Library Journal* used librarians as its reviewers—generalists speaking to other generalists. In more recent years, undoubtedly under the influence of CHOICE, it has acquired a number of academics as reviewers. It does review from galleys and is thus able to be close to book publication dates in much of its reviewing. It covers essentially the same subjects as *Booklist*. The reviews, like those in *Booklist* and CHOICE, are limited to 150-175 words and are printed as submitted by the reviewers. There is thus a great variation in style. The reviews are all signed, and librarians often come to have their favorite reviewers, whose work they follow from one issue to the next. By contrast, librarians also often have a list of reviewers whom they do not trust. It is hard to generalize about *Library Journal* reviews; some are of outstanding quality, while others show a lack of knowledge of a specific subject field. With all its faults, *Library Journal* remains a very popular source of reviews, especially for the public library.

Children's Book Review Media

I have mentioned that *Booklist* has a highly respected children's book section, currently edited by Betsy Hearn, and that both *PW* and *Kirkus* also devote a large amount of their space to children's books. (In 1977 *PW* reviewed 561 juveniles and *Kirkus* 1,250.) There are also several specialized reviewing sources that limit themselves to this type of material. First we should mention *School Library Journal*. It reviews by far the largest number of children's books (some 2,297 in 1977), because it tries to review every such title published in the United States. Since its coverage is all-inclusive, it naturally expresses both favorable and negative opinions about books. Just as with adult books reviewed in *LJ*, the reviews are written by librarians working in the field. Thus a very practical point of view is brought to the reviews. However, since there are many different reviewers, *School Library Journal* has the concomitant disadvantage of much variation in quality.

The staff of the *Booklist* reviews about half again as many children's books (1,423 in 1977) but publishes only reviews of books it can recommend. It is no longer as conservative as it once was in the types of books it recommends, to the chagrin of some of its readers, but this has made it a much more lively publication. Following numerically after *SLJ* and *Booklist* come the *Bulletin of the Center for Children's Books* of the University of Chicago and *Horn Book*, with 828 and 496 reviews in 1977, respectively. The *Horn Book* was founded in 1924 and is somewhat conservative in appearance and contents. In recent years it has lost some of its leadership to other publications, most notably the *Bulletin of the Center for Children's Books*, which was started in 1947. The *Bulletin's* extremely thoughtful and well-written reviews by Zena Sutherland, who is advised by a six-member committee meeting weekly, carry all the prestige of its parent body, the University of Chicago. It should surely be consulted by anyone selecting children's books because of the authoritativeness of its opinions. It often focuses on new trends or on subjects not generally dealt with in the other children's book review media.

Since 1970 the Council on Interracial Books for Children has published *Interracial Books for Children Bulletin*, which analyzes all types of library materials for stereotypes, distortions, and omissions about women, blacks, Chicanos, Asian Americans, Puerto Ricans, and native Americans. It appears eight times a year, and many issues center on one specific topic. It has proved a valuable aid in balancing some of the more conservative children's review publications.

Reference Book Reviews

One of the most important types of books to all libraries is reference materials. Because of the often great expense of an individual item, reviews are probably more often consulted for this type of book than for any other. While all the library review media cover reference books extensively, there are several specialized sources that offer further guidance. The most important of these is *Reference and Subscription Books Reviews (RSBR)*, formerly known as *Subscription Books Bulletin*. It is the work of a committee of the American Library Association and was for a long time published as a separate journal. In more recent years it has been published in *Booklist*, but it still remains a separate publication with its own editor and staff and lies outside the responsibilities of the *Booklist* editor, who merely provides space in the journal for it. This separation is important to keep in mind, for the methods of selection and reviewing practiced by *RSBR* are quite different from those utilized by *Booklist*. First of all, the selection and reviewing are done by a fairly large committee, representative of the profession as a whole. All the longer reviews are the work of several people; only shorter works or new editions of works previously evaluated at length are given to one person to review. Since obtaining a committee review of a large reference set such as an encyclopedia is a time-consuming job, *RSBR* reviews are often delayed as much as a year or more following publication of a work. The detail and care with which reference works are reviewed makes waiting for these reviews very worthwhile in the case of expensive sets. Reference book publishers hold this committee in awe and await with some fear and trepidation its verdict on major reference publications. Some publishers have been known to with-hold sets from review by the committee, not wishing to risk condemnation of a marginal product. Since reviews are months in the works, the committee frequently publishes lists of those books it is in the process of examining as well as lists of reference books it does not plan to review. At one time, the committee reviewed a very limited number of large reference works. Over the past several years, how-ever, it has published a much greater number of shorter reviews. These resemble in many ways the reviews appearing in other library journals.

In addition to *RSBR*, the American Library Association, through its Reference and Adult Services Division, publishes other reviews of reference books. These appear in *RQ*, the division's membership journal, and are likewise the work of practicing reference librarians. Charles Bunge edits an excellent column, "Current Reference Books," in each monthly issue of the *Wilson Library Bulletin*. *Reference Services Review*, edited by Edward Wall and published by Pierian Press, also includes reviews of reference books within its pages. *ARBA*, the *American Reference Books Annual*, published by Libraries Unlimited, offers belated coverage once a year of a very large number of reference books, as well as citations of other reviews appearing elsewhere. Twice a year, *College & Research Libraries* publishes a supplement to the standard *Guide to Reference Books*, currently edited by Eugene Sheehy. It is closely followed by most book selectors, whether in academic or public libraries. It is notable for the inclusion of outstanding foreign reference tools and of material suitable for very large research libraries that may not be reviewed elsewhere.

Scientific and Technical Book Reviews

The selection of good scientific and technical books has often posed a problem for public and school libraries. Thus the launching in 1965 by the American Association for the Advancement of Science of *Science Books* (now known as *Science Books & Films*) was warmly greeted by librarians. The first editor, Hilary Deason, brought it instant acclaim, and the present editor has continued the high standards initially set. *Science Books & Films* was consciously modeled on the success of CHOICE, utilizing college faculty members for most of its reviewers. Subject expertise was the essential criterion, as what had been lacking in the reviewing of so many science books for libraries was the knowledge of whether the contents of a book, particularly popularizations or children's books, were scientifically sound or not. *Science Books & Films* differs in a few ways from CHOICE, however. It now includes films, as the new name indicates, and its reviews are signed. Furthermore it covers science books and films for all age levels from primary school through college. It is published quarterly and in 1976 published about 1,000 reviews. Its modest cost puts it within the reach of all libraries, and it is especially useful as a buying guide in small and medium-sized public and academic libraries. It cannot be too highly recommended.

Another helpful publication for libraries is the New York Public Libraries' monthly *New Technical Books*, published since 1915. Subject emphasis is on the pure and applied physical sciences, mathematics, engineering, industrial technology, and related disciplines, but interdisciplinary works cutting across both physical and natural sciences are now included. Whereas in the early days most of the material included was of a fairly advanced nature, an attempt has been made in recent years to include publications of interest to small and medium-sized public and academic libraries. The reviews are the work of the staff of NYPL's Science and Technology Division.

Reviews of Reprints and Small Press Publications

Two types of books that present problems to all library book selectors are reprints and the publications of small presses. CHOICE, for a period of half a dozen years or so in the late 1960s and early 1970s, reviewed large numbers of reprints. This was at the height of the reprint boom. With a subsequent squeeze in the amount of space available in the magazine and a decrease in the reprint market, these reviews were drastically reduced in number and are now limited to large series. Meanwhile, there appeared in 1955 the *Reprint Bulletin— Book Reviews*. In its earlier incarnation, *Reprint Expediting Service Bulletin*, it merely attempted to encourage the reprinting of needed works; in recent years it has turned into a journal publishing some 900 reviews of reprints a year. Organized along the lines of CHOICE and *Library Journal*, it utilizes outside reviewers—both librarians and academics—to do its reviewing. It has unfortunately remained largely unknown to the profession. No large-scale advertising campaign ever seems to have been attempted, and its poor typographic appearance (mimeographed with unjustified right-hand margins) has probably brought it few subscribers. It remains a useful source of information in a field largely ignored by other review journals.

With the advent of socially conscious librarians in the late 1960s, many became concerned about the failure of most libraries to provide alternative materials, representing opinions and culture outside the mainstream of commercial publishing. One of the most difficult things was to find any listing or evaluation of such materials. By their very nature, such publishers avoided association with the standard bibliographic tools or review media. One of them, however, Len Fulton of Dustbooks, came to the rescue and began publication in 1967 of the *Small Press Review*. While Bill Katz, in a column published from time to time in *Library Journal*, also sought to bring this material to the attention of librarians, Len Fulton's publication has been the main continuing source of information about such publications. It deserves the attention of all wishing to collect nonestablishment publications.

Reviews of Foreign Publications

The obvious sources for information about books published in a foreign language are review journals in the country of origin.

Unfortunately most U.S. libraries, other than the large research libraries, usually do not have the resources to satisfy such needs. Furthermore the need for foreign-language materials is of several different kinds. Academic libraries need materials to support the teaching of foreign languages and literatures and must occasionally purchase basic foreign-language reference works. For their needs *TLS*, as previously mentioned, is of great value. For foreign literature the best U.S. source of information is *World Literature Today* (formerly titled *Books Abroad*). It covers many different languages and, while somewhat late in its reviewing, due no doubt to the delays inherent in getting review copies of foreign books, it provides knowledgeable reviews by academics.

In public libraries, materials needed for various ethnic groups have traditionally been limited to recreational materials and perhaps a few basic reference tools. In recent years, however, new immigrants to this country and to Canada have increasingly been educated persons wishing to keep in contact with their original culture. Providing in-depth materials for these newcomers has presented a problem for public libraries. Leonard Wertheimer's *Books in Other Languages*[4] is a helpful guide to librarians faced with this new challenge. Need for light reading of a recreational nature is satisfied largely by the lists prepared under the direction of Earle M. Gladden, Supervising Librarian of the Donnell Foreign Language Library, New York Public Library. These lists are published regularly in *Booklist*.

Finally, mention should be made of another review source, which, while dealing with English-language publications, can technically, at least in the United States, be considered a foreign publication. This is *British Book News*, published by the British Council in London. The unsigned reviews are prepared by librarians and academics throughout England and provide high-quality opinions of a selection of the best current British publications. Its nominal cost places it within the range of all U.S. libraries. Librarians could use it much more than they now do, as a supplement to our own reviewing sources.

Professional and Scholarly Book Reviews

Book reviews appear in a vast array of professional and scholarly journals. These are prime sources for research and special libraries that have the time and personnel to examine the myriad journals in all the major academic fields. To the average public or college librarian this task is too great and, at least in most colleges, is left to the faculty. Librarians should be aware, however, that such publications exist and

[4]Leonard Wertheimer, *Books in Other Languages*, 4th ed. (Ottawa, Ontario: Canadian Library Association, 1979).

that some of them carry great weight within specific subject fields. They are of two types. The first is the regular scholarly journal, such as the *American Historical Review* or *PMLA* (*Publications of the Modern Language Association*), which carry book reviews as one part of their publishing program. Others are devoted exclusively to book reviews. Some outstanding examples of this type of publication are *Contemporary Psychology*, *Journal of Economic Literature*, *Educational Studies*, and *Philosophical Books*. The difficulty with these scholarly journals is the great time lag between the appearance of a book and the publication of a review. The time lag varies from field to field. At present it is only six months to a year in history, but in literature it is usually one to two years and in philosophy it can be anywhere from two to four years. There is no pressure in an academic field to make a hasty judgment of a new book, but as a result of these time lags, some books go out of print before they are reviewed in the scholarly journals. For libraries, these journals are useful primarily as follow-ups, for building collections retrospectively.

Reviews of Other Types of Printed Materials

Most of my comments about reviewing so far have dealt primarily with books. But library collections today contain, or should contain, many other types of materials. Let us now examine what reviewing is available for these other types, beginning with other kinds of printed materials. We will discuss periodicals and serials, government documents, and music.

Periodicals and serials are reviewed regularly by a limited number of sources. First and foremost is Pierian Press's *Serials Review*, begun in 1975. This quarterly reviews new periodicals of all types and subjects, as well as indexes, abstracts, bibliographies, handbooks, yearbooks, and other reference tools serially published. Furthermore it reviews new cumulative and other published indexes to periodicals, newspapers, and serials and identifies where a periodical is indexed or abstracted. It also indexes reviews of periodicals and serials appearing in some 200 other publications. It is thus the primary source of reviews for any periodical, newspaper, or serial.

Library Journal and CHOICE carry monthly columns reviewing selected new periodicals and serials, each of them edited by the author of a basic list of periodicals. Bill Katz, the author of *Magazines for Libraries* (3d ed., 1978), supplies *LJ* with its monthly feature, "Magazines." This lists new periodicals of interest to public, school, and college libraries. Evan Farber, the author of *Classified List of Periodicals for the College Library* (5th ed., 1972), assisted by present and former members of his Earlham College library staff, supplies

CHOICE with a similar monthly column, "Periodicals for College Libraries." One characteristic of all the reviews of periodicals and serials is that reviewers usually wait for several issues of a periodical to appear before attempting a review. Too many periodicals launched with considerable fanfare fall victim to lack of funds or lack of reader interest and disappear after only one or two issues. It is also necessary to see whether a periodical continues its original policy and coverage or takes a new direction after the initial issue. Farber provides a list of new periodicals as soon as information about them becomes available but waits for a year or two before passing judgment. Most of the reviews in Katz's column are likewise of periodicals that have been in existence at least a year. As we shall see when discussing the selection of periodicals, a great deal of emphasis is placed by most libraries on whether indexing of that periodical is available. Farber indicates in his column where periodicals are indexed—as does, of course, *Serials Review*. All the reviewing sources for periodicals and serials often run combined reviews comparing several periodicals on one topic—particularly topics of current interest, such as the environment or women's studies. This type of comparative reviewing is very helpful in building strong collections.

Government documents have long posed a problem to the reviewing media, as the U.S. Government Printing Office has never seen the necessity of publicizing the existence of government publications beyond a listing in the *Monthly Catalog* (and sometimes not even there) and refuses to supply review copies to any of the review journals. Reviewing of government documents has had to be limited to librarians who had access to a government depository collection. Only occasionally does a government agency supply copies of a particular book to the review media. This has meant that CHOICE, which uses primarily teaching faculty as its reviewers, has been handicapped in its reviewing of government documents. Columns written by documents librarians do appear regularly in *Booklist, RQ,* and *Wilson Library Bulletin*. Most recently (in 1977) the quarterly *Government Publications Review* began a "selected annotated listing of high interest documents." Coverage is worldwide, and although these listings cannot really be classified as reviews, by their very selective nature they are an aid to collection development.

Many public and academic libraries have long maintained collections of sheet music and scores. The general book trade and library review media do not usually cover such materials. The best source of reviews of classical music of all types is *Notes*, the very fine quarterly journal of the Music Library Association. One issue may contain reviews of as many as fifty different compositions, most of them lengthy and detailed. It should be mentioned here that *Notes* is an excellent source of reviews of books in the field of music as well. Books in all languages and from all over the world are reviewed. While there is an overlap of coverage (primarily with English-language materials) with the general library review media such as CHOICE, the reviews in *Notes* tend to be longer and more detailed. As with many scholarly journals, however, the reviews often appear late. *Notes* has a number of other noteworthy features (which will be discussed later) that make it essential for all but the smallest public or academic library.

Microform Reviews

Microfilm, microcards, and microfiche have come to fill important needs in library collections in recent years. Microfilms have almost completely replaced the bulky bound volumes of newspapers in most libraries, as well as many bound files of periodicals. Microcards seem to have passed their heyday and are being replaced by microfiche. The reviewing of microtexts presents two problems to reviewers. Not only the contents but also the technical qualities of the product must be examined and evaluated. Usually one reviewer is not competent to do both. Printed introductions or aids sometimes accompany the microtexts, and these too must be reviewed. Because of the high cost of many microtext projects, a knowledgeable appraisal of a publication is of great value to libraries. Unfortunately their high cost also prevents many microtext publishers from giving away review copies. Thus other arrangements must be made to compensate reviewers. Some publishers provide a credit up to a certain amount toward the purchase of a set by a reviewer's library. In most cases, the publisher requests the return of the review set after the review has been prepared.

The major source of reviews of microtexts is *Microform Review*, published quarterly since 1972. Because of the high quality of its reviews, other review journals, such as CHOICE, have hesitated to enter this field. We find here the ideal assessment of both the content and the technical qualities of each publication. The technical qualities are assessed by the renowned expert Hubbard Ballou of Columbia University. The contents of each publication are evaluated by a respected scholar in the field, following the pattern of CHOICE. Reviews are lengthy and detailed, often covering two or three pages.

Reviews of Audio-Visual Materials

Comprehensive sources for reviews of audio-visual materials of all types are few. Most review sources in this area limit themselves to one type of material. Two sources specifically aimed at libraries' needs, *Booklist* and *Previews*, cover films (8 mm and 16 mm), filmstrips, slides, video recordings and cassettes, media kits, games, and spoken recordings. Both omit music recordings.

Booklist inaugurated its audio-visual reviews in 1969, although an ALA Audio-Visual Committee had been issuing 16 mm film reviews for some time before that date. As with book reviews, the A-V reviews in *Booklist* are prepared by an in-house reviewing staff, with the aid of some outside consultants. Films for all age groups are reviewed, as well as those suitable for all types of libraries. Some 1,756 items were assessed in 1977. In reviewing A-V materials, the technical qualities as well as the contents of the media are assessed. An attempt is also made to indicate the age group for which the material is suitable. As with *Booklist*'s book reviews, only A-V materials that generally can be recommended are listed in the semimonthly issues of the journal. There is a tendency, however, to be a little more critical than with the book reviews. Subject coverage is wide-ranging, and the reviews are carefully prepared. The results are most suitable for the public or school library; college librarians complain that too many films and other materials are recommended for college-age students that, upon closer scrutiny, are not particularly suitable for this audience. They have long sought a medium that would review A-V materials just for this type of user, but to date no organization has had the funds to launch such a venture.

Previews grew out of the A-V reviews in *Library Journal* and *School Library Journal*. These reviews were withdrawn from *LJ* and *SLJ* in 1972 to form a separate journal which is now issued nine times a year, monthly from September through June. As with the reviews in *LJ* and *SLJ*, evaluation is done by outside reviewers, usually librarians actively engaged in audio-visual work. Again the audience is primarily the school and public library, with more emphasis probably on the former. Approximately 900 to 1,000 reviews are published annually.

Films

While the number of review media interested in more than one kind of A-V medium is very limited, there are a number of specialized journals reviewing one type. We will discuss several that offer guides to current 16 mm and 8 mm films. The Educational Film Library Association has offered a review service since 1946. *EFLA Evaluations* are the work of committees scattered throughout the country. Every title is evaluated by at least two committees before the reviews are synthesized and published. Each review entry contains information on format, producer, director, price, release date, and critical comment on the content and the technical quality, awards won (if any), subject matter, grade level, and audience suitability. The quality of the reviews varies, as is true with any service that is the work of volunteers. *EFLA* also publishes *Sightlines*, a quarterly which reviews 8 mm and 16 mm films for school and library use. Each issue focuses on a different theme, such as black and ethnic films, family life, and creative curriculum films.

Another library group, the Film Library Information Council, began in 1967 to publish reviews of 16 mm films of primary interest to public libraries in the *Film Library Quarterly*. Another review medium for films which also covers filmstrips is *Film News: The International Review of AV Materials and Equipment*, published six times a year since 1939. Reviews include descriptive and evaluative annotations of format, running time, producers, content, technical quality, and subject area pertinence of each film or filmstrip.

One of the most popular review sources for films and filmstrips (as well as for slides and other projected material) is *Landers Film Reviews*, published ten times a year. Again the audience is schools and public libraries. Each entry includes the following items: running time, format, release date, producers, purchase/rental price, grade level, contents summary, and a critical review. Film distributors are charged a fee for a review of their film. Finally, mention should be made of the monthly column "Cine-Opsis," appearing in the *Wilson Library Bulletin*. Unfortunately the column reviews only four to eight films each month. It is aimed at the small and medium-sized library. Only favorable reviews are published, and each issue usually concentrates on one topic of current concern.

Recordings[5]

For review purposes, recordings must be divided into three groups, each with its own review sources. These are (1) classical music recordings, (2) popular music recordings, including jazz, blues, rock and roll, and folk music, and (3) spoken recordings (poetry, plays, and instructional recordings). The last category is reviewed regularly in *Booklist* and in *Previews*. Contrary to usual *Booklist* policy, most of the spoken recordings are reviewed by outside consultants. Both audiocassettes and phonodiscs are included.

With music recordings, the picture changes drastically. There it is necessary to go to journals published for the hobbyist, the private record collector, or the music lover. Coverage is on the whole very

[5]For a much more detailed discussion than can be presented here of sources for reviews of popular and classical music recordings, see Carol Lawrence Mekkawi, "Music Periodicals: Popular and Classical Record Reviews and Indexes," *Notes*, 34 (Sept. 1977) 92–107.

good. The first record collections developed in libraries were almost exclusively of classical music. Later some libraries branched out into jazz. More recently libraries have attempted to collect all types of music. Three good sources of classical record reviews can be recommended to the average public or academic library. They are *High Fidelity*, *Stereo Review*, and *Gramophone*—the first two published in the United States, the last in Great Britain.

Both *High Fidelity* and *Stereo Review* review about forty classical recordings, in both disc and tape format, each month. There is considerable overlap, although just enough difference in the recordings selected for review so that most libraries should subscribe to both. *Stereo Review* tends to be a little more middle-of-the-road in its tastes than *High Fidelity*, but on the other hand, it covers some of the very fine, inexpensive recordings of the Musical Heritage Society, which are usually reviewed nowhere else. *High Fidelity*'s fine reviews are cumulated each year in the annual publication *Records in Review*, a series that has been in existence since 1955 and supplies a good retrospective ready-reference set for libraries.

One may wonder why a British publication, *Gramophone*, should be included here as an essential reviewing source for U.S. libraries. First of all, as I mentioned in Chapter Three, musical recording is an international business, and most classical recordings are issued by various companies (many of them linked in huge monopolistic cartels) throughout the world. While it is necessary for the U.S. librarian to "translate" the issuing company from a British to a United States firm when using the reviews in *Gramophone*, the overall quality and comprehensiveness of its reviews make the effort worthwhile. Most of the reviews are comparative. *Gramophone* includes an average of 110 classical record reviews in each of its monthly issues, thus covering a far greater number of recordings than any U.S. publication. Its arrangement and indexing features are also far superior to those of any U.S. review source in the field, and since it accepts subscription payments in dollars drawn on local U.S. banks, U.S. libraries have little excuse for not obtaining it.

While *Gramophone* is almost exclusively devoted to classical recordings, both *High Fidelity* and *Stereo Review* include popular records as well. In the past these tended to be middle-of-the-road items, but early in 1977 *High Fidelity* announced that it was expanding its popular coverage to include many more rock, soul, disco, and country-music recordings. For in-depth reviewing in the popular field, however, it is necessary to turn to more specialized sources. These include *Billboard* (although its reviews are promotional rather than evaluative), *Creem*, and *Rolling Stone*. *Creem* and *Rolling Stone* are the main sources for reviews of rock and roll music. Both started as counterculture publications in the 1960s and *Creem* may still be a little too far out for some conservative libraries, but for thoughtful reviews of this type of music, they cannot be equaled.

INDEXES TO REVIEW SOURCES

With such a multiplicity of review sources, librarians or library school students may well wonder how they can locate a review of a specific book or other item. Such questions come up not only in the selection process but also in answering innumerable student requests for reviews of books or other materials that they have been asked to read or examine.

For many years, the H. W. Wilson Company's monthly *Book Review Digest* was the primary source of information. Unfortunately the coverage of the *Digest* has always been highly selective. Limited space has meant that certain criteria for inclusion have had to be established. At the present time, for a work of fiction to be included, four reviews must have appeared within eighteen months following publication in the selected group of periodicals covered by the *Book Review Digest*. For nonfiction the total number is only two. For those books selected, a brief summary of the plot or contents is prepared, and citations to all the reviews found in *BRD*'s list of publications searched are listed. Certain of these reviews are also digested so that a fairly good picture of the temper of the reviews can be gained without going back to the originals. While the coverage of *BRD* has increased drastically since the mid-1960s, there are many books for which the required number of reviews cannot be found, at least within the time frame allowed. To remedy this, the Wilson Company launched in January 1976 a new monthly publication entitled *Current Book Review Citations*. Its announced purpose was to index the book reviews appearing in some 1,300 periodicals—all those listed in the Wilson indexes as well as all those appearing in *Booklist*, CHOICE, *Library Journal*, and *School Library Journal*. While providing a valuable service, *Current Book Review Citations* has not yet come up to expectations, especially when compared with its rival, *Book Review Index*, published by Gale Research bimonthly since 1965. *Book Review Index*, after a healthy start, was forced to suspend publication in the early 1970s. It has since been revived and the gap filled in. It provides an easily used and very accurate index to reviews appearing in a wide variety of publications. While the total number of publications covered (1,200 at last count) is slightly smaller than in *Current Book Review Citations*, the publications seem to be indexed in greater depth. With the added attraction of speedier coverage, *Book*

Review Index seems to be the first source to consult for any book review and the first-priority purchase for all types of libraries.

The New York Times Book Review has long been a major source of information for all libraries. Thus it was good to see the publication in 1973 of the five-volume *New York Times Book Review Index*, covering the reviews published in *The New York Times* between 1896 and 1970. Since *Book Review Index* did not begin publication until 1965 and *Book Review Digest* has always been very selective, the *New York Times Book Review Index* has provided a valuable tool for libraries.

In addition to these general tools, there are various special subject indexes to book reviews. Phillip Thomson has been publishing *Index to Book Reviews in the Humanities* annually since 1960. Its primary value is in its coverage of many literary quarterlies and other journals. *Technical Book Review Index* has been published since 1935 (first by the Special Libraries Association and more recently by a commercial publisher), giving helpful coverage in the technical and scientific fields. More recently another commercial publisher, Carrollton Press, has issued two multivolume indexes to book reviews in scholarly and professional journals: *Combined Retrospective Index to Book Reviews in Scholarly Journals, 1886–1974*, covering the fields of history, political science, and sociology, and *Combined Retrospective Index to Book Reviews in Scholarly Humanities Journals, 1802–1974*. The first of these covers 472 journals and the second 173. These should prove gold mines of information, as most of these reviews have been very hard to trace.

For periodicals and serials the main index to reviews is the "Serial Review Index," appearing as part of each quarterly *Serials Review*. Reviews in more than 200 periodicals and review journals are covered.

For nonprint media the primary source since 1970 has been the annual *Media Review Digest*, published by Pierian Press. It currently indexes reviews of all types of nonprint media appearing in 150 periodicals, offering 50,000 to 60,000 review citations per year. For recordings alone, there are two primary sources. Dean Tudor and Andrew Armitage have published an *Annual Index to Popular Music Record Reviews* since 1973. This is a unique compilation, with many admirable features that are useful in many types of libraries. *Notes*, the previously mentioned quarterly publication of the Music Library Association, publishes two indexes to record reviews. The first of these, "Index to Record Reviews," edited by Kurtz Myers, has been published since 1948 and covers classical music recordings. A more recent addition to the journal is "Popular Music . . . Records Recently Reviewed," edited by Robert M. Jones. Still fairly modest in extent, it cannot yet rival the annual coverage of Tudor and Armitage. The

Kurtz Myers "Index" is extensive indeed, covering an average of 320 recordings per issue. Happily the entire series has been cumulated in a five-volume set published by G. K. Hall. This should prove to be a basic tool for years to come.

BIBLIOGRAPHY

Popular Review Media

Atlantic Monthly. Boston: Atlantic Monthly Company, 1857– . (Monthly.)

Books of the Times. New York: Arno Press, 1978– . (Monthly.)

Commentary. New York: American Jewish Committee, 1945– . (Monthly.)

Harper's. New York: Harper's Magazine Company, 1850– . (Monthly.)

Los Angeles Times Book Review. Los Angeles: Times-Mirror Publishing Company, 1882– . (Weekly.)

Nation. New York: Nation Associates, Inc., 1865– . (Weekly.)

New Republic. Washington, D. C.: New Republic, 1914– . (Weekly.)

New York Review of Books. New York: NYREV, Inc., 1963– . (22 issues per year.)

New York Times Book Review. New York: New York Times, 1896– . (Weekly.)

Newsweek. New York: Newsweek, Inc., 1933– . (Weekly.)

Saturday Review. New York: Saturday Review Magazine Corporation, 1924– . (Bi-weekly.)

Time. New York: Time, Inc., 1923– . (Weekly.)

Times Literary Supplement. London: Times Newspapers, Ltd., 1902– . (Weekly.)

General Book Trade and Library Review Media

Booklist. Chicago: American Library Association, 1905– . (Semimonthly.)

CHOICE. Middletown, Conn.: CHOICE, 1964– . (11 issues per year.)

Kirkus Reviews. New York: Kirkus Service Inc., 1933– . (semimonthly.)

Library Journal. New York: R. R. Bowker Company, 1876– . (Semimonthly.)

Publishers Weekly (PW). New York: R. R. Bowker Company, 1872– . (Weekly.)

Children's Book Review Media

Center for Children's Books Bulletin. Chicago: University of Chicago Press, 1945– . (Monthly, Sept.–June.)

Horn Book. Boston: Horn Book, Inc., 1924– . (6 issues per year.)

Interracial Books for Children Bulletin. New York: Council on Interracial Books for Children, 1970– . (8 issues per year.)

School Library Journal. New York: R. R. Bowker Company, 1954– . (Monthly, Sept.–May.)

Reference Book Review Media

American Reference Books Annual. Littleton, Colo.: Libraries Unlimited, 1970– . (Annual.)

College & Research Libraries. Chicago: Association of College and Research Libraries, 1934– . (Bimonthly.)

RQ (Reference Quarterly). Chicago: American Library Association, Reference and Adult Services Division, 1960– . (Quarterly.)

Reference Services Review. Ann Arbor, Mich.: Pierian Press, 1973– . (Quarterly.)

Reference and Subscription Book Reviews. Chicago: American Library Association, 1930– . (Biennial; appears semimonthly in *Booklist*.)

Wilson Library Bulletin. New York: The H. W. Wilson Company, 1914– . (Monthly.)

Science and Technical Books Review Media

New Technical Books. New York: New York Public Library, 1915– . (Weekly.)

Science Books and Films. Washington, D.C.: American Association for the Advancement of Science, 1965– . (Quarterly; variant title: *AAAS Science Books and Films*.)

Reprints and Small Press Publications Review Media

Reprint Bulletin. Dobbs Ferry, N.Y.: Glanville Publishers, Inc., 1955– . (Quarterly.)

Small Press Review. Paradise, Calif.: Dustbooks, 1967– . (Monthly.)

Foreign Publications Review Media

British Book News. London: British Council, 1940– . (Monthly.)

World Literature Today. Norman, Okla.: University of Oklahoma Press, 1927– . (Quarterly; formerly *Books Abroad.*)

Professional and Scholarly Book Review Media

American Historical Review. Washington, D.C.: American Historical Association, 1895– . (5 issues per year.)

Contemporary Psychology. Washington, D.C.: American Psychological Association, 1956– . (Monthly.)

Educational Studies. Ames, Iowa: American Educational Studies Association, 1970– . (Quarterly.)

Journal of Economic Literature. Nashville, Tenn.: American Economic Association, 1963– . (Quarterly.)

Philosophical Books. Leicester, England: Leicester University Press, 1960– . (3 issues per year.)

PMLA (Publications of the Modern Language Association). New York: Modern Language Association, 1884– . (6 issues per year.)

Periodicals and Serials Review Media

"Magazines" in *Library Journal.*

"Periodicals for College Libraries," in CHOICE.

Serials Review. Ann Arbor, Mich.: Pierian Press, 1975– . (Quarterly.)

Government Documents Review Media

Government Publications Review. Elmsford, N.Y.: Pergamon Press, 1974– . (6 issues per year.)

Music Review Media

Notes. Ann Arbor, Mich.: Music Library Association, 1942– . (Quarterly.)

Microforms Review Media

Microform Review. Westport, Conn.: Microform Reviews, Inc., 1972– . (Quarterly.)

Audio-Visual: General Review Media

Booklist. Chicago: American Library Association, 1905– . (Semimonthly.)

Previews. New York: R. R. Bowker Company, 1972– . (Monthly, Sept.–May.)

Audio-Visual: Film Review Media

"Cine-Opsis," in *Wilson Library Bulletin.*

EFLA Evaluations. New York: Educational Film Library Association, 1946– . (10 issues per year.)

Film Library Quarterly. New York: Film Library Information Council, 1967– . (Quarterly.)

Film News: Incorporating Learning Resources of Canada: The International Review of AV Materials and Equipment. New York: Film News Company, 1939– . (5 issues per year.)

Landers Film Reviews. Los Angeles: Landers Associates, 1956– . (5 issues per year.)

Sightlines. New York: Educational Film Library Association, 1967– . (4 issues per year.)

Audio-Visual: Record Review Media

Billboard. Los Angeles: Billboard Publications Inc., 1894– . (Weekly.)

Creem. Birmingham, Mich.: Creem, 1969– . (Monthly.)

Gramophone. Middlesex, Eng.: General Gramophone Publications, Ltd., 1923– . (Monthly.)

High Fidelity. Great Barrington, Mass.: ABC Leisure Magazines, Inc., 1951– . (Monthly; cumulated annually as *Records in Review.*)

Rolling Stone. New York: Straight Arrow Publishers, 1967– . (Semimonthly.)

Stereo Review. New York: Ziff-Davis Publishing Company, 1958– . (Monthly.)

Indexes to Review Media

Armitage, Andrew, and Dean Tudor. *Annual Index to Popular Music Record Reviews*, 1972– . Metuchen, N.J.: Scarecrow Press, 1973– . (Annual.)

Book Review Digest. New York: The H. W. Wilson Company, 1905– . (Monthly.)

Book Review Index. Detroit: Gale Publications, 1965– . (Bimonthly.)

Combined Retrospective Index to Book Reviews in Scholarly Humanities Journals, 1802–1974. Arlington, Va.: Carrollton Press, 1978.

Combined Retrospective Index to Book Reviews in Scholarly Journals, 1886–1974 (History, Political Science and Sociology.) Arlington, Va.: Carrollton Press, Inc., 1978.

Current Book Review Citations. New York: The H. W. Wilson Company, 1976– . (Monthly.)

Index to Book Reviews in the Humanities. Detroit: Phillip Thomson, 1960– . (Annual.)

"Index to Record Reviews" in *Notes.*

Media Review Digest. Ann Arbor, Mich.: Pierian Press, 1970– . (Bimonthly.)

New York Times Book Review Index, 1896–1970. New York: New York Times, 1973.

"Popular Music . . . Records Recently Reviewed" in *Notes.*

"Serial Review Index" in *Serials Review.*

Technical Book Review Index. New York: JAAD Publishing Company, 1935– . (Monthly; compiled and edited in the Technology Department, Carnegie Library of Pittsburgh.)

SUGGESTED READINGS

Book Reviewing: A Guide to Writing Book Reviews for Newspapers, Magazines, Radio, and Television by Leading Book Editors, Critics, and Reviewers, ed. by Sylvia E. Kamerman. Boston: The Writer, Inc., 1978.

"How-to-do-it" for all librarians faced with writing book reviews. These twenty-one chapters include essays by such critics as Robert Kirsch (*Los Angeles Times*), Doris Grumbach (*Saturday Review*), and Christopher Lehmann-Haupt (*New York Times*). Also provides insight into how the major general review media operate.

Encyclopedia of Library and Information Science, vol. 25 (1978). S.v. "Reviews and Reviewing, Introduction," by Robert Stueart; "Reviews and Reviewing of Multimedia Materials," by Estelle Jussim; "Children's Book Reviews and Reviewing," by Priscilla Moulton.

Each of these articles provides an overview of the development and present character of reviewing. The principal sources of reviews are listed and brief evaluative comments provided. As a guide to further reading, there are short bibliographies at the end of each article.

"A Look Inside the *New York Review of Books*," *Publishers Weekly,* 205 (Mar. 11, 1974), 37–40.

A short exposition of the reviewing practices of the *New York Review of Books.* Includes background on its origins and relationship to the book trade. There is a special comment on the connections between *NYRB* and *Kirkus Reviews.*

Stuttaford, Genevieve. "A Short Review of the Magazine Reviewers," *Publishers Weekly,* 206 (Dec. 2, 1974), 38–41.

A survey of book editors and reviewing practices in the mass circulation magazines. Among issues discussed are the relationship of reviewing to book sales, the problem of timeliness of reviews, how books are selected for review and assigned to reviewers, and the quality and character of reviews.

Weyr, Thomas. "The Making of the *New York Times Book Review*," *Publishers Weekly*, 202 (July 31, 1972), 36–49.

This article was occasioned by the appointment of John Leonard as editor of *NYTBR*. The author discusses how reviewing is done at *NYTBR*, attitudes of book trade people and authors toward the magazine, problems in deciding who should review which books, and the position of the "Best Sellers" list.

CHAPTER SEVEN
Aids to Retrospective Collection Development

Books, periodicals, and other library materials, once they have been listed in the trade and national bibliographic sources and reviewed, become part of the bibliography of a subject area or a particular type of material. They take on a life of their own. If they have been found to be of little value, they will soon be consigned to oblivion; nothing more will be heard of them, and they will soon be withdrawn from the marketplace. The only sign of their having existed will be entries in the various retrospective bibliographies, such as *Cumulative Book Index* and the *National Union Catalog*. If, however, they are excellent works, they will soon be cited over and over again in lists of "best books" or as parts of "basic collections."

Lists of best books have existed since the beginning of the history of books and printing. Many of the earliest bibliographies were not inclusive lists but rather attempts to select the most worthwhile books on a particular subject. In modern times, such lists have been compiled for various purposes and various groups of people. Some are intended for booksellers—to tell them what to stock in their stores in order to include more than just the current best sellers. *The Reader's Adviser*, now in its twelfth edition, edited by Sarah L. Prakken and others (3 vols., Bowker, 1974–1977), had as its initial purpose just such a goal, although it has proven to be useful beyond the confines of the book store and is so marketed today. Other lists have been compiled for the general reader—at various age levels—with the intent of offering advice on what to read. These lists all have a didactic purpose; they are attempts to raise the level of reading, to woo the reader away from the trivial to something more "worthwhile" and "substantial," to the classics of literature and other fields, it is hoped. A good example of such a list is *Good Reading: A Guide for Serious Readers*, edited for many years by J. Sherwood Weber and now in its twenty-first edition (Bowker, 1978). Many such lists are intended for the scholar or student in a particular subject area and are published in the form of subject bibliographies. Such subject bibliographies may be elementary and therefore very selective, or they may attempt to cover a field in depth and be as inclusive as possible. A good example of a selective subject list is Edna Louise Lucas's *Art Books: A Basic Bibliography on the Fine Arts* (New York Graphic Society, 1968), while an example of a much more comprehensive list is the *Harvard Guide to American History*, edited by Frank Friedel (rev. ed., 2 vols., Harvard University Press, 1974). Even more specialized historical bibliographies can be seen in those published by Oxford University Press (under the direction of the American Historical Association and the Royal Historical Society of Great Britain), which cover only one period of British history—for example, the *Stuart Period, 1603–1714*, edited by Mary Frear Keeler (1970).

A book may be so outstanding that it wins a prize, such as the Newbery or Caldecott awards for children's books or a Pulitzer Prize or an American Book Award. Library associations and library journals are fond of drawing up lists of the "best books of the year." In fact, it sometimes seems as though librarians do little else than compile lists of the "best" books—best for particular types of libraries, for particular age groups, or for particular types of readers, such as the blind or handicapped. One special kind of list that has broad appeal for librarians is the starter list, which aids persons beginning a new library collection or building a collection in a new subject area. Examples of such lists are the Public Library Association's Starter List for New Branch and New Libraries Collection[s], entitled *Books for Public Libraries: Non-Fiction for Small Collections*, or the *Opening Day Collection* for community college libraries, published by CHOICE. Librarians find that all these lists, no matter what their source or original purpose, are useful in building collections. Thus they avidly seek out new lists or new editions of older ones of proven value.

Who compiles these lists? Many of them, as we have already indicated, originate with library associations or library journals. Many of them are produced locally by libraries for use within their own systems, either by staff or for patrons. These often find their way into publications such as the *Vertical File Index* or into various library periodical listings; eventually they come to be known and to have wider use outside the local area. Many, and many of the best and most useful, are the product of professional and scholarly associations that feel the need to control the bibliography of their subject area, to indicate strengths and weaknesses in available publications, and to offer guidance to those working in the field. Individual publishers, such as the aforementioned Harvard or Oxford University presses, often provide the impetus for such works. And finally, individual scholars, because of their personal interests, may be the source of a particular list, which will eventually be published in some form. Some of the most useful bibliographies compiled by such scholars have come to publishers over the transom.

Lists of best books or subject bibliographies appear in all types of formats. They may be full-fledged books or even multivolume sets, such as *Books for College Libraries* or the H. W. Wilson Catalog series. Others may opt for a more modest paperback format in order to keep the price down. Examples of these are the previously mentioned Lucas's *Art Books*, as well as F. W. Bateson and H. T. Meserole's *A Guide to English and American Literature*. Others may be offset from typewritten copy and issued as pamphlets (examples being the Mathematical Association of America's lists for two- and four-year college library collections). Frequently lists are published as articles in professional and library journals. All of the major library and review journals offer such lists—some of them, such as CHOICE, on a regular basis, others from time to time as they see a need to be filled. Finally, there are the separate lists put out by individual organizations and libraries. These are often discovered by accident, as there is no regular listing of such materials anywhere, although *Vertical File Index* does pick up some of the more extensive ones.

The arrangement of lists of recommended or best books varies widely, from straight alphabetical listings by author or title to various subject arrangements. With subject arrangements the Dewey Decimal Classification may be adopted (as in the H. W. Wilson Catalog series) or the Library of Congress Classification (as in *Books for College Libraries*), or an idiosyncratic or homemade scheme may be used. The range of possibilities is unlimited, and all have been tried. Arrangement is an important feature for librarians to consider if the list is to be used as a selection guide, as the arrangement will determine how easily a list may be checked against a library catalog or shelf list to find out which materials are already on hand. The amount of bibliographic information given in lists also varies greatly. Librarians, of course, want as complete bibliographic information as possible to avoid the need to look up data for placing an order or for checking the library catalog. In fact, some excellent lists may not be used at all if their arrangement or lack of bibliographic data create too many searching problems. Just as with publishers' catalogs, librarians wish for the complete author's name, title, publisher (with complete address if the publisher is obscure), publication date, and price (if any). Notes as to content are a bonus. The existence of an index and the type of index may also influence the use of a particular list. For example, the use of the first edition of *Books for College Libraries* was seriously hampered by the omission of titles from the index. Since only authors' names were given, it was often necessary to search many different pages to find the book wanted. Fortunately the second edition remedied this omission by including a full title index.

One perennial problem with lists of recommended or best books is that they quickly go out of date and must be revised or supplemented. As with encyclopedias and other reference books, various methods have been used to keep lists up to date. The most common is to issue revised lists periodically. This is easy to do if the list is brief, but if the list is extensive, this may not be financially feasible. In such cases, supplements are the usual answer. H. W. Wilson combines the two methods, issuing a number of annual supplements to its Catalogs (usually up to a maximum of four or five) and then revising the whole work. The purchase price of the original volume usually includes the forthcoming supplements. Other publishers or organizations market the supplements separately. The second edition of *Books for College Libraries* was purposely issued in six volumes in order to facilitate revision of one volume at a time; unfortunately lack of funds has so far prevented regular revision. Some of the more ephemeral lists are just that—lists for the moment—and do not merit revising or supplementing. Other topics and lists take their place as the interests of the library's public changes.

In addition to the various lists of recommended or best books, there are guides to sources for various types of materials for various age groups. These give lists of organizations—associations, publishers, libraries, etc.—where one may obtain needed materials. As with the lists of materials themselves, these go rapidly out of date and must be supplemented or revised periodically.

SOME OUTSTANDING LISTS

We shall now discuss some well-known basic lists, as well as guides to sources of materials. The selection included here reflects the personal views and prejudices of the compiler regarding usefulness for a particular type of library. It should therefore be looked upon as only a list of possible suggestions. Librarians will want to be on the lookout for other lists that they may consider just as useful. In any case, a list such as this is bound to be out of date as soon as it is published and must be supplemented by more current material. Our purpose here is to give the novice some idea of the range of materials that have been and are currently available. Similar lists, both better and worse than the ones listed here, are issued all the time.

General Lists and Guides

First let us consider some guides and lists of interest to several types of libraries and different age groups. Following a discussion of these, we will go on to more specialized lists for specific types of libraries, types of materials, and various subject fields.

The Reader's Adviser: A Layman's Guide to Literature. Edited by Sarah L. Prakken, F. J. Sypher, and Jack A. Clarke. 12th ed. 3v. New York: R. R. Bowker Company, 1974–1977.

Probably the best-known list of recommended books is *The Reader's Adviser*, which began in 1921 as *The Bookman's Manual*, edited by Bessie Graham. It retained that title until the ninth edition in 1960. Over the years it has had various editors, with each volume in the current edition being the responsibility of a different person. The original edition was meant to be of value to "readers, booksellers, and librarians," but the current edition is probably of more value to the general reader and librarian than to the bookseller since so many reference books are included, enough to qualify it as a miniature Sheehy. It is a selective list, purporting to "include the best of the 365,000 volumes listed in *Books in Print* for 1973–1974." The emphasis in the subjects covered has always been heavily literary. In fact, two of the three volumes in the current set are devoted to literature in its various forms, as the titles of the individual volumes indicate: Volume 1: *The Best in American and British Fiction, Poetry, Essays, Literary Biography, Bibliography and Reference*, and Volume 2: *The Best in American and British Drama and World Literature in English Translation*. It is left to Volume 3, *The Best in the Reference Literature of the World*, to cover all other subjects. This imbalance is one of the two major criticisms of *The Reader's Adviser*, the other being the increasing tendency to list scholarly and technical books in a guide intended for the average reader. No clear distinction is made in the annotations between scholarly and more popular works. As with any list, a critic can point to some strange omissions, but on the whole, *The Reader's Adviser* maintains a very high standard of excellence both for its coverage and for the quality of the bibliographic information and the annotations. It is particularly valuable for its extensive coverage of foreign literature in translation. All in all, *The Reader's Adviser* is a valuable source of advice for the development of library collections in a variety of types of libraries.

Good Reading: A Guide for Serious Readers. Ed. by J. Sherwood Weber. 21st ed. New York: R. R. Bowker Company, 1978.

While *Good Reading* is intended to stimulate the reading interests and enjoyment of an individual, its various editions have served as aids to book selection within the small and medium-sized library— school, college, and public. The twenty-first edition is the first new one in a decade and has been radically revised and updated. Some thirty-five book lists have been developed in all areas of reader interest—from history and geography to literature to the social and natural sciences. Attempts have been made to indicate the best editions and translations of a work and to state the level of difficulty. Bibliographic information is given in full, and a work available in paperback is so noted. This is an admirable starter list for almost any small library. Larger libraries will want every title listed for their collections.

We have noted in passing that various journals regularly include lists of recommended books. While *American Libraries* and *Library Journal* do so only sporadically, two prominent library journals do it on a regular basis. CHOICE includes in each of its eleven yearly issues a retrospective bibliographic essay on a topic of current interest. Some of these essays have also been made available in pamphlet form, often in revised editions. Recent topics include "Energy Politics," "The Institution of the Modern Presidency," and "The Feminine Presence in Literature." Another journal that regularly offers guidance in book selection is the *Wilson Library Bulletin*, which once a year offers three or four lengthy bibliographic essays. While the lists in *Library Journal* and *American Libraries* do not appear on a regular basis, they are often of great value; recent examples are "Medical Texts for Public Libraries" and "Physical Fitness Books" (*Library Journal*, Oct. 15, 1978, and June 15, 1979). *Publishers Weekly* from time to time also offers reading lists, and although these tend to be nonselective, they can be useful guides to what is available on a certain topic. In 1978 *PW* published lists on homosexuality and on running and other aerobic exercises.

The annual lists of best books have also been mentioned. The list most widely known in library circles is undoubtedly the "Notable Books for the Year," chosen annually by the Notable Books Council of the American Library Association. Members of the council represent various types of libraries, and while they have sometimes been criticized for avoiding the more controversial titles, in general their selections merit serious consideration for purchase by most libraries.

Their track record for picking winners over the years has been as good as that of any other body. Their annual lists usually include 30 to 50 adult titles. Another much more lengthy list is that prepared by the editors of CHOICE each year and published in the May issue. This list of "Outstanding Academic Books" runs from 500 to 600 titles and is a selection of the best academic books from among the 6,500 usually reviewed each year in CHOICE. Since the Notable Books Council tends to pick more popular types of materials, this list offers libraries a different type of "best book." Admittedly the list is very long, but it contains much of permanent value for the larger public and academic library. Children's librarians watch eagerly each January for the announcement of the winners of Newbery and Caldecott awards. Even those books that achieve only "nomination" status are bought by most libraries. The American Book Awards have had a checkered career, having been sponsored or administered at various times by the American Publishers Association, the American Library Association, and the National Institute of Arts and Letters. The categories have also varied considerably from year to year. They currently number over twenty. As with the Newbery and Caldecott awards, the nominations are widely publicized before the judges make their final choices, and these lists of nominated books (usually about five in each category) offer useful guides for purchase for libraries.

Public Libraries

Public Library Catalog. 7th ed. New York: The H. W. Wilson Company, 1978. Annual supplements.

Fiction Catalog. 9th ed. New York: The H. W. Wilson Company, 1977. Annual supplements.

The most widely used selection tools for building retrospective collections in the public library field are undoubtedly the two Wilson Catalogs: the *Public Library Catalog* for nonfiction and the *Fiction Catalog.* In addition, H. W. Wilson publishes a *Children's Catalog* (to be discussed later in connection with children's books), as well as a *Senior High School Library Catalog* and a *Junior High School Library Catalog.* All the Wilson Catalogs are produced in the same manner— by a committee of librarians and library school teachers. As would be expected of any work produced by a committee, the results often reflect the lowest common denominator. Nothing that will offend anyone gets in. Also, traditional titles, those that have been on lists of best books for years, continue to be included, although librarians in the field may realize that they are no longer read and should have been replaced. Such is the nature of all committee-produced lists.

Only individuals, responsible to themselves alone, can afford to go out on a limb and include some controversial titles. But in all fairness, it must be stated that lists of best books must consist of those that have achieved the status of classics and that are widely considered important. In spite of any criticisms leveled at the *Public Library Catalog* and the *Fiction Catalog*, they remain useful tools for the selection and evaluation of basic collections.

The *Public Library Catalog* includes nonfiction arranged by subject under Dewey Decimal Classification numbers. Complete bibliographic information is given, as well as annotations on the content of each work. Sometimes critical comments are noted; if so, the source is always carefully stated. As with all H. W. Wilson indexes and catalogs, there is a thorough author, title, and subject index, with the addition, in this case, of an analytical index for parts of books. The current edition is the seventh, published in 1978. It includes 8,045 titles. Each year a supplement is published to bring the work up to date. Four annual supplements, adding a total of 3,200 titles, are included in the volume's purchase price, after which a new edition is issued and the whole process begins again. The *Public Library Catalog* is supplemented, in turn, by the *Fiction Catalog*, now in its ninth edition (1977). This latest edition lists 4,734 titles of the best fiction in the English language. Translations from foreign tongues are included. Arrangement is alphabetical by the author listed on the title page. As with the *Public Library Catalog*, out-of-print as well as in-print works are included, since inclusion in one of the Wilson Catalogs is almost sure to bring a work back into print again. The *Fiction Catalog* includes an analytical index to composite works and offers a valuable subject index to the content of the novels listed. Thus it serves as a valuable reference tool for persons seeking novels about a particular topic, person, or place.

As was mentioned earlier, there is another type of work useful for new public libraries. This is *Books for Public Libraries: Non-Fiction for Small Libraries*, issued by the Starter List for New Branch and New Libraries Collection Committee of the Public Library Association and now in its second edition (American Library Association, 1975).

Academic Libraries

Voigt, Melvin, and Joseph H. Treyz. *Books for College Libraries*. Chicago: American Library Association, 1967.

Books for College Libraries: A Core Collection of 40,000 Titles. 2d ed. Chicago: American Library Association, 1975. 6 vols.

CHOICE. *Opening Day Collection*. 3d ed. Middletown, Conn.: CHOICE, 1975.

Academic libraries have had lists of "basic books" available as guides since 1931, when Charles B. Shaw, then Librarian of Swarthmore College, published *A List of Books for College Libraries*. In 1940 a supplement covering the years 1931 to 1938 was published. The impetus for publishing these lists was a series of grants from the Carnegie Corporation to strengthen college library collections in the dark days of the Depression. They were to be used as evaluation tools and as buying guides. Approximately 14,000 titles suggested by some 200 college professors, librarians, and other experts were included in the basic volume and another 3,600 in the supplement. When college libraries began to expand after World War II, a more extensive, more up-to-date list was needed. Unfortunately, the American Library Association, which had published the Shaw lists, was a long time in developing another one. Into the gap stepped Harvard University, which published the catalog of its undergraduate Lamont Library in 1950. This was a much longer list, totaling some 39,600 titles. In spite of its weaknesses (limited coverage of fine arts and education and the listing of whatever edition existed in the Lamont Library), it proved to be a valuable tool for selection and evaluation and was widely used. A similar list originated from the University of Michigan Undergraduate Library in 1958, this one available only on microfilm or cards.

In the mid-1960s the University of California approached the American Library Association with a proposal to publish its list of books for three new campuses in that state—Irvine, Santa Cruz, and San Diego. This list of 53,400 titles was eventually accepted for publication by the ALA, after revision by faculty members and librarians suggested by the staff of CHOICE. Thus began *Books for College Libraries*. *BCL* was meant to satisfy the needs of students in an institution that relied heavily on use of the library. It was also intended to satisfy the general intellectual curiosity of students beyond the regular curriculum and their recreational reading needs. The size and balance of the first edition of *BCL* were similar to those of the Lamont and Michigan catalogs. No items published after 1964 were included; it was felt that those titles would be listed in CHOICE, which began that year. There were difficulties with the inadequate index in the first edition, which did not include titles in any form. The second edition of *Books for College Libraries* was issued in 1975 in six volumes. This time the total number of titles was reduced to a more manageable 40,000. The work was produced from computer tapes and included for the first time the complete Library of Congress catalog entry (with subject headings and tracings). As with the first edition, arrangement was by Library of Congress Classification number. More detailed indexing was provided, including a complete title index. While it was hoped that the publication of the work in separate parts would permit revision of individual subject volumes as needed, funds have to date not permitted such revision. At the moment the basic coverage, when supplemented by CHOICE, seems to be adequate for academic libraries. For a starter collection, CHOICE has issued three editions of an *Opening Day Collection* for community college libraries. It has enjoyed considerable popularity not only among academic libraries but in high schools and public libraries as well.

Pirie, James W., ed. *Books for Junior College Libraries*. Chicago: American Library Association, 1969.

Bertalan, Frank J., ed. *The Junior College Library Collection*. New ed. Newark, N. J.: Bro-Dart Foundation, 1970.

Lunsford, Effie B., and Theodore J. Kopkin. *A Basic Collection for Scientific and Technical Libraries*. New York: Special Libraries Association, 1971.

Mapp, Edward. *Books for Occupational Education Programs: A List for Community Colleges, Technical Institutes and Vocational Schools*. New York: R. R. Bowker Company, 1971.

Reinhart, Bruce. *The Vocational-Technical Library Collection*. 2d ed. Williamsport, Penn.: Bro-Dart, Inc., 1974.

Community or junior colleges have long felt the need for a list of basic books different from the lists prepared for four-year institutions. An early list was that of Charles B. Mohrhardt. The lists in use today are those noted above. The American Library Association followed up on the first edition of *BCL* by issuing *Books for Junior College Libraries*, edited by James W. Pirie. This, like the Bertalan list published by Bro-Dart, was limited to the liberal arts sector of the community college curriculum, thus omitting half of many of the colleges' curricula. Bertalan further limited himself to what was in print at the time his lists were prepared. A total of 19,000 titles is claimed by Bertalan and 20,000 by Pirie. The gap in the coverage of technical materials has been filled by the three other titles listed. While the Lunsford and Kopkin list appears to be for special libraries, it actually includes 2,500 titles (books and periodicals) for the engineering technician level. To date, only one of these lists has been updated, although again CHOICE can be considered to cover much of the current material needed by community colleges. All these lists are beginning to show their age, and a consistent pattern of revision such as is practiced with the H. W. Wilson Catalogs needs to be established.

Jones, Emily S., ed. *College Film Library Collection*. Williamsport, Penn.: Bro-Dart Inc., 1972. 2 vols.

The basic lists for academic libraries cover only books. Thus there has been a great need for a basic collection of audio-visual materials. Emily Jones includes some 1,900 16 mm films, 5,700 8 mm films, and 600 filmstrips in her collection. Arrangement is by subject, and annotations are provided.

School and Children's Library Collections

Children's Catalog. 13th ed. New York: The H. W. Wilson Company, 1976. Annual supplements.

Gillespie, John T., and Christine Gilbert, eds. *Best Books for Children: Preschool through Middle Grades*. New York: R. R. Bowker Company, 1978.

Quimby, Harriet B., and Rosemary Weber. *Building a Children's Literature Collection*. Rev. ed. Middletown, Conn.: CHOICE, 1978.

The basic list for children's collections in public libraries, and one that is also useful in elementary school libraries, is the H. W. Wilson *Children's Catalog*. The arrangement is the same as for the adult Wilson Catalogs, but both fiction and nonfiction are included together in the children's volume. At one time some items were starred as being especially important, but that feature has been dropped in the most recent editions. More than 5,400 titles are included in the thirteenth edition. An additional 2,200 titles will be added in the four annual supplements.

Best Books for Children has been published in revised editions periodically by Bowker since 1961. The latest edition, edited by John T. Gillespie and Christine Gilbert, includes approximately 7,000 titles, a considerable expansion from previous editions and one that makes this list more comprehensive than the *Children's Catalog*. Arrangement is by subject. There is a good mix of old and new titles. Most helpful is the handling of such difficult topics as sex-role images and ethnic minorities. Some librarians prefer this guide to the more traditional and conservative *Children's Catalog*.

Harriet Quimby and Rosemary Weber's *Building a Children's Literature Collection* first appeared as two bibliographic essays in CHOICE in 1974. It was an attempt to assist in upgrading· teaching collections of children's books. Since the second essay was "A Suggested Basic Collection of Children's Books," the work quickly caught on as a guide to building children's collections in school and public libraries as well. As a result of its popularity, the authors prepared a revised and expanded edition in 1978. It includes more than 1,200 titles, thus forming a core collection or starter list.

As has been suggested above, the lists of best books for children are supplemented by several lists for the same age group. These, however, are addressed to the elementary school library rather than the public library. They can often be used interchangeably, however.

Among the principal guides for elementary school libraries are the following:

The Elementary School Library Collection: A Guide to Books and Other Media, Phases 1-2-3. Lois Winkel, editor, assisted by Margaret Edsal. 12th ed. Newark, N.J.: Bro-Dart Foundation, 1979.

Hodges, Elizabeth D. *Books for Elementary School Libraries: An Initial Collection.* Chicago: American Library Association, 1969.

National Council of Teachers of English. *Adventuring with Books: A Book List for Pre-K—Grade 8.* New ed. Urbana, Ill.: The Council, 1977.

American Association of School Librarians. Committee on Paperback Lists for Elementary Schools. *Paperback Books for Children.* New York: Scholastic Book Services, 1972.

Brown, Lucy Gregor. *Core Media Collection for Elementary Schools.* 2d ed. New York: R. R. Bowker Company, 1978.

The most extensive list of materials, both book and nonbook, for elementary school libraries is the Bro-Dart *Elementary School Library Collection*. New editions appear approximately every year. The list is graded for first and subsequent purchase (Phases 1-2-3). The first group of titles in Phase 1 represents a basic or minimum collection. In the eleventh edition 9,662 books and 1,665 audio-visual items are listed. The list is classified, with author, title, and subject indexes. Annotations are included, as are grade and reading levels. Complete bibliographic information is supplied in catalog card form. The integrated listing of all types of media is unmatched in any other library tool and makes this a first-priority selection guide.

Another classified list, this one limited to about 3,000 books, corresponding to Phase 1 of the Bro-Dart volume, "an initial collection," is Elizabeth Hodges's *Books for Elementary School Libraries*. Of about the same size (2,400 volumes) is the NCTE list, *Adventuring with Books*, which sets out to suggest books that "combine the qualities of entertaining reading with literary merit." The AASL list makes available information on 700 recommended titles that can be found in paperback. Finally Lucy Gregor Brown has produced a list of some 3,000 media items suitable for grades K through 6. Included are films, film loops, recordings, study prints, and other A-V materials. This list focuses on post-1970 materials, although attention is paid to earlier classic titles. (An earlier edition of this work appeared under the title *Resources for Learning*, edited by Roderick McDaniel.)

Junior High School Library Catalog. 3d ed. New York: The H. W. Wilson Company, 1975. Annual supplements.

National Council of Teachers of English. Committee on the Junior High School Book List. *Your Reading: A Book List for Junior High Students*. New ed. Urbana, Ill.: The Council, 1975.

Senior High School Library Catalog. 11th ed. New York: The H. W. Wilson Company, 1977. Annual supplements.

National Association of Independent Schools. Library Committee. *Books for Secondary School Libraries*. 5th ed. New York: R. R. Bowker Company, 1976.

National Council of Teachers of English. Committee on Senior High School Book List. *Books for You: A Reading List for Senior High School Students*. 6th ed. Urbana, Ill.: The Council, 1976.

Beginning with the ninth edition, the Wilson standard catalog for the upper grades was split into two separate publications: one for grades 7 to 9 and the other for senior high schools. *The Senior High School Library Catalog* now includes many adult and young adult books, reflecting the needs of many high school curricula. The *Junior High School Library Catalog* has 3,791 titles (with an additional 2,200 in the supplements); the *Senior High School Library Catalog*, 5,281 titles (with 2,500 to be added in the supplements). The NCTE continues its recommended reading lists for these grade levels with much the same criteria as for the elementary grades. The National Association of Independent Schools, however, presents a different point of view. These schools, whose students usually go on to college, need a more sophisticated and advanced list of books to satisfy their higher academic requirements. Thus their list of some 6,300 titles includes much adult-level material.

Lists of Particular Types of Materials

Periodicals and Serials

Just as different lists of basic books or core collections have been developed for various types of libraries, so have they been compiled for various types of materials. The first that we shall consider is periodicals and serials. There are three basic guides for the selection of periodicals: one of a general nature, the second for college libraries, and the third for school media centers.

Katz, William, and Berry G. Richards. *Magazines for Libraries*. 3d ed. New York: R. R. Bowker Company, 1978.

Farber, Evan I. *Classified List of Periodicals for the College Library*. 5th ed. Westwood, Mass.: F. W. Faxon Company, 1972.

Richardson, Selma K. *Periodicals for School Media Programs.* Chicago: American Library Association, 1978.

Magazines for Libraries is an excellent guide to some 6,500 periodicals that Katz and Richards consider suitable for the general reader, whether in a school, academic, or public library. Besides the usual bibliographic information, Katz and Richards indicate where a particular magazine is indexed. Their annotations are forthright and attempt to pinpoint the use of a particular title for a specific type of library. Farber, on the other hand, is much more limited in his coverage; only about 1,000 titles are considered suitable for the liberal arts curriculum of the undergraduate college. Again an indication of where a periodical is indexed is given, along with a clear summary of a periodical's contents, its point of view, and its value. Both Katz and Richards and Farber attempt to keep their lists current by publishing regular updates in library periodicals, Katz and Richards in the *Library Journal* and Farber in CHOICE.

Richardson lists more than 500 periodicals suitable for use in school media centers in support of curricula studies or as leisure reading for students. *Periodicals for School Media Programs* includes a very wide range of subjects in both popular and scholarly treatments. Richardson's annotations are lively and to the point and give essentially the same information as in Katz and Richards and Farber, plus indications of grade level. A subject index and an annotated list of periodical indexes are included as appendices.

Marshall, Joan K., ed. *Serials for Libraries: An Annotated Guide to Annuals, Directories, Yearbooks, and Other Non-Periodical Serials.* Santa Barbara, Calif.: ABC-Clio/Neal-Schuman, 1978.

A recent addition to guides is Marshall's *Serials for Libraries,* which evaluates more than 3,000 titles. These have been chosen for their relevance for school, academic, and public library collections.

Reference Books

Sheehy, Eugene P. *Guide to Reference Books.* 9th ed. Chicago: American Library Association, 1976. *Supplement.* 1980.

American Library Association. Ad Hoc Reference Books Review Committee. *Reference Books for Small and Medium-Sized Public and Academic Libraries.* Ed. by Larry Earl Bone. 3d ed. Chicago: American Library Association, 1979.

Enoch Pratt Free Library, Baltimore. *Reference Books: A Brief Guide.* 8th ed. Ed. by Marian V. Bell and Eleanor A. Swidan. Baltimore: The Library, 1978.

Kister, Kenneth F. *Encyclopedia Buying Guide: A Consumer Guide to General Encyclopedias in Print.* 2d ed. New York: R. R. Bowker Company, 1978.

Kister, Kenneth F. *Dictionary Buying Guide: A Consumer Guide to General English-Language Wordbooks in Print*. New York: R. R. Bowker Company, 1977.

All librarians are familiar with the *Guide to Reference Books*, which has been through many editions under several different editors. It is probably the most widely used tool in developing reference collections. Its very size, however, may intimidate some persons. Thus it is helpful to have other, more selective guides, such as those published by the ALA Ad Hoc Reference Books Review Committee and the Enoch Pratt Free Library. While the ALA list was developed specifically as a buying guide, the primary intent of the Enoch Pratt list has been to help library users find their way among the various reference tools. It is, however, an exceedingly well-chosen list and can profitably be used as a selection guide by most small libraries, whatever their type. The two Kister volumes are the latest guides to encyclopedias and dictionaries for both librarians and the general public. (Earlier guides were often the work of S. Padraig Walsh.) Kister gives criteria on how to judge dictionaries and encyclopedias; detailed descriptions of the works evaluated in each volume; evaluations of their good and bad points; and finally, a comparison among the various works available. This detailed, comparative evaluation is unfortunately not available for most other types of library materials. Would that it were!

Audio-Visual Materials

In conjunction with our discussion of lists of recommended materials for particular types of libraries, we have mentioned two lists which deal exclusively with A-V materials: Emily Jones's *College Film Library Collection* and Lucy Gregor Brown's *Core Media Collection for Elementary Schools*. Other than these, there are no good inclusive guides to films or other visual materials that offer selective lists of recommended works. Most existing guides are merely inclusive listings of all that is available.

In the field of music recordings, however, the picture is quite different. A series of guides for the record collector have been published since the 1930s. One of the earliest of these was B. H. Haggin's *Music on Records* (Oxford University Press, 1938). This was followed by a series of books written by David Hall, the last of which, *The Record Book-International Edition: A Guide to the World of the Phonograph*, was published by Oliver Durrell in 1948. Two current guides to classical music recordings are:

Greenfield, Edward, et al. *The Penguin Stereo Record Guide*. 2d ed. New York: Penguin Books, Inc., 1977.

Halsey, Richard Sweeney. *Classical Music Recordings for Home and Library.* Chicago: American Library Association, 1976.

The Penguin Stereo Record Guide has been compiled by three contributors to that most prestigious of current record reviewing sources, *Gramophone.* The recommendations take into account the technical quality of the recordings as well as the quality of the performance itself. While the selection is admirable, it is unfortunately, for U.S. libraries, based on what is available currently for purchase in Great Britain. Thus the coverage of American music is very poor. There is some talk of attempting to remedy this lack by adding an American editor for future editions. If so, this could prove to be among the best guides. Fortunately we have an excellent alternative in Halsey's *Classical Music Recordings for Home and Library.* Halsey gives the novice great help in choosing compositions for a basic record collection and indicates which recording of each composition is best.

Subject Guides

As was mentioned earlier in this chapter, there are many bibliographic aids to developing collections in specific subject areas. Some of these have been produced primarily for libraries, but many are intended as guides for the student and scholar in the field. All of these make admirable selection guides for libraries. They exist at all levels; some comprehensive and addressed primarily to the advanced scholar, while others are selective and intended for the beginner or the basic collection. Some outstanding examples of subject lists are included here. This is a very selective list, examples having been chosen for the excellence of their contents, the diversity of their authorship or sponsorship, and the variety of their presentation. Additional bibliographic aids can be traced through most of the guides to reference materials, such as Sheehy. The various library review media, particularly CHOICE, attempt to bring new ones to the attention of librarians. Every good book selector is constantly on the watch for new guides to the literature of a field.

Multi-Topic Subject Lists

U.S. Library of Congress. General Reference and Bibliography Division. *A Guide to the Study of the United States of America: Representative Books Reflecting the Development of American Life and Thought.* Washington, D.C.: Government Printing Office. *Supplement, 1956–1965.* 1976.

American Universities Field Staff. *A Select Bibliography: Asia, Africa, Eastern Europe, Latin America.* New York: American Universities Field Staff,

1960. *Cumulative Supplement, 1961–71*. New York: American Universities Field Staff, 1973.

One of the finest selection aids that has ever been published is the Library of Congress's *Guide to the Study of the United States of America*. All aspects of American civilization are covered in the thirty-two chapters prepared by the experts of the Library's reference staff. The original volume covers more than 6,500 titles, almost all richly annotated. The supplement covers another decade's publications. Any book selector can learn a great deal from perusing this admirable guide.

In the 1960s and early 1970s many libraries made a great effort to upgrade their collections of material on the Third World. To aid this effort, the American Universities Field Staff published a series of publications that suggested priorities for acquisition by marking the titles with a letter code. It is to be regretted that this excellent guide has not been continued in recent years and is now beginning to show its age. It still is useful however for filling in older materials as background to present-day studies in an area where many public and academic library collections are weak.

Ethnic Studies

Duran, Daniel. *Latino Materials: A Multi-Media Guide for Children and Young Adults*. Santa Barbara, Calif.: ABC-Clio/Neal-Schuman, Inc., 1978.

Johnson, Harry A. *Multimedia Materials for Afro-American Studies*. New York: R. R. Bowker Company, 1971.

Rollock, Barbara. *The Black Experience in Children's Books*. New York: New York Public Library, 1974.

Whereas a decade ago libraries were concerned with building collections of material on the Third World, today they are probably more interested in gathering materials on the various ethnic minorities in this country, another area in which many collections are underdeveloped. Duran lists books, periodicals, and films concerning Chicanos and Puerto Ricans, the latter accounting for 75 percent of the Spanish-speaking population in the United States. Much of this material has never been reviewed or listed in the established review media, so it will be new to many librarians. Duran helpfully indicates where this material may be purchased. The New York Public Library has published lists of children's books for and about blacks for a number of years. The early editions were prepared by Augusta Baker, the latest by Barbara Rollock. Items are carefully annotated. Harry Johnson, with the aid of several collaborators, has compiled a list of films, filmstrips, and other nonprint materials that will aid in building collections in the areas of Afro-American, Asian-American, native Indian, and Spanish-speaking studies. The material is carefully graded. Other lists such as these are appearing all the time.

Humanities

Rogers, A. Robert. *The Humanities: A Selective Guide to Information Sources*. 2d ed. Littleton, Colo.: Libraries Unlimited, 1979.

There is no good general list for the humanities other than those found in *Books for College Libraries* and the Wilson Catalogs. Rogers's textbook for library science courses in the bibliography of the humanities lists mainly reference works and periodicals. There are few monographs. The areas covered are philosophy, religion, the visual arts, the performing arts, and language and literature. Fortunately most of these subject fields have good individual guides of various types that can be used for collection building.

FINE ARTS

Ehresmann, Donald H. *Decorative Arts: A Bibliographic Guide to Basic Reference Works, Histories, and Handbooks*. Littleton, Colo.: Libraries Unlimited, 1977.

Ehresmann, Donald H. *Fine Arts: A Bibliographic Guide to Basic Reference Works, Histories, and Handbooks*. 2d ed. Littleton, Colo.: Libraries Unlimited, 1979.

Muehsam, Gerd. *Guide to Basic Information Sources in the Visual Arts*. Santa Barbara, Calif.: J. Norton, ABC/Clio, 1977.

The field of fine arts has several bibliographic guides that can be used for collection development. Three of the most useful ones are listed here. The two by Ehresmann are simply annotated bibliographies, while Muehsam's is in the form of bibliographic essays. Each lists more than 1,000 titles, with Ehresmann (in his *Fine Arts*) offering as an appendix a "Selected List of Fine Arts Books for Small Libraries," some 235 titles of a general-interest, nonscholarly type. Ehresmann's *Decorative Arts* offers a unique guide to books in such diverse fields as folk art, ceramics, clocks and watches, costumes, jewelry, lacquer, musical instruments, and textiles. Muehsam, a librarian and fine arts scholar, offers a wealth of knowledge of fine arts literature in a discriminating volume that can serve as an instruction manual on how to conduct research in the fine arts as well as a bibliography of source materials. The bibliographic essays are supplemented by an alphabetical list that simplifies checking.

LITERATURE

Bateson, Frederick Wilse, and Harrison T. Meserole. *A Guide to English and American Literature*. 3d ed. London: Longman, 1976.

Gohdes, Clarence. *Bibliographical Guide to the Study of the Literature of the U.S.A.* 4th ed. Durham, N.C.: Duke University Press, 1976.

Kennedy, Arthur G., and Donald B. Sands. *A Concise Bibliography for Students of English*. 5th ed. rev. by William E. Colburn. Stanford, Calif.: Stanford University Press, 1972.

The field of language and literature has so many bibliographic guides for collection development that it is difficult to know which ones to recommend. In the end, it seems mainly a matter of personal preference. Until this latest edition, Bateson covered only English literature, and while the coverage of the twentieth century could be considered a trifle eccentric, the earlier years were admirably covered in discriminating essays that reflected Bateson's many years of work on the *Cambridge Bibliography of English Literature*. The addition of Meserole's essay on American literature cannot be considered a success. It represents a British view of American literature, with many well-known authors left out and the scholarship on those included not on the same level as Bateson's on English literature. Still this remains a useful work for English literature because of its discriminating comments on the best editions of an author's work and on the best critical works. Gohdes likewise presents annotations on most of the titles he recommends, but Kennedy and Sands merely list titles with no comments. Gohdes covers a wide range of topics on the fringes of American literature—much background material—while Kennedy and Sands stick to the language and literature. Many other guides exist. The well-known ones include those by Richard Altick and Andrew Wright, Inglis Bell (a list that includes Canadian literature as well), and Donald F. Bond.

MUSIC

Winesanker, Michael. *Books on Music: A Classified List*. [s.l.]: Texas Association of Music Schools, 1979.

Music Library Association. Subcommittee on Basic Music Collection. *A Basic Music Library: Essential Scores and Books*, ed. by Pauline Shaw Bayne. Chicago: American Library Association, 1978.

Both of the above lists are the work of associations whose members are concerned about the content of library collections and who attempt to upgrade that content by publishing buying guides. Winesanker's list is essentially a rearrangement in classified order and an updating of the National Association of Schools of Music's *A List of Books on Music*. Some 1,500 titles are included. Unfortunately there are no annotations. The MLA list is intended not for music schools but for small and medium-sized public and academic libraries as a complement to a basic record collection. As its subtitle indicates, it includes both music scores and books. A basic reference collection in the field is suggested as well as a list of basic periodicals and yearbooks.

RELIGION

Adams, Charles J., ed. *A Reader's Guide to the Great Religions*. 2d ed. New York: The Free Press, 1977.

These scholarly essays by eleven American and Canadian authorities in the field of religion are an outstanding guide to the literature about the principal religions of the world. There is no separate list of titles, as in Muehsam, thus creating some checking problems. However, this work offers so much help for collection building that it is worth the effort involved in drawing up lists of titles for purchase. The second edition adds quite a bit of new material.

Social Sciences

White, Carl M., and Associates. *Sources of Information in the Social Sciences: A Guide to the Literature*. 2d ed. Chicago: American Library Association, 1973.

Hoselitz, Bert F. *A Reader's Guide to the Social Sciences*. Rev. ed. New York: The Free Press, 1972.

Unlike the humanities, the social sciences are blessed with not one but two excellent guides to the literature. While both date from the early 1970s, it is good to know that the White volume is currently undergoing revision under the direction of William Webb and a new edition is scheduled for publication in early 1981. In contrast to Rogers's book in the humanities both White and Hoselitz have the advantage of having called upon experts to write about the literature in their field instead of offering one person's opinion of a wide variety of subjects. Hoselitz is in essay form and therefore a little hard to check, but the White volume consists of individual author entries with annotations. The subjects covered in each volume vary slightly, with White being somewhat more inclusive.

BUSINESS

Daniells, Lorna M. *Business Information Sources*. Berkeley, Calif.: University of California Press, 1976.

Harvard University. Graduate School of Business Administration. Baker Library. *Core Collection, An Author and Subject Guide, 1978–79*. Boston: The Library, 1978.

Daniells, head of the Reference Department at the Harvard Business School library, has compiled an annotated list of books in the field of business and management that is essential as the starting point for anyone wishing to build a business or management collection. The first part lists various types of reference works; the second part is arranged by subject (specific management functions). The library where Daniells works also publishes periodically a selected list of recent books, a core collection, which serves as a further buying guide.

ECONOMICS

Leamer, Laurence E., and George G. Dawson. *Suggestions for a Basic Economics Library: A Guide to the Building of an Economics Library for School, Classroom or Individual*. 5th ed. New York: Joint Council on Economic Education, 1973.

Another list concerned with building collections, this one includes annotations for some 250 to 300 books at approximately the secondary school level. The items are ranked for priority of purchase as well.

GEOGRAPHY

Lewthwaite, Gordon R., et al. *A Geographical Bibliography for American College Libraries*. Rev. ed. Washington, D.C.: Association of American Geographers, 1970.

Harris, Chauncy D. *Bibliography of Geography, Part I, Introduction to General Aids*. Chicago: University of Chicago, Department of Geography, 1976. (Research Paper No. 179.)

A decade ago, the Association of American Geographers published this excellent list of books for a basic geographical library. It needs updating now, but because of its outstanding quality, it can still be used as a buying guide for older basic materials in larger libraries. The University of Chicago's initial volume is probably too highly specialized for the average library, being directed at the graduate university level. For those libraries, however, it is a thorough listing of important reference materials. It is hoped that other types of materials will be covered in subsequent volumes.

HISTORY

American Historical Association. *Guide to Historical Literature*. New York: The Macmillan Company, 1961.

Like English and American literature, the field of history is rife with bibliographic guides, many of them limited to specific countries or to particular historic periods. Only the most famous guide is listed here as a reminder of what the field has to offer. It should be noted that although this guide was produced by the American Historical Association, it covers the history of all countries in all periods. It is basic to the building of any collection in this field.

Science and Technology

Deason, Hilary J. *The AAAS Science Book List: A Selected and Annotated List of Science and Mathematics Books for Secondary School Students, College Undergraduates and Nonspecialists.* 3d ed. Washington, D.C.: American Association for the Advancement of Science, 1970. *Supplement,* 1977.

Deason, Hilary J. *The AAAS Science Book List for Children: A Selected and Annotated List of Science and Mathematics Books for Children in Elementary Schools.* 3d ed. Washington, D.C.: American Association for the Advancement of Science, 1972.

Chen, Ching-Chih. *Scientific and Technical Information Sources.* Cambridge, Mass.: The M.I.T. Press, 1977.

The difficulty with lists in the fields of science and technology is that they are outdated almost as soon as they are published. Therefore the review periodical *Science Books and Films* is probably of greater use in building collections than any of the retrospective lists mentioned here. Still, most libraries need a small core of older materials, and the sources listed above should prove helpful. Deason's two lists for differing age levels have the same backing as *Science Books and Films,* the American Association for the Advancement of Science, which in itself gives prestige to the lists. The list for secondary school and college students (also useful for adult collections in public libraries) has been doubled by the issuance of a supplement. Together these two lists present more than 5,000 suggested titles. The Chen volume is a successor to Frances B. Jenkins's *Science Reference Sources,* which went through five editions. Chen includes monographs as well as reference works, some 3,650 titles arranged in various subject categories. It emphasizes works from the period 1970–1976. Undoubtedly it will be issued in revised editions, as was the volume by Jenkins.

ASTRONOMY

Seal, Robert A. *A Guide to the Literature of Astronomy.* Littleton, Colo.: Libraries Unlimited, 1977.

This is useful guide to current materials on astronomy and

closely related fields. Astronomy has lacked such a bibliography for many years, so this work is very welcome.

BIOLOGY

Commission on Undergraduate Education in the Biological Sciences. *Guidelines and Suggested Titles for Library Holdings in Undergraduate Biology*, ed. by Joan C. Creager. Washington, D.C.: The Commission, 1971.

This is another example of a professional body's attempt to offer guidance in the development of library collections in its field. It lists approximately 875 books and periodicals that were suggested by biology professors. Similar compilations by chemistry and physics professors were published in the 1960s, but these are now out of date and have not been revised. Only mathematics teachers (see below) carry on the work regularly and consistently for all school levels.

CHEMISTRY

Antony, Arthur. *Guide to Basic Information Sources in Chemistry*. New York: Jeffrey Norton, Inc., 1979.

To fill a major gap, a science librarian from the University of California, Santa Barbara, has written a guide to chemistry bibliography for students and other librarians. While the last chapter is on search strategy, the others deal with the sources themselves and therefore constitute a good selection tool.

MATHEMATICS

Mathematical Association of America. Committee on the Undergraduate Program in Mathematics. *Basic Library List*. 2d ed. Washington, D.C.: The Association, 1977.

Mathematical Association of America. Committee on the Undergraduate Program in Mathematics. *A Basic Library List for Two Year Colleges*. Washington, D.C.: The Association, 1971.

Schaaf, William L. *High School Mathematics Library*. 6th ed. Reston, Va.: National Council of Teachers of Mathematics, 1976.

Wheeler, Margariete Montague, and Clarence Hardgrove. *Mathematics Library—Elementary and Junior High School*. 4th ed. Reston, Va.: National Council of Teachers of Mathematics, 1978.

Librarians are extremely fortunate that over the years the Mathematical Association of America and the National Council of Teachers of Mathematics have taken on the responsibility of improving mathematics collections in school and college libraries by regularly issuing lists of suggested titles. The MAA's lists are particularly interesting, including an innovation that other science lists could well adopt. Since the major scientific publishers all issue basic textbooks covering the same material in many areas and since these rival textbooks are often of similar quality, it is foolish to single out the work of one publisher as the only book that should be purchased. The MAA lists cover that situation by suggesting that one of two or three titles be purchased.

CONCLUSION

Finally, a word should be said about the use of these lists in collection building. Much of what is stated here has been said before, but it bears repeating. These lists should always be looked upon as suggestions for buying, never as essential purchase lists from which one dare not deviate. Every library has its own needs at any time. It is hoped that somewhere a guide exists to help the librarian fill those needs, whether for current or retrospective material. As will be mentioned in Chapter Twelve, bibliographic guides can be useful in assessing a collection by indicating what titles cited by reputable authorities the library does or does not possess. The actual checking of library catalogs and shelf lists against bibliographies, while a tedious process, lies at the heart of collection building. Not until one finds out what is lacking in a collection can the process of building begin. To a true collection developer, such work will prove fascinating for what it reveals and what it suggests as remedies. Finally, any list of materials, for whatever purpose first conceived, is valuable for the collection builder. All roads lead to the same end—the choosing of materials to enhance a collection.

PART THREE
Building Collections

CHAPTER EIGHT
Selection: Theory and Principles

Many readers will feel that we have been a long time getting to the subject of selection, surely the heart of any textbook on library collection development. In the past, most textbooks on this subject have discussed principles of book selection in the opening chapter. As I have mentioned, I believe that before attempting any selection, one must know the product and how it came into being. Furthermore one must know how to find out about the existence of that product, since it cannot be selected if no one knows it exists. These topics have been covered in detail in Parts One and Two. In Part Three we shall examine the "how" of the matter, beginning with some basic principles and criteria for the selection of library materials. In presenting these principles and criteria, we shall examine all types of library materials together rather than separating book and nonbook materials, as has so often been done in the past. When one examines selection principles and criteria, it becomes evident that while differing formats require different standards in judging them, these are usually in addition to the basic elements and not in place of them. Collections should be thought of as entities composed of many different formats, but all formats should be judged by the same standards.

Those who are new to materials selection in libraries want, and anticipate that they will be given, hard and fast rules for selection—definite guidelines that can be followed, at least in the majority of situations. Unfortunately this is not the case. Selection is an art, not a science. All we can do here is to outline the various theories of selection, explain the problems that are likely to be encountered, offer something of our own philosophy of selection, and then encourage individuals to develop their own. Furthermore a philosophy of materials selection does not spring up full-grown; it matures slowly as the person acquires more and more experience in the field. In addition, even after the development of a personal philosophy of selection, much of its application and use will depend on the actual situation in which the librarian works. Different types of libraries require different types of selection policy; even within the same type of library, no two libraries will ever be exactly the same. Every library reflects its history, the expectations of its founding body, and the desires of its clientele. Also every library reflects in its holdings the philosophies and the work of all its former staff members, at least those charged with selection and acquisition. If a library has been directed or if its collection has come under the influence of one person for a long period, one can usually see that individual's personality reflected in the collection. Every item in a collection is the result of a conscious act, a decision to acquire something for a definite purpose. As such, every decision is individual, and the result is a unique collection. No two library collections are ever exactly the same.

GENERAL PRINCIPLES

Demand versus Value or Quality

If one examines the writing that has been done on selection of library materials over the past half century,[1] it quickly becomes evident that there are two basic schools of thought. One of these is the demand theory; the other is the value or quality theory. These two theories can be considered as opposite ends of a spectrum. Most librarians today do not opt exclusively for one theory. They adopt a position somewhere between the two; exactly where will depend on personal beliefs and usually on the situation in which the librarian works. Let us now examine these two theories.

The demand theory was first put forth in some detail by Lionel

---

[1]An excellent detailed summary of the principal theories of selection from McColvin (1925) to Broadus (1973) can be found in G. Edward Evans, *Developing Library Collections* (Littleton, Colo.: Libraries Unlimited, 1979), pp. 137–156.

McColvin, the English librarian, in *The Theory of Book Selection for Public Libraries* (1925). McColvin believed strongly that public libraries (unlike national or research libraries) were established in response to public demand. As such, it was their duty to provide the services required of them by the public, by the taxpayers, who were paying for them. McColvin felt that the library should first ascertain what the demand was and then satisfy that demand. The subject content of a collection would therefore be determined by the demands being made upon it and not by some predetermined plan to encompass all subjects. The amount of demand in any subject area would determine the depth of the collection, given the availability of material in that subject area. It might be possible, or even preferable, to satisfy public demand by supplying duplicate copies of the same book or a small group of books rather than by buying one copy each of numerous works on the topic. McColvin realized that the public's idea of what was important and valuable did not always coincide with that of the librarian. Therefore he sought to balance these two factors by assigning numerical values to various subjects (according to their importance) and other numerical values based on the number of requests for books on a particular subject. These two numbers would be multiplied to obtain a "representative number." As can be seen, there are a number of pitfalls in applying McColvin's scheme. The most important element, however, is the need for a great deal of sociological and economic research in order to determine the needs of the community as completely as possible.

While the details of McColvin's demand theory have been discarded today, many of its elements continue to find wide acceptance. Those who subscribe to this theory believe strongly that librarians have no right to impose their personal preferences on others and to decide what others shall read. Do librarians always know what is best for others? Are they omniscient? Librarians should provide the books and other materials that people want; after all, they are paying for them. If librarians become too elitist and create collections that are far over the heads of their patrons or far outside their areas of interest, then they should not be surprised if they soon have no patrons to serve. Eventually they may not even have any financial support. Some librarians rationalize "giving in" to the demand theory by saying that if patrons do find what they want in a library, even if that something is of no literary or subject value, they may later, just by frequenting that library, be drawn to read something better and thus to appreciate the finer things in life.

The greatest difficulty with the demand theory, as we have mentioned, is ascertaining what the clientele of a library needs and wants. In a special library and in most academic and school settings, this is not too difficult. In an academic setting, the curriculum of the institution will be the controlling factor. In a special library, the product or services rendered by a company or firm will usually determine the nature of the demands placed upon the collection being built. It is in the public library that selection becomes most difficult. Here it is necessary to undertake a detailed study or survey of the community being served. Often librarians do not have all of the expertise needed to undertake such a survey. If so, outside advice should be sought. Sociologists or urban planners may be one source of such help; librarians who have done such surveys may be another.

There are other problems with the demand theory. What is "true" demand, and what is demand that has been artificially stimulated? Publicity can easily stimulate demand; even opposition to something can create it. A small group of people within a community can make so much noise that the library can come to believe that they represent a larger group than they actually do. They can create what are later perceived to be artificial demands. There is also the problem of the duration of demand. Everyone is aware of how quickly a best-seller fades into oblivion. Is a library to satisfy the short-term demand for many copies of a particular title at the expense of the long-term benefits to be derived from buying single copies of many different books?

One element that is often ignored in connection with the demand theory occurs in the academic or school setting. It can occur in the special library setting as well. It involves who actually selects materials for the collection. In many academic and school libraries, the faculty and teachers pretty much dictate what shall be added to the collection. Thus the librarian merely reacts to the demands of the faculty and has little to say. This situation largely disappeared in college and university libraries in the 1960s and early 1970s, as library budgets became larger and better able to cope with demands. Most faculty demands could be met with a portion of the library materials budget, leaving the library staff plenty of money for their own selections. With the return of a tight money situation in the late 1970s, a reversal has begun to take place. Over the next few years, most academic libraries will be hard put to satisfy even the demands of the faculty. In school settings, teachers have always pretty much controlled what is bought for the library. The librarian has been limited to supplying information on what is available and what it is possible to obtain; the final choice has been left up to those who would be using the materials in their classrooms. While it is true that in these situations librarians seem to be following the demand theory, in actuality those doing the selection—faculty and teachers—are probably as much concerned about value and quality as any librarian.

They are constantly on the lookout for the best that can be obtained on any topic. It is only in the range of materials being sought—neglect of some fields entirely or, at least, certain aspects of them that do not interest a particular faculty member—that the librarian's philosophy of collection development may come into conflict with the faculty's. This is an interesting aspect of the situation, which proves once again that all is not black or white, but rather a mixture of gray.

Those persons espousing the value or quality theory believe that the library is an institution that exists to educate its patrons and to bring about a better world. This is part of the traditional American belief in human perfectability. This theory can be decried as elitist, but it has substantial support within the library world. Just look at the lists of best books and core collections that exist. All of them represent what one or more persons felt to be the quality materials on a subject—what every library worth its salt ought to have on its shelves, whether the books were ever used or not. Librarians subscribing to the value theory have long found great support in Helen Haines's *Living with Books: The Art of Book Selection* (2d ed., 1950). Thirty years later, this book is still valuable for today's materials selectors and repays close reading. Haines believes strongly that libraries should select materials that will develop and enrich the lives of their patrons. Selection should also be positive, not negative. In other words, a book, record, or film should have a purpose for being in the collection, not merely be added on the grounds that it will do no harm.

If one is to practice quality selection, one must have extensive subject and book knowledge. The selector must know the classic works in any field, what has stood the test of time. The selector must also keep up with current trends of thought. Like the demand theorist, the quality theorist must know the community to be served. Only then can materials be selected that will cover all the needs of the community, for some needs are always unexpressed. Only the squeaky wheel gets the grease unless one is careful. Again Haines attempts to provide for potential as well as actual readers. Where Haines disagrees most with the demand theory is in her feeling that the library should select some materials for their permanent value, even if they are not much used. Those advocating the quality theory also maintain that it is usually possible to find quality materials to satisfy the demands of most patrons. This is largely true when it comes to a particular subject area, although there are certain areas (pseudoscience, for one) that some librarians feel should be ignored. It is more difficult when patrons request a particular title, usually a best seller, or something in the news that may have little permanent value. Then quality selection comes into direct conflict with demand.

One solution is to try to satisfy such demands as inexpensively as possible, either by buying paperback editions rather than hardbound books or by renting rather than buying them. In giving in to demand, most quality selectors feel that they are compromising their standards, but they may justify it by hoping that the partron will eventually be led to read something better.

Any selector who opts for quality faces the problem of inadequate subject knowledge. No one person can know everything. Such a selector is closely bound to selection aids—the current review media and the retrospective selection guides. Selectors who merely react to demand have no need to ascertain what the experts have thought about a particular work. If selectors rely on such selection aids, they must get to know these tools—their strengths, their weaknesses, their biases. A quality selector is also more likely to go outside the library field for help in developing a collection—seeking the advice of experts on campus or within the company or office, as well as using the bibliographic tools of a particular subject area. A true quality selector is always seeking to acquire new knowledge—subject knowledge and book knowledge. The task never ends, as the world and patron needs are always changing.

Most library materials selectors today must usually make some compromise between the theories of demand and value. Most feel that the library is there to serve its customers and that collections should be built around their needs rather than some theoretical needs which exist only in the mind of the selector. Most selectors, of whatever persuasion, feel that all aspects of a question should be represented in a collection, although it is difficult sometimes to obtain works of equal value or worth on both sides. Demands need to be faced with the realization that patrons do not always have as much knowledge of what is available as the librarian, and if they did, they might prefer something else. Just as most selectors believe in providing a wide range of materials on topics in demand, they feel that some attempt should be made to serve the few patrons who have specialized interests or needs (although in times of tight budgets this is becoming increasingly difficult to do). Selectors must be resigned to the fact that they will have to live in a state of tension between the demands of their patrons and their own concepts. Life will never be easy, but it should be interesting.

Criteria for Judging Materials

If one is to apply the quality theory to materials selection then there must be some criteria to use in measuring materials. Below is a list of qualities that should be weighed and questions that should be asked to determine whether an item merits inclusion in a collection. (Similar or related criteria are grouped together.) While not every criterion listed here is relevant for every type of library material, most are applicable in one way or another.

Authoritativeness
• What is the background and reputation of the author or creator? Of the publisher? Of the sponsoring body?

Accuracy
• How accurate is the information presented? (Expert opinion is usually needed here.)

Impartiality
• Are all sides of a question presented fairly, or is there evidence of bias? Hidden bias or openly admitted bias?

Recency of data
• How up-to-date is the information? In revised editions, how much revision has been done?

Adequate scope
• Are all important aspects of the topic covered, or are some slighted or left out?

Depth of coverage
• Does the work go into enough detail, or is it superficial?

Appropriateness
• Is the work presented at a level (vocabulary, visual, etc.) that can be comprehended by the intended user?

• How suitable is the length? Will the user's attention span be overtaxed?

• How suitable is the medium for the presentation of this subject?

• Is the work suitable for group or individual use? Or both?

Relevancy
• Is the work relevant to the user's experience? Can they relate to it?

• How useful will the data be to intended users?

Interest
• Will the work hold the user's interest by appealing to the imagination, sense of curiosity, human needs, etc.?

• Does the work offer an intellectual challenge?

Organization
• Is the work developed in a logical fashion?

• Are all parts pertinent?

Style
• Is the style of presentation appropriate to the material?

• Is the style comprehensible to the intended user?

Aesthetic qualities
• Does the work offer a genuine artistic experience?

Technical aspects
• How faithful to the original are illustrations, visual matter, or sound? What is the degree of clarity? Is everything in focus?

• What is the relationship of the size of the images to the original? Is this clearly indicated in some way, or is there possible confusion?

• Are all elements well synchronized?

• Are transitions from one scene to another (in a film) well done?

Physical characteristics
• Is the typeface well chosen and of the right size?

• Are the paper and binding or the film or vinyl of good quality?

• Is the work well designed? Attractively packaged?

• How easy is it to use the work? To repair the work?

• How durable is the work?

Special features
• Are bibliographies, appendices, notes, and guides to the material included?

• Is the work part of a multimedia package, with supporting elements available?

Library potential
• How does this work fit into the collection that already exists?

• Does it balance another work of differing viewpoint or merely add more of the same?

• How frequently will this work be used?

Cost
• Is there a less expensive substitute that will serve the same purpose?

• Would it be less expensive in the long run to purchase this item or to rent it?

• What are the costs of any equipment needed to use this work? Does the library already own such equipment?

• What are the processing costs? The storage costs?

• How permanent is the content of this work? Will it soon become obsolete because of the visual matter or content?

• Is the medium well established in the marketplace, or is it one that may be changed or replaced in the near future?

If the above questions are posed for most types of materials, the essential factors in selection will have been adequately considered.

However, there is one type of printed material that needs additional thought: periodicals. Surprisingly little has been written about the differences in selection between books and periodicals. Since both are printed materials and since periodicals are not new to libraries, most persons take it for granted that in selection the same factors prevail. This is not quite true. When one selects a book, a film, or a record, there is a one-time cost for a single unit. When one selects a periodical, a long-term commitment is usually being made. Furthermore periodicals are often not selected until they have been in existence for some time. Back issues, unfortunately, are not always kept in print. Thus the selector is faced with the problem of obtaining the earlier issues or of starting the library's holdings with what is currently available. Ongoing or periodic evaluation is also needed for journals since their nature often changes radically over time.

Another factor that must be considered with periodicals is the cost of binding or microfilming and storing the year's issues. If kept in their original form, periodicals take up much more space than do most books. Access to the content of periodicals is another issue. Most libraries do not attempt to index the content of periodicals; they rely instead on published indexes. Therefore whether a periodical is indexed in a published source is often a determining factor in selection. Whether a periodical is to be indexed is often determined by how many libraries possess it and want it indexed. Thus a vicious circle can develop: no one selects the periodical because it is not indexed, and then the periodical is not indexed because no one owns it!

Unlike most books, sample copies of periodicals can be obtained from the publisher; thus selection decisions can be made with the product in hand. One final point should be made concerning periodicals. More than with any other type of material, selection is usually made with the resources of neighboring libraries in mind. The existence of many union lists of periodical holdings makes this possible. For periodicals that will not be used too frequently, it makes sense to attempt to set up cooperative arrangements for borrowing copies rather than entering a long-term subscription.

With microforms we enter an area in which the technical qualities of the product are as important in selection as is the content. Microforms require not only special equipment to be viewed but also expertise to make the necessary technical judgments about their quality. Even when all this is available, no librarian has the time to examine each frame, fiche, or reel to look for missing pages, blurred images, and other problems. Therefore, with microforms, great reliance has to be placed on the review media, particularly *Microform Review*.

Finally, technical qualities, as well as content, are equally important in selecting most audio-visual materials. Librarians are usually more knowledgeable about judging printed materials than nonprint materials. But with practice, expertise can be gained. The reader is referred to the many audio-visual textbooks, one of which is listed in the *Suggested Readings* at the end of this chapter, for help in developing such expertise. Audio materials are not usually available for previewing before purchase, and selectors must rely on the various review media in deciding what to acquire. The unit cost of visual materials, particularly films, is so great, however, that no publisher expects libraries to purchase such materials sight unseen. Most publishers make preview copies available, either on their own premises or through loan. Since the commitment to buy a film is a major expenditure of funds, films in most libraries are usually selected by a committee.

SELECTION AND THE COMMUNITY OF USERS

Selection never occurs in a vacuum. It is made in terms of the users of a library, in terms of the existing collection, and in terms of other collections in the area that can be drawn upon. In addition, one should consider not only persons presently using the collection but those who should be using it. In weighing these factors, the following questions need to be asked: For whom are we building the collection? How are the materials used? What materials are essential for those uses? Of these three questions, the most difficult to answer is probably the second, as little significant research has been done on how people use library materials. It should be possible, however, to ascertain fairly easily for whom the collection is being built. Every library has an institutional or community setting within which it must function. This setting determines the library's purpose and the content of its collections. Within an academic or school setting, it is easy to determine who the library's users are. They are students and faculty. Some academic institutions also serve outsiders, but usually outsiders who have the same needs as the institution's primary clientele. At least, little conscious effort is made to shape an academic library's collections other than for its primary users. Within an academic institution, forces outside the library usually determine the extent of the collection by establishing what subjects are to be taught and at what depth and level. The same is true for special libraries, most of which likewise exist within an institutional setting, albeit often a commercial one. Again the institution decides what will be collected and for what purpose.

The public library, however, is unlike any of the above. While it exists within a community, it is usually an independent body, often with its own board of trustees. Furthermore the range of people within the community that it may be called upon to serve varies enormously. It is never the neat, homogeneous body that one finds in a campus or school setting. Therefore it is essential that the public library know as much as possible about the community it is trying to serve. Often communities change, and libraries, as established bodies, may fall out of step with their needs. Thus every public library should make a continuing effort to gather information about its community. Sometimes this effort is aided if other governmental agencies are involved in urban or rural planning. These agencies often collect large amounts of useful sociological and economic data that the library can interpret for its own benefit. If not, then the library must consider doing its own community analysis or survey. Such a task is not easy. Few manuals or guides exist. Often the employment of an outside consultant and expert may be the best answer. What types of data are essential to a thorough community survey? They include the following: historical data (background information, how things came to be as they are), legal data (anything affecting the operation of the library), geographic information, demographic data (particularly projections of future growth), political information (strength of parties in the area, their attitude toward libraries, etc.), economic data, communications facilities (radio, TV, etc.), social and educational opportunities, cultural and recreational sources, and finally, other community information services that may exist.

Information may be gathered in many different ways. Key persons may be called upon to supply most of the data, open forums may be held, or a full-fledged survey may be undertaken. In most situations a combination of these methods will be used. What is important is that the library not take for granted that it already knows what the community is like. The average public library comes in daily contact with only a small segment of the area's population. Within this closed little world, it is very easy to lull oneself into believing that everything is known about the community that should be known. Every library must make a conscious effort periodically to see whether it is indeed fulfilling the needs of its community.

COOPERATION AND BALANCE

One of the elements mentioned above that should be investigated in any survey is other sources of information within the community. No library exists today in isolation from others in the area. At one time, some librarians thought that it was possible to build self-sufficient collections that would serve all the needs of their users. Gradually these librarians began to admit that a few things might need to be borrowed on interlibrary loan. Today most librarians realize that with the explosion in knowledge and in publication that has occurred in the twentieth century, it is impossible for any library to satisfy its users completely. Some form of cooperation is necessary between libraries of differing types and sizes. Increasingly consortia or cooperative systems are being formed. Even without such legally binding arrangements, librarians are increasingly aware of what is available in other collections and do their selecting with this in mind. The ideal arrangement is, of course, for some sort of formal agreement within a group of libraries as to what each is to buy. Some nationwide plans, such as the Farmington Plan, have attempted grandiose schemes and have generally failed. What has succeeded have been more modest plans at the local level, particularly when state or federal funds have been available, above and beyond the regular budgets of the local libraries, to finance the purchase of materials. In a few cases, independent agencies have been created to undertake cooperative acquisitions with pooled funds, buying materials that are rarely used and can therefore easily be shared. Periodical subscriptions are often the starting point for cooperation among a group of libraries, with agreements being made to assure that at least one copy of a periodical is available in an area. Other cooperative agreements are made in connection with storage facilities.

In Connecticut the public libraries have divided up the Dewey Decimal Classification system, with each library agreeing to serve as a source of last resort for particular portions of the scheme. When any library is disposing of its last copy of a title, it first offers the work to the library responsible for that subject area. Thus at least one copy of a work should remain within the state's public library system. Further, libraries that have accepted responsibility for certain subject areas often make special efforts to collect in depth in these areas without waiting for the arrival of duplicates from other libraries. Other examples could be cited of special libraries in an area entering into agreements with the public library or with a major academic library nearby to pass on materials that the special library no longer needs for its immediate use in return for access to these and other materials when needed. Unfortunately these modest attempts at cooperative collection development have received little publicity in the library literature. Most librarians consider them of too little national importance to warrant publicity. Thus some people may be left with the impression that cooperative collection development is doomed to failure. In spite of the failure of the Farmington Plan and

LACAP (the Latin American Cooperative Acquisition Plan), much good work continues to be done in this area. With increasingly tight budgets, cooperative collection development certainly seems to be the wave of the future.

Selection in a resource-sharing situation, whether it be within a library system or among independent libraries, is often different from selection for an individual library's immediate clientele. Since the patrons often live far away and are thus somewhat removed, selection may be even more difficult. Great coordination is necessary if cooperative acquisition is to be a success. Knowing what other libraries in the area do and do not have is essential. Often selection for resource sharing is done at far greater depth than selection for the home library, and proper subject expertise is essential. While many resource-sharing plans rely on existing collections, much effort is currently being made to strengthen local collections beyond what is needed locally. It is axiomatic that cooperative selection should never be undertaken at the expense of local needs. Additional funding (state or federal monies, it is hoped) should form the basis of such programs. (The subject of resource sharing is explored further in Chapter Thirteen.)

We have mentioned that selection is always affected by what already exists in a particular collection. Few librarians today have the novelty of starting a collection from scratch. Most are faced with the successes and failures of their predecessors and must work within these confines. Any collection is a dynamic organism, continually changing and growing. A well-selected item added to a collection enhances other items in that collection. An item is never an isolated work; it is related to others. In any collection a work will supplement, complement, or fill in other works. A collection is an aggregate of titles, each of them unique, but it is more than that; it is an aggregate that has a life of its own. The great library collections developed over the ages have achieved stature because they are more than collections of individual works. It is the bringing together of related materials, which reveals unsuspected relationships in thoughts and ideas, that makes a great collection. To the dedicated book selector and developer of collections, there is no greater thrill than seeing a collection emerge that has individual character and life. Every selection made is one more building block in developing a collection.

Finally it cannot be stressed enough that the selector should constantly strive for balance in the collection, to present all points of view in as equitable a manner as possible. Often this will seem an impossible task, but it should always be the goal. It is particularly true in public and school libraries, perhaps less so in academic research and special libraries. In general public libraries, balance should be sought not just within individual fields but among all fields of knowledge as well. Personal interests must not be allowed to focus collection building too narrowly. The needs of all users should be served.

SELECTION IN DIFFERENT TYPES OF LIBRARIES

The actual practice of selection varies from one type of library to another. We have mentioned the control that some academic faculty and school teachers have on the materials selected for libraries in their institutions. It is only in public libraries that librarians are free to choose. In almost all other types of libraries, the users have some say—small or large—in the selection of materials. In academic or special libraries, the users may play this role because they are the only ones with the expertise to judge the quality of the material to be acquired or the only ones who are aware of the specialized needs they face in their daily work. Over the last two decades, however, academic and special libraries have increasingly sought to employ subject experts as bibliographers or selection officers. While they do not entirely replace faculty or staff selection of material, they are often able to anticipate demands. Also they are more often able to oversee the development of an entire collection—to see the bits and pieces that are lacking—than is the faculty member or researcher whose interests are limited to one narrow area. In the end, however, the process remains a cooperative one, with everyone contributing some expertise. Librarians should never think that they know everything there is to know about the book world. They should always be willing to accept the advice of an expert and even to go out of their way to seek it when necessary.

One great difference in selecting materials for a special or research library as compared with a public library is the desire of many research institutions to acquire all the material available on a certain subject—the good, the bad, the indifferent. It is felt that all is grist for the scholar's mill and that future generations will be grateful for the library's having preserved the average, run-of-the mill items as well as the masterpieces. When selection is done in this fashion, subject areas are selected for collection development rather than individual titles. Decisions also have to be made about the depth of collecting in various fields. All will not be collected to the same depth, as no library has unlimited funds or unlimited space. Indeed the primary factors that limit gathering-in plans are funds and space. Special libraries also undertake this type of selection, although they usually limit themselves to a few fields of interest.

Even public libraries do a certain amount of this type of collecting, often limited to local history or genealogy. In effect, though, any subject with a local tie can be treated in this fashion—business, industry, art, music, or the works of local authors. In these cases, the public library is often serving an archival function, more akin to that of a museum, of preserving the heritage of the local community.

Selection also varies according to the size of the library. Small libraries with small materials budgets have a much more difficult time selecting materials than do larger institutions that have the luxury of acquiring the majority of current materials as they become available. The small public library, with its very mixed clientele and limited budget, is probably in the most difficult position of all. At least school, academic, and special libraries have more or less well-defined and homogeneous clienteles.

A further difference in collecting in various types of libraries occurs because of the changing nature of some types of collections versus the stable nature of others. Research libraries that collect in great depth and for the future needs of scholars do not face the same problems as public libraries, which emphasize current information needs. In public libraries there is much more of a turnover in the collection than in a research library. But the greatest turnover of all may occur in special libraries, where, if something is not of current interest to the company, out it must go to make way for something that is. The reason is that company libraries usually occupy very expensive rental space, and there is a decided limit on what can be housed. Some special libraries find it cheaper to discard an item and repurchase it later than to house it unused for two or three years. Thus a librarian with research library experience who goes to work in a special library may have to make many psychological adjustments in the new job situation.

One problem peculiar to public libraries is the large amount of duplication that is often practiced. In systems with branch libraries, all the branches will be buying some of the same materials. In fact, in some systems the main library must own a copy of a work before the branch libraries are allowed to buy it. The problem in such systems is thus compounded, as selection must be made first for the central collection (often a large collection divided into subject departments with specialized interests) and then for the branches with their more general needs. Public libraries also have the problem of light reading—westerns, mysteries, science fiction, and formula books such as romances of the Barbara Cartland variety. How much time and effort—and how many dollars—are to be spent on acquiring this type of material? Its inclusion in a public library collection can be justified only on the basis of satisfying public demand. (Paperbacks and rental or leased collections have provided the answer for some public libraries.)

SUBJECT AREAS THAT PRESENT SELECTION PROBLEMS

Once a selector has solved the problems presented by specific types of materials and by the constraints of particular types of libraries, another problem area remains: the innate characteristics of certain subjects, which create difficulty in selecting materials successfully. Everyone knows that if you wish to avoid a fight, you should stay away from politics and religion. Just as these two areas present constant difficulties in everyday life, so do they create problems in library materials selection. The primary reason is that so much emotion and personal feeling goes into the discussion of these two subjects. Some scholars maintain that religion cannot be considered a scholarly discipline, like art history or musicology, because religion demands a creedal commitment from its believers that is incompatible with free scholarly inquiry. Whether one accepts that statement or not, it is true that much writing in religion and in politics tends to be polemical—one person trying to convince another of the right position. Both areas present inherent problems of bias and the possibility of propaganda. With political groups, and even more so with religious groups, there are so many separate bodies, each with its own system of beliefs, that libraries are faced with a bewildering array of publications. Much of this material is very narrow and parochial. Its quality also varies much more widely than in other fields. The result is that many libraries shy away from making purchases. In these areas the library should seek out the best factual information and make a particular effort to have material on all sides of a question.

The main difficulties in areas of the social sciences other than political science are due largely to the fact that practitioners seem to be caught up in their own little world, speaking to their peers in a private jargon that no outsider can understand. A number of years ago, a Yale University Press editor spoke despairingly of her efforts to put a social science book into plain English so that it would have the wider audience that she felt it deserved. She was opposed by the author, who insisted that she would lose the respect of her colleagues in the profession if she were to publish a "popular" book. This is a sad commentary on social scientists but one that is all too true. Furthermore there is little cumulation of knowledge in the social sciences, as there is in the pure sciences, where the most recent book in a field will usually summarize what has been discovered and go on from there. In the social science world, there are myriad schools of thought and much obsolescence.

After the social sciences, the pure and natural sciences are a welcome relief. There currency counts above all else. Most scientific knowledge is first made known through technical reports and journal articles. Only at a later stage is it incorporated into monographs. Any science monograph older than five years should be looked at very carefully and considered for replacement. After ten or twenty years, it is probably fit only for historical use. Two areas in the sciences present particular problems for the public librarian. First are the areas of pseudoscience, such as astrology and the occult, and borderline areas in which there is still a good deal of sensational publication, notably parapsychology. It is in these areas that expert advice is needed and where a publication such as *Science Books & Films*, sponsored by the American Association for the Advancement of Science, is invaluable. CHOICE, over the years, has also attempted to clarify some of these areas, particularly parapsychology. It has an arrangement with one of the leading scholars in the field, who sorts through the vast literature on the subject and selects worthwhile material for review. The second problem area is another one in which *Science Books & Films* can be of great help: popularizations. For too long, librarians have looked at the style in which a popularization was written and not at the content. The great danger with popularizations is not that they offer wrong facts but that they simplify complex subjects to such an extent that they give wrong impressions and thus contribute to the misunderstanding of the subject.

In the area of technology, many community college libraries and public libraries are faced with another type of problem: the lack of material or very limited material on trades and technical skills that are widely taught. Often technical training manuals and films are the only resources available. In some areas, such as the trucking industry, librarians have complained that they cannot find anything of value. This challenges the ingenuity of the selector to locate materials to satisfy these demands. Certainly most of the material that is available must be found outside the normal publishing channels.

To return full circle to the humanities, there are other areas that present problems besides religion. While art books generally represent a good investment, as they remain useful for a long time and are not quickly outdated, their evaluation is not easy. The problem is with the illustrations. The general public wants the brightest-colored illustrations it can find, while the scholar, believing that all color reproductions are distorted in some way, prefers black-and-white illustrations. The problems of evaluation do not end there, however. The relationship of the size of the reproduction to the size of the original artwork is of capital importance. Unfortunately many books do not supply that important data. In addition, reproductions are sometimes cropped and do not show the entire painting, or part of it is lost in the binding process. Often no mention is made of the fact that only a portion of the original is being reproduced.

With the field of music, book selection does not present any particular problems, since the amount of publication is not overwhelming. Most libraries now also accept the necessity of having record collections. The problems arise with collections of music itself. Since most music publishing is done by companies other than book publishers, many librarians do not know where to find music scores. Furthermore they do not know the differences in the various score formats. Music dealers are constantly facing the problems of such meaningless orders as "Wagner, Richard. *Die Meistersinger*. 75¢." Does the library want a full orchestral score of this opera, a vocal-piano score, a miniature study score, or what? Even a miniature score will cost more than 75¢. Fortunately the dealer who recounted this story remembered that it was possible to purchase a miniature study score of just the Prelude to *Die Meistersinger* for this price and offered this to an eventually satisfied customer. Libraries that purchase scores should find someone on their selection staffs who is knowledgeable about such matters. There is really nothing complicated about acquiring scores, and they are a type of material that should not be neglected if materials on music are being collected.

A problem of balance does often arise in the fields of music and fine arts. Libraries—public, school, academic—have often tended to stress the acquisition of classical music and traditional art over more popular forms. Only in recent years has the study of popular culture become respectable in academe. Likewise, only in recent years has collecting pop music, rock, and country and western music or the art of Walt Disney or Norman Rockwell become acceptable in many libraries. What should be sought is balance in any fine arts or music collection and the selection of the *best* of all art forms.

Finally we come to the field of literature. Most librarians have little difficulty in this area. Many were literature majors in college and feel comfortable about making the necessary judgments. For the novice, however, it is not always that easy. First of all, one cannot ask: Is it accurate? Is it up to date? Is it authoritative? None of these criteria apply to fiction, drama, or poetry. Instead judgments become matters of taste and aesthetic response, none of which is susceptible to objective verification. There is, of course, the reputation of the author and sometimes of the publisher to fall back on. If a selector is uncertain, he or she can wait and see what the reviewers and later the critics think about a work. There is also the problem of judging the light, recreational novel, the detective story, and the western, as well as the serious novel. Each presents different problems. In the long run, nothing can substitute for experience—the experience of what has been accepted as great literature in the past and the wants and needs of library users.

SOME FINAL WORDS OF ADVICE

In concluding this chapter on materials selection—its theory and practice—I should like to offer a few words of advice, reemphasizing some of the points I have tried to make. It is hoped that readers will find some guidance in these precepts.

The goal of any library materials selector should be the optimum collection possible for any given community of users (or possible users). This is a goal that, though often unattainable, should always be striven for. There are all sorts of excuses that can be given for failure—lack of time, lack of money, lack of space—but this still does not negate the fact that library selectors have a mission they should constantly try to fulfill. Libraries are service institutions, and librarians are there to serve. But in serving a community of users, the needs of the individual user should never be forgotten. In this age of mass media onslaught, the library is often the only refuge of the lone individual seeking facts or inspiration. The needs of this person must never be neglected.

In building collections, it must never be forgotten that reading, viewing, and listening can all be done for different purposes: factual, educational, cultural, recreational. The purpose differs with the user. In other words, a work in a collection never has a single use or purpose; it is multidimensional, depending on the individual user's needs. Therefore different levels and styles of materials, and different approaches to a subject, are needed.

A selector should strive for a balanced collection. That is, materials should be available on all sides of a question. Only in this way can the selector hope to avoid imposing personal beliefs and prejudices on a collection; only in this way can bias be avoided. The selector faces a real dilemma when nothing of quality or value can be found to represent one side of a question. Some compromises may then be in order, but is not this far better than the selection of material presenting only one point of view, as if that point of view were the only valid or accepted one? The right to varying opinions on a topic is a cornerstone of our democratic society and one that must be constantly fought for.

It should be realized that completeness is unattainable, even when building collections in minute subject fields. There will always be something that escapes the selector's net. Librarians should be on guard against a common mania of their profession—a desire to complete sets and series for the sake of completeness, with no regard for the usefulness of these additional volumes. Many basic lists fall prey to this mania, recommending everything written by an author rather than suggesting a judicious selection. Every work should have to justify its existence in a collection.

In stressing the need for a balanced collection, I do not mean to imply that no specialization is allowable. Special in-depth collections bring distinction to a library and enable it to serve some people that other libraries cannot. The point is that in most institutions special collections must be the frosting on the cake, not the meat and potatoes. They must never be developed at the expense of the day-to-day needs of the community being served. Of course, if the purpose of a library is to serve specialized needs, then that is another matter. All its energies will be devoted to that purpose and peripheral areas ignored. Still, within its own specialized areas, it too will need to develop a balanced collection.

Beginning selectors should be humble and realize that all quality judgments are relative; they are all to some extent personal. When one talks also of lasting values, one should realize that only time will tell whether a work has such qualities. And along with the problem of making a quality judgment is often the dilemma posed by the need to accept something of poor quality simply because nothing else is available on the subject. This dilemma offers no easy or satisfactory solution.

A further point that deserves reiteration is that the selection process is dynamic. It has its own ongoing momentum. It is also a process in which all parts are interrelated; nothing exists in isolation. Every item selected affects those already in the collection. A new work may replace an old standby and cause it to fall into disuse. A new work may call attention to a previously neglected work, offering new insights and a reevaluation of its worth and use. Nothing is static in the world of materials selection. Therein lies the challenge and the excitement.

Finally all selectors need to formulate a personal philosophy of selection as clearly as possible. They need to be aware of what they are doing and why. They cannot afford simply to drift from one situation to another. Institutions must formulate their own selection policies (as we shall see in Chapter Eleven), and if individuals are to contribute to the shaping of such policies, they must have a stance of their own. But beyond this, persons who work at materials selection have to be sure of their own beliefs, or they will constantly be torn to and fro in the daily battle of what to accept and what to reject.

SUGGESTED READINGS

For the historical background of much of the material in this chapter, the reader is referred to the following major works (listed in chronological order):

McColvin, Lionel R. *The Theory of Book Selection for Public Libraries*. London: Grafton, 1925.

Drury, Francis. *Book Selection*. Chicago: American Library Association, 1930.

Haines, Helen. *Living with Books*. 2d ed. New York: Columbia University Press, 1950.

Since many librarians do not have the technical expertise to judge nonprint materials as well as they do printed ones, it is suggested that they study a basic textbook on A-V materials such as the following:

Brown, James W., Richard B. Lewis, and Fred F. Harcleroad. *AV Instruction: Technology, Media, and Methods*. 5th ed. New York: McGraw-Hill Book Company, 1977.

More advice about specific criteria to be used in selecting all types of media (print and nonprint) is to be found in

Gillespie, John T., and Diana L. Spirt, *Creating a School Media Program*. New York: R. R. Bowker Company, 1973. Appendix III.

For more information on community analysis, see:

"Community Analysis and Libraries." Issue ed. by Larry Earl Bone. *Library Trends*, 24 (Jan. 1976).

This issue contains important articles by Lowell Martin, Margaret Monroe, and Arthur A. Kunz.

CHAPTER NINE
Selection Procedures

Now that we have studied the basic philosophy of selection—what should be done—let us turn to how selection is carried out in various types of libraries. We know how to find out about the existence of materials—through trade bibliographies, announcements, and advertisements. We know how to determine how good or how poor the materials may be—through reviews. We have learned how to judge the quality—or lack thereof—ourselves. We have also studied some problems peculiar to different kinds of libraries and subjects. Now we need to look at the routine of selection. Who does it, and how it is done.

WHO DOES THE SELECTING?

Who does the selecting? Much depends on the size of the library. Let us start with large libraries. In research libraries not attached to academic institutions, the professional staff are all experts in their fields; they may even be leading scholars. They do their own selection, with perhaps the occasional help of outside colleagues. In university libraries, the faculty formerly did most of the selection. The task has now grown so big, however, that most university libraries employ subject bibliographers whose primary and often exclusive task is to develop the library's collections. In many institutions, the first of these bibliographers were the librarians in charge of the various subject branch libraries (chemistry, music, fine arts, etc.). Most universities now employ subject bibliographers as part of an acquisitions or collection development department in the main library. Although they may often consult faculty on purchases to be made, the main task of selection is theirs. In large public libraries, subject department heads are often charged with systemwide responsibility for selection in their respective subject fields. In addition, there may be one or more general selectors, especially for branch libraries.

In medium-sized libraries the picture changes somewhat, as less subject expertise is found among the staff members. In college libraries, great reliance may still be placed on the faculty, particularly in areas where the staff is weak. Some faculty members are only too happy to participate in such a plan; others shrug off the responsibility. In this case, the librarians will be forced to fall back on the printed review media. School libraries like to involve teachers in the selection process, feeling that teachers tend to make greater use of materials they are familiar with and have helped to select. In medium-sized public libraries, less subject expertise is available. Usually all professional staff members participate in selection. Sometimes subjects are assigned according to the interests of the individual staff members; at other times, staff members will be responsible for selection for their departments only—reference, children's, etc.

Small libraries present the greatest problem. Often these are one-person operations (or at least with only one or two professionals), and almost complete reliance must be placed on the printed media. A few cooperative arrangements have been made in some areas whereby librarians of small libraries are permitted to attend the book selection meetings of larger libraries nearby. (This is feasible only in large metropolitan areas.) In other parts of the country, some small libraries have banded together and hold monthly book selection meetings to pool their knowledge.

HOW SELECTING IS DONE

Purchases

Now that we have answered the question of who does the selecting, we must turn our attention to how it is done. The usual way, as indicated by the structure of this book, is to rely upon the printed word—announcements, advertisements, and most importantly, reviews of new materials. Much material can be given instant rejection or acceptance from such sources. In large libraries, it is often as much a matter of rejecting irrelevant or unessential materials as it is of determining precisely what individual items are to be added. In small libraries with very limited budgets, more excellent possible additions to the collection will be found than can ever be purchased. It then becomes a matter of determining which of these will be most in demand and should be acquired.

Beyond this basic method of selection, there are many variations. The most desirable way of selecting materials, as has been stated several times, is to examine the books or other types of materials before deciding whether to add them to the collection. However, only with very expensive materials (films and reference books such as encyclopedias) are publishers or producers willing to supply libraries of all sizes with examination or approval copies free of charge. In recent years, large libraries have worked out two methods of satisfying this desire to examine materials before making acquisition decisions. These are blanket order plans and approval plans. Blanket order plans call for the publisher to supply a library with one copy of every item as soon as it is available to bookstores and reviewers. The library agrees to keep all of these items and in return receives a larger than usual discount. Thus, if one item is found to be unsuitable for the collection, it can be discarded with no overall financial loss to the library. Some of these plans are called *Greenaway Plans,* after the former director of the Free Library of Philadelphia, who first conceived of the idea. The idea behind such plans (at least in public libraries) is that the library can decide how many duplicate copies to order for the branches with the book in hand. The main library also has the book available for patrons very promptly. Naturally care must be taken to choose only publishers whose output is of sufficiently high quality so that most of the items received will be suitable for retention. Blanket orders have been instituted not only with trade publishers but also with university presses. Blanket orders may also be placed with dealers. University libraries use this method most often to acquire materials from overseas. In this case, no idea of duplication is intended. The selection task is simply delegated to another person—this time someone outside the library. Great care must be taken, of course, in selecting such dealers. However, it is often the only way to obtain materials from out-of-the-way places.

Approval plans differ from blanket order plans in that the library has the option of returning any items it does not find suitable for its collection. This type of plan is most often used by academic libraries, although a few larger public libraries have also tried it. The great danger with approval plans is that the library will fail to examine the material received with any care and will simply automatically add all the items to its collections, whether they are suitable or not. (Approval plans can be instituted with either publishers or dealers.) With both blanket order plans and approval plans, libraries usually place certain restrictions in advance on the types of materials they will accept—age and reading levels of the material, subject areas, types of bindings, etc. The subject specifications are often worked out in detail in a "profile," which must be constantly updated as the library's needs and interests change. Most problems concerning approval plans occur in this difficult area of developing an adequate profile of a library's needs.

Once materials are actually received for inspection, who looks at them? In public libraries it is the staff: heads of departments, heads of branches, and members of any permanent selection department. In academic libraries it is also the staff (department heads, other professional staff, but especially the subject bibliographers spoken of in the previous chapter). In addition, faculty members may be called on, although this is often difficult to do on a continuing basis because of the great amount of material acquired by a major academic library.

Small libraries, whether college libraries or public libraries, do not usually find it possible to participate in approval plans or blanket orders. Some public libraries may have subscriptions to book clubs, thus delegating a portion of their selection responsibilities to someone outside the library (just as large academic and research libraries do with book dealers overseas). Again great care must be taken to make sure that most of the titles chosen by a particular book club are those the library needs. Book clubs usually give more substantial discounts than do regular book dealers, but the quality of the book-club edition may be inferior to that of the regular trade edition, and the book may not stand up too well under hard library use. Another possibility open to the librarian of a small library is to examine books on display at a library convention. There is a Combined Books Exhibit (including periodicals) at all national library meetings, and at many state meetings as well. Such an exhibit includes the major publications of the current year, and perhaps the previous one as well, from the major trade and university publishers. It is an excellent device much appreciated by librarians from smaller libraries. Many of them save a major portion of their budget for expenditure after they have examined the books on display. This type of display is particularly useful for items which have received conflicting reviews or about which the librarian has some doubt.

In public library systems, there is the unique problem of a "secondary" level of selection for the branch libraries after the main library has made its initial selection. In this connection, many library systems assign books for review to various staff members, thus producing an in-house review to go along with any published reviews that may be available. The advantage of such in-house reviews is that they can be tailored to the local situation. They also usually contain a comparative element indicating that if people liked a certain previous book, they will like this one (or vice versa). Staff reviewing is very time-consuming, and not all libraries feel that it adds much to the printed reviews—except perhaps in timeliness. Whether a large public library system resorts to staff reviewing or not, some provision is usually made for regular book meetings, where the subject department heads may be brought in to discuss new books in their areas of expertise and/or where branch librarians may discuss works assigned to them for examination and review. Most public libraries will make available the main library's copy of a book to the branch librarians for examination. Along with the book will usually go any reviews available. Academic libraries are seldom faced with wide-spread need for duplication, as their branch libraries are limited to special subject fields. Thus there is no need for staff reviews, book meetings, or book examination rooms (except possibly for books received on approval).

Some large school districts maintain districtwide evaluation and selection centers. Within these centers selection committees may operate, or committees may be formed at the individual school level. Within such committees, attempts are usually made to involve not only media center personnel and teachers but students and parents as well (the latter often at the policymaking level). The "Policies and Procedures for Selection of Instructional Materials" adopted in 1976 by the American Association of School Librarians states that "while selection of instructional materials involves many people (library/media specialists, teachers, students, supervisors, administrators, and community persons), the responsibility for coordinating the selection of most instructional materials and making recommendations for acquisition rests with certificated library/media personnel" (See Appendix 1, p. 280). In some schools the media personnel control the selection of materials, with only minimal participation by teachers or others. In these cases, they are operating much as do librarians in other types of libraries, where only one or two librarians are working alone.

In regard to various types of materials, there is basically no difference in how most of them are selected. Most of the problems involved are innate to the type of material itself; for a thorough discussion of these, the reader is referred to Part One of this book. Reference has been made, however, to the fact that government documents are poorly reviewed. The problem of selection varies enormously between libraries that have been designated as government depositories and those that have not. Government depository libraries have the right to receive free of charge a large proportion of the documents issued by the U.S. and some state governments. Selection is usually made by entire series rather than by individual document. Sometimes a sample copy of a publication in the series will be made available and sometimes not. When a government depository library discovers that it has not been receiving a particular series that it now finds useful, it is not possible to get free copies of the previous items in the series. Individual items may never be acquired separately except through outright purchase. Libraries that are not government depositories do not have this problem, but they do have the problem of finding out about the existence of the documents themselves. The government does little publicity. Libraries must rely on the *Monthly Catalog* and *Selected Government Publications* and upon the few review columns that appear in library journals.

Gifts

Up to now, we have spoken of the selection of materials largely in the context of purchasing. Libraries, however, have other sources of materials, principally gifts. Gifts may be in the form of money or more often of materials. The latter pose a serious problem for the library. Monetary gifts are always welcome. Through such generosity, the library is often able to add an expensive item that it otherwise could not afford. Many such gifts may be in the form of memorials to a deceased person, and it is simple courtesy to insert a special bookplate stating that fact in the books purchased. Gifts of materials, however, may present a public relations problem. They often are of a type or kind that cannot be added to a collection if the library applies the same standards to the gifts as it does to a purchase. The books may be outdated, in poor physical condition, or duplicates of items that the library already possesses in sufficient quantity. Often no more than a quarter or a third of the total gift may be suitable for addition to a collection. When accepting gifts, libraries need to insist that they be allowed to dispose of the material as they see fit. Many times unwanted items can be given to other libraries; most often they can be disposed of in a library book sale, the proceeds then being used to purchase new books. Most donors will accept such an arrangement, knowing that their gift will eventually benefit the library.

Libraries can sometimes be the recipients of valuable collections that have little to do with their aims as an institution. It is difficult to suggest to donors that another library might be a better home for a valuable collection, especially when the donor has ties to an institution and wants the collection to go there and nowhere else. Scholars, however, are not helped by the wide dispersal of related materials. Public libraries, in particular, need to exercise great care in accepting special collections, unless they come with endowment funds for their future support and maintenance. Even then, most public libraries should not be in the business of maintaining specialized scholarly collections. They belong elsewhere.

One type of material which often comes as a gift is valuable to public as well as academic libraries. This is material that deals with local history, culture, or literary life. As was mentioned in the previous chapter, different standards apply to the acceptance of such material. In other cases, a donor will offer material that will enhance existing purchases or turn a skimpy collection into an in-depth one. If the subject of the collection is appropriate to the library, then it should be welcomed. Donors may also offer books from earlier periods, allowing the library to replace well-worn copies with better ones. Or donors will offer works that are out of print and that the library has been unable to obtain or to afford. It must always be kept in mind, when accepting any gift, that gifts do cost money. They cost money in sorting and selecting those items to keep. They cost money for storage. They cost money for cataloging and processing. Nothing is truly free.

One final remark concerning the selection of gifts. This is one area where the retrospective guides really prove their worth when the librarian is unfamiliar with a particular title. The guides alone can tell a librarian whether a particular work is of permanent value. Naturally book reviews are also helpful in deciding what to retain.

Exchanges

Books and periodicals may also often be obtained through exchange with other libraries. Libraries of all types and sizes participate in exchange unions within the United States and Canada. It is usually most profitable for a library to join one which is made up of similar institutions. The material to be exchanged will then most often be what is sought. Exchange unions operate under all sorts of conditions and regulations, but generally the library that has duplicate or other material that it is willing to give away free or for the price of transportation (all that is usually asked) will simply list that material and mail the lists to members of the exchange union. The first library requesting a particular item then receives it. The one problem of selection from such lists is that they must be perused promptly and selections made as soon as possible; otherwise someone else will get the item desired. Usually only one copy of a particular item will be available.

Large research libraries practice a different kind of exchange—with libraries in foreign countries, particularly countries where purchase of materials is difficult. Often libraries in these countries have materials that cannot be obtained commercially and are only too happy to exchange these for American books or periodicals. Libraries that participate in such exchanges often have to buy books and periodicals to satisfy the needs of their foreign exchange partners. They do not rely solely on duplicate items from their own collections. It is in fact a kind of barter arrangement imposed upon large libraries by currency restrictions or the vagaries of publishing activities in Third World and Communist-bloc nations. Selection in such exchange situations depends largely on what is available. Great flexibility and considerable persistence are required in this type of work. Such operations often take months and even years to accomplish, so patience is also needed. There can be great rewards for the selector who becomes knowledgeable in this area, however.

Out-of-Print Materials

Out-of-print (OP) materials are basically selected in the same way as in-print materials. In fact, most out-of-print materials are first selected as in-print materials, and only later is it determined that they are no longer available from the publisher or a current book dealer. It is then necessary to turn to the secondhand or rare book market. Since locating an item in the secondhand market is not as easy as when a book is in print (for one thing, all libraries will be competing for a very few copies; maybe only one or two will be available), libraries usually reconsider their decision to purchase. Only after it is determined that the work is truly essential will the search for a secondhand copy proceed. Cost will undoubtedly be a factor, as scarcity of an item inevitably inflates the price.

Out-of-print items may not be found readily or promptly, thus requiring files of desiderata to be kept. Persons charged with selection need to review such files regularly to determine whether the library still needs an item sought for but not yet found. Often it will be discovered that an item is no longer needed or that another book has been obtained that satisfies the need. Academic and research libraries are constantly involved in selecting and seeking to obtain out-of-print materials. Public libraries are involved to a lesser extent. Again the size of the library is an important determining factor. In many small libraries, if an item is found to be out of print, the order is canceled and the library turns to another source for the information needed. If this is simply because the librarian does not know how to obtain out-of-print materials, this is hardly a desirable solution. It is hoped that the decision will be made on the grounds of real need, and whenever necessary, the appropriate channels will be used to obtain the out-of-print item.

What are these appropriate channels? First of all, it must be reiterated that the selection of out-of-print materials involves one overriding problem—the scarcity of the item being sought. Usually the source of supply will have only one copy of an item; therefore, just as with exchanges, the library selector must act promptly if that one copy is not to wind up in other hands. Out-of-print book dealers regularly issue catalogs of materials they have for sale. Rare items also find their way into book auctions. Selectors peruse these lists and catalogs for items that they are seeking and make a prompt offer. Sometimes this is done by telephone or telegraph to ensure that selectors get their bid in first. Selectors can also work the opposite way. They can issue want-lists to dealers or advertise their needs in *The Library Bookseller* (formerly called *TAAB*) or in *AB Bookman's Weekly*. There are also some "search services" that will undertake to locate items a library needs. Care should be taken, if a library chooses to search itself, that the want-lists are given to one dealer at a time (with a stated time limit for supplying available or found items). Otherwise the library will find that rival dealers are competing for the same book and, because of the ensuing competition, upping the price in the process. Selectors who choose to advertise have to wait for offers to come in. The problem then becomes one of judging whether to accept the first offer or wait for one at a better price. The one at a better price may never come along, and meanwhile, the one offered previously may go to someone else.

Selectors of out-of-print material have additional factors to consider that selectors of in-print material never have to worry about. The first factor is the condition of the item. Secondhand material has often seen some use, sometimes hard use, and the library must know its present condition. The second factor is the edition being offered. With in-print materials, it is always understood that the latest edition will be supplied. With out-of-print materials, any edition can be offered for sale. Selectors must be very careful that what they want is exactly what is being offered. Catalogs from auction houses usually specify edition and condition. Catalogs from secondhand dealers vary greatly in the information they provide and the care with which they are prepared. Over time selectors get to know dealers whom they can trust. Otherwise it is always "buyer beware."

Rental Collections

Finally there are times when a library neither buys an item nor obtains it by gift or exchange but instead leases it for a limited period. The public library is the type of library that does this most often. Leasing plans, such as those offered by the McNaughton Company, provide duplicate copies of current best-sellers to public libraries, thus relieving them of the necessity of purchasing many copies of items that have a relatively short lifespan. Once the demand has ceased, the books are replaced by other in-demand items. Under most of these plans, the library has the option to purchase one or more of the copies it has leased after a certain period, should it desire to add these to the permanent collection. A few reference works, particularly the *Rand McNally Commercial Atlas,* are also obtained by libraries on a lease plan and must be returned at a certain time and replaced by newer editions.

However a library obtains its material and whoever participates in the selection process, the end product should be the same—the building of the best collection possible to serve that library's clientele.

SUGGESTED READINGS

Ford, Stephen. *The Acquisition of Library Materials.* Rev. ed. Chicago: American Library Association, 1978.

The process of selecting materials leads into the area of acquisitions. The book by Ford will supply all the basic knowledge needed in this area. Its bibliographies will suggest further sources of information.

McCullough, Kathleen, et al. *Approval Plans and Academic Libraries: An Interpretive Survey.* Phoenix, Ariz.: Oryx Press, 1977.

A recent survey of approval plans. Particularly valuable are the three "Authors' Responses," which examine approval plans from the point of view of an acquisitions librarian, a subject specialist, and a book dealer.

CHAPTER TEN
Weeding and Storage

If material is constantly added to a collection and nothing is ever removed—except what is lost or stolen—there comes a time when the library simply runs out of space. But more importantly there comes a time when access to the materials in a collection becomes so difficult that users fail to find what they need and may stop using the collection altogether. In earlier days, when collections were smaller and the annual publishing output was less overwhelming, the tendency was to seek more space. In most cases, this is no longer possible. Even if funds are available, space adjacent to present library quarters often is not. Thus a library is faced with the problem of removing material to allow space for new material and easier access to the collection. This process is usually referred to as *weeding* a collection. Weeding is defined by H. F. McGraw as "the practice of discarding or transferring to storage excess copies, rarely used books, and materials no longer of use."[1] While library standards for all types of libraries have long advocated weeding and most library science

[1]H. F. McGraw, "Policies and Practices in Discarding," *Library Trends*, 4 (Jan. 1956), 270.

textbooks recommend it, in practice very little weeding is done. Many librarians put off weeding until they have completely run out of space and then do it hastily, subjectively, and with no organized plan. As a result, libraries of all types, particularly public and college libraries, often contain quantities of unused, unneeded, and unwanted materials. If librarians are to build collections for use, then they must be concerned with keeping these collections in the best possible condition. This involves removing materials when they are no longer needed.

PROBLEMS WITH WEEDING

Why do librarians resist weeding? There are many reasons. One of the most obvious is that Americans have always considered size to be synonymous with greatness. The biggest has to be the best. Therefore rivalry between institutions has resulted in a mentality in which libraries have sought to add as many volumes to their collections as possible and never to discard anything. Sometimes this concern with size has been connected with an attempt to impress accrediting agencies, whose representatives, in visiting the libraries, often looked at the statistics of holdings rather than examining the shelves for quality and currency of materials. Another reason for not weeding is simply lack of time. There are too many other pressing duties, and so weeding goes to the bottom of the list of priorities. It is deemed much more important to get something cataloged and onto the shelves, crowded as they may be, than to think about removing something. Cost is also a factor; staff time, particularly professional staff time, does not come cheap. Some believe that it is more costly to remove items from the shelves (with all the changes in record keeping implied) than to let the materials occupy shelf space. This may be correct if one is dealing with transferral to storage, but it is not necessarily so if true discarding is the objective. In any case, who stops to think of the cost in time and effort to the library user, whose search is hampered by unwanted and useless material on the shelves?

Another reason is that weeding is not easy. If it is difficult to select materials for a collection in the first place, it is just as difficult to weed them. It is the same process in reverse and should be carried out with the same care. The greatest constraint, however, is the feeling that a library collection is a sacred trust and must not be disturbed. This comes from a tradition of preserving materials for the future use of scholars and has little to do with the basic philosophies behind present-day public, school, college, or special libraries. It is appropriate only in university and research collections. And even there, not all materials may require the same ease of access. Some are better placed in storage, thus making the most used materials more accessible. Librarians who feel that library collections must be maintained exactly as they were created forget that many books wear out and others disappear or are stolen. Thus no collection ever remains the same. Adding items to a collection drastically changes the relationships of items already in the collection, as I have already pointed out. Finally, librarians are reluctant to admit that they (or one of their predecessors) made a mistake. They hope against hope that time will prove them right and that someone will find an item useful. But how long should one wait? How much better to admit that no one can be 100 percent right all the time and get rid of the useless item.

Whenever weeding is discussed, differences between types of libraries play a big role. School libraries in general are small, and most of them are fairly new; as a result, they do not contain large quantities of material for weeding. The same is true, at least for the present, of community college libraries. In both cases, use should be the deciding factor, and no thought should be given to preserving materials for archival or historical purposes. If the curriculum has changed, then the collection should change also. In special libraries, where space is often at a premium and where the service factor is most important, collections are usually kept small and up to date, and every item on the shelves must justify its presence. If there is any type of library in which weeding is part of the daily routine, it is the special library. The big problems come with public and university library collections. The problems in these two types of libraries are almost diametrically opposed, but some of the solutions now being proposed are bringing them closer together.

Let us first consider the public library. It is in many ways the simplest, and the solutions are fairly well standardized. The former *Minimum Standards for Public Libraries* (American Library Association, 1966) stated clearly (no. 36) that "Systematic removal of materials no longer useful is essential to maintaining the purposes and quality of resources." Public libraries should be stocked with materials for use. When obsolete, unused material is removed the collection may be decreased, but it will also be improved. Research has shown that circulation often increases after weeding. People are able to find what they want more easily. The shelves often look more attractive and enticing with all the old drab items removed. Up to the last decade or so, weeding in a public library usually meant destroying or selling the item removed. In more recent years, with the establishment of library systems and networks, it is more likely that weeded materials will be offered to the next highest level and that somewhere within the system or network, there will be a final resting place for the "last" copy. This permits the elimination of many duplicates but the assurance that at least one copy will always be available nearby. With the development of library systems or of a central collection within a city, one can think of branch or regional libraries as trying to meet the basic demands placed upon them and using the central library to satisfy specialized and infrequent demands. This permits much more extensive weeding at the local level.

HOW IS WEEDING DONE?

In the past, weeding was a very subjective process and remains so today in many libraries. The following criteria are frequently used:

• appearance
• condition
• duplication
• older outdated editions
• poor content
• age
• use

It is fairly easy to weed out unattractive works, but since their content may be useful, is this any way to do it? As for books in poor condition, these have usually been heavily used. Thus they are candidates for replacement rather than weeding. The books that just sit on the shelves unused will take a long time to deteriorate noticeably. Duplicates no longer needed (old best-sellers are an excellent example) and older editions which have been replaced by newer ones are prime candidates for weeding and are easy to spot. When it comes to possible poor content, the librarian is faced with the time-consuming task of ascertaining whether this is really so. This means checking lists of best books, subject bibliographies, and book reviews. It is the selection process in reverse, and it is the proper thing to do. Two other factors, however, have been much studied in recent years and can help considerably in the process of weeding. They are an examination of the age of a work and a study of its use.

Over the past two or three decades, there has been considerable study in academic libraries of the use of library materials. This research has been summarized in Stanley J. Slote's *Weeding Library Collections*. Slote has done further research in the public library field and has come up with an interesting method of weeding that deserves some discussion here. Earlier academic library researchers

(Grieder, 1950: Fussler and Simon, 1969; and Trueswell, 1965, 1966, 1969)[2] attempted to prove that the use of a book in the past was an indicator of its probable use in the future. Slote's research tends to substantiate their findings, and he bases his system of weeding on what he terms *shelf-time period*—that is, the estimate or measurement of the length of time a book remains on the shelf between successive uses. This requires a circulation system which records date of use. The old Newark card system was fine. Computer-based systems also work well. The problems arise with the transaction-type system used in many libraries today. This type of system makes no mark in the book itself and keeps no record that can be retrieved for analysis by title. Slote proposes to overcome the handicaps of such a system by placing a simple mark in the books as they circulate or, better still, by placing a dot on their spines. After an extended period, the books without marks or dots will be in the minority and easily identifiable. These will be the ones not used and thus prime candidates for weeding. Since Slote believes that any collection should answer 95 percent of the demands made upon it, he would wait until 95 percent of the items in a particular subject category were marked and then withdraw the other 5 percent. It should be noted that different parts of a collection usually have differing rates of usage. Thus a collection cannot be examined as one large block; it must be broken down into more or less small subject categories.

Another criterion often used in weeding is age of the materials. This has been applied especially to periodicals and to the fields of science and technology. First an optimum age must be determined beyond which materials are no longer or infrequently called for. This is done by citation analysis and varies from field to field. It works quite well in science and technology, where there seems to be a fairly consistent pattern of use. It works less well in the social sciences and not at all in the humanities, where the publication date of a work seems to have no correlation with scholars' needs. A philosopher may be more interested in Plato and Aristotle than in Jean-Paul Sartre or Teilhard de Chardin. This is not usually true of scientists and engineers. The one great problem with using age as the sole weeding criterion is that in any field the classics would get weeded. Therefore this system has to be supplemented by subjective judgment. Slote, on

[2]Herman H. Fussler and Julian L. Simon, *Patterns in the Use of Books in Large Research Libraries* (Chicago: University of Chicago Press, 1969); Elmer M. Grieder, "The Effect of Book Storage on Circulation Service," *College & Research Libraries*, 11 (Oct. 1950), 274–276; Richard W. Trueswell, "Determining the Optimal Number of Volumes for a Library's Core Collection," *Libri*, 16 (1966), 49–60; Richard W. Trueswell, "A Quantitative Measure of User Circulation Requirements and Its Possible Effect on Stack Thinning and Multiple Copy Determination," *American Documentation*, 16 (Jan. 1965), 20–25; Richard W. Trueswell, "User Circulation Satisfaction vs. Size of Holdings at Three Academic Libraries," *College & Research Libraries*, 30 (May 1969), 204–213.

the other hand, claims that continuing use of the classics will prevent them from showing up as candidates for weeding in his system. Much of the preliminary work in Slote's system (and he would probably say all the work) can be carried out by nonprofessional staff, thus decreasing the cost of this method of weeding.

STORAGE OF MATERIALS

Now let us turn to university and research libraries. Here, in contrast to public libraries, there is little desire to limit collections to current materials. Public libraries are expected to discard little-used materials; research libraries seldom do. Yet research libraries are faced with the problem of ever-increasing numbers of publications and proliferating subject fields. Collections constantly increase, but space rarely does. So, they too are faced with weeding. While the methods described above are all applicable to weeding in research libraries, and in fact the two best ones (age and usage) have been researched largely in academic libraries, the goals of most academic libraries in weeding are different from those of public libraries. Research libraries weed for storage rather than for discard. This factor creates a major difference in what is done and how decisions are reached. Therefore, let us examine what is involved in storing library materials.

The fact that research libraries do need to preserve books for the use of future generations of scholars means that they have been the principal types of libraries exploring various alternative means of storage. The ideal solution is, of course, the construction of new library buildings or additions to present structures to house the collections as the need arises, but construction has always lagged behind needs. What, then, are the alternatives? First, there is the possibility of compact storage. This means shelving by size to reduce the waste space between shelves, shelving books on their edges instead of upright, narrowing the aisles between stack ranges, and finally, installing various types of compact shelving. Compact shelving comes in various forms, much of it on rollers or tracks, so that ranges of stacks can be pushed close together when not in use and one range pulled out when needed.

Compact shelving can be installed in existing library buildings and thus increase the number of books that may be stored there. Compact storage can also be installed in another building, either nearby or at a remote location. This brings us to the possibility of separate storage (warehouse) libraries. Such library facilities have been constructed by individual institutions, such as Princeton University, or by groups of libraries acting in concert to solve a common problem. Such has been the case with the New England Deposit

Library in Boston and the Center for Research Libraries (formerly the Mid-West Inter-Library Center) in Chicago. The Hampshire Inter-Library Center in western Massachusetts has never erected or rented a separate building for storage but has instead relied on empty space available at one of the member institutions.

The Center for Research Libraries has been the most successful cooperative storage venture in the United States. It had three original purposes (which went beyond the mere storage of materials). They were (1) to provide cooperative custody, organization, housing, and servicing (and for some materials, ownership) of little-used research materials; (2) to encourage and even implement coordination of the collection policies of the member libraries; and (3) to explore the possibilities of cooperative bibliographic services among members. Most of the work of the center has to date been concentrated on the first of these objectives, although there has been a spillover into the second category because of the types of materials that have been housed at the center. From the beginning, the center has sought to obtain ownership of the materials transferred to it in order to eliminate duplicates. In recent years, the center has shifted its emphasis from deposits of little-used materials to the cooperative acquisition of such materials. Thus the member institutions no longer have to worry about acquiring such things as German doctoral dissertations or many foreign newspapers and can devote their funds to other types of materials.

The construction and use of various storage libraries have resulted in certain findings concerning the use of such facilities. Any decision to store library materials is usually met with resistance from patrons (if they are aware of it), particularly university scholars. Therefore it is essential that any storage facility be as close to the campus as possible (if it cannot be established on campus) and that prompt delivery service be provided. Furthermore the idea that storage libraries should be buildings where the patron was kept out of the collection has largely been abandoned. Scholars often find it easier to travel to the storage libraries than to have the materials brought to them, and they should be provided with reading facilities. If it is feasible (i.e., if the collections are arranged in any subject order), researchers should also be allowed into the stacks even if the aisles are very narrow and the storage space is not very attractive.

ADDITIONAL CONSIDERATIONS IN WEEDING AND STORING

No library exists in isolation today. Even small public libraries are now parts of local, regional (county), state, and even national networks. Academic libraries are heavily involved in networks, and some states, such as New York, have grouped all types of libraries into cooperative networks so that all citizens may have access to the materials they need for their work and enjoyment. Networks bring about a sharing of resources and in many cases the acquisition of additional resources that would otherwise not be available. Therefore any plans for weeding at the local level should take into account the needs of neighboring libraries and of any networks to which a library belongs. To return to a thought expressed earlier, discarding has now largely been superseded by arranging for the items to be offered to the next higher echelon, with the goal of keeping at least one copy of a work available for use in an area.

Weeding is influenced by whether an item is to be discarded or transferred to storage. Different conditions demand different decisions. With both discarding and transferring to storage, there are sometimes legal barriers. If the storage facility is within the same library system, there are usually no problems, but if it involves another library or a cooperative facility, there may be difficulties. With discarding the problems may be even greater. Some public institutions are forbidden by law from donating or destroying what is considered public property without considerable red tape. In some cases, destroying a work may be the only solution allowed. Therefore it is necessary for cooperative storage libraries to have flexible policies as to ownership of materials. Even if a library has the authority to dispose of materials as it sees fit, there are sometimes strings attached to materials that were received as gifts. Finally there is the public relations aspect of the matter. The public does not usually understand the concept of outdated materials, particularly if such materials are still in good physical condition. If a library elects to destroy certain materials by carting them off to the town dump, it had better be sure that they are not discovered by some irate citizen who will arouse public opinion against the wanton destruction of public property, even if it is legal. Some libraries dispose of unwanted materials by selling them to secondhand book dealers or to the public. If this is done, then all marks of ownership should be obliterated; otherwise, the books may find their way back to the library that discarded them. Some librarians recommend the recycling of unwanted materials as one good way of obliterating all marks and of making sure that the books do not end up in the hands of irate citizens.

In conclusion, the importance of weeding must be stressed. It is the reverse of selection and should be done with just as much care. Once it is realized that a library should be a planned collection, not a haphazard one, and that the library is there to serve its patrons as best it can, then it follows that weeding is an integral part of maintaining a collection. Weeding is just as creative an activity as selection. Furthermore the needs of most library clienteles change over the years. New subjects are introduced into academic or school curriculums and older ones are dropped. The library's collections need to reflect such changes. In public libraries the interests of patrons change constantly. Often neighborhoods change, and the persons currently frequenting the library are very different from those of a decade ago. Library collections need to keep up with such changes. To reiterate an idea presented in Chapter Eight, the community of users should determine the collection, what is selected, and what is discarded. Otherwise the collection will fail to serve its purpose.

SUGGESTED READINGS

Weeding

Evans, G. Edward. "Limits to Growth or the Need to Weed." *California Librarian*, 38 (Apr. 1977), 8–16.

An overview of the weeding problem. Without offering specific prescriptions, this article discusses the pros and cons of weeding in various types of literature and the relationship of weeding to collection development.

Slote, Stanley J. *Weeding Library Collections*. Littleton, Colo.: Libraries Unlimited, 1975.

The basic text on weeding. Reviews all the research on the topic up to 1975 and recommends practical solutions. Extensive bibliography.

Storage

"Book Storage." Issue edited by Mary B. Cassata. *Library Trends*, 19 (Jan. 1979).

The major aspects of the storage problem are covered in nine papers.

CHAPTER ELEVEN
Collection Development Policies

Every library should have reasons for selecting materials for its collections. Furthermore it should be able and willing to write down these reasons in a *collection development policy*. (The terms "selection policies" and "acquisition policies" are often used as synonyms for "collection development policies." However, the last is a more encompassing term and is more appropriate for our discussion, since collection development involves more than just selection and/or acquisition, as we have seen in the preceding chapters.) A collection development policy is a written statement that is both a planning tool and a communications device. It is meant to clarify objectives and to facilitate coordination and cooperation, both within a library or library system and among cooperating libraries within a region. If it is well done, it should serve as a day-to-day working tool that provides the necessary guidelines for carrying out the majority of tasks within the area of collection building.

PURPOSE

In the 1950s and early 1960s, collection development policies (usually then called simply *selection policies*) were written as part of a defense

221

against censorship and in support of intellectual freedom. The McCarthy era had brought many attacks on certain books and periodicals in library collections, and librarians felt the need for a written statement of why the library was collecting such materials that could be shown to complainants. Library staff members also felt the need of support from governing boards and so attempted to get these bodies to adopt written selection policies that would be available as backup in the event of a crisis. In the late 1960s and early 1970s, libraries that worked out collection development policies did so more from a concern for social responsibilities. Often the writing of a collection development policy was part of an overall study of whether the library was serving the entire community it was meant to serve or just the select few who made the effort to use it. Did the collections contain materials for all segments of the community or only for the intellectually superior? In the second half of the 1970s the rationale behind collection development policies shifted once again. This time, diminishing funds for library collections brought about the need to assure that all funds were being expended as wisely as possible, that there was indeed a rational plan of action that could be defended before budgetary authorities and the public.

A collection development policy can be a set of theoretical goals or a statement of actual practice. Ideally it is a set of goals based on actual practice—that is, something that can be put into action but at the same time will challenge the staff to better performance. It should be more than just a public relations gimmick, as some of the early selection policies unfortunately were—mere flag waving to keep the wolves at bay. It should be a day-to-day working tool, something that provides the answers to most of the problems encountered in the daily routine. If a collection development policy is to be successfully written, it requires input from both the library staff at all levels and the library's clientele (if possible, potential users as well as actual users). Eventually the policy should be submitted to the library's governing body and adopted by them as official library policy. In the course of submission there may have to be revisions, but a policy that is satisfactory to both staff and governing board should be worked out; one that does not have the backing of the governing body is of little use in the long run.

Why are collection development policies needed? There are a number of good reasons:

1. A collection development policy forces the library staff and the governing body to think through the goals of the library and, in putting them down on paper, to commit themselves to these goals. Libraries need to identify the long- and short-range needs

of their clienteles and to establish priorities for the allocation of funds to meet these needs.

2. A collection development policy helps assure that the library will seriously commit itself to serving all parts of the community and not content itself with serving only its current clientele.

3. A collection development policy helps set quality standards for the inclusion and exclusion (selection and weeding) of materials.

4. A collection development policy informs users, administrators, governing bodies, and other libraries in the area of the scope and nature of the collection. This facilitates coordination of collection development among different institutions within an area or region.

5. A collection development policy helps minimize personal bias on the part of the individual selectors. When a librarian has to defend certain selections in terms of agreed-upon criteria, there is much less likelihood that personal likes and dislikes will be imposed on the collection. An imbalance in one area is soon perceived as out of line with overall policy.

6. A collection development policy serves as a good in-service training tool for new staff members.

7. A collection development policy helps assure continuity when staff and governing boards change. It is difficult for new staff members to orient themselves quickly to a new collection, particularly if it is one of any depth or size. Guidelines as to what has been done in the past and why are an enormous help, if only in deciding to adopt a new policy. They may also spare the library staff unwarranted criticism from new board members, who may also wonder why something is or is not being done. The problem of continuity in selection has always been a problem. It affects both public libraries, in which only staff changes affect collection development, and academic libraries, in which each change of faculty in a field may greatly affect the collecting in that area.

8. A collection development policy provides a means for the staff to evaluate its own performance periodically. It is also a tool for the public or the governing body to use to evaluate the performance of the library ·staff—a very important point in these days of increasing public accountability.

9. A collection development policy also helps to demonstrate to the public that the library is running a businesslike operation, which is vitally important in public relations.

10. A collection development policy provides information that will assist in the budgetary allocation process.

11. A collection development policy contributes to internal operating efficiency in that many routine decisions can be made once and

for all and need not be considered every time they arise. Staff members, particularly those of lower status, are often very appreciative of such policy decisions, which make life much simpler for them.

12. Finally, a collection development policy can serve as a tool for meeting the objections of individuals or groups concerning the purchase or rejection of specific titles. It also provides guidelines for the handling of such complaints, thus forestalling ad hoc decisions made on the spur of the moment, when calm and collected thought are not likely to prevail.

CONTENT

What do collection development policies contain? They should, first of all, concern themselves with the clientele to be served and their characteristics. What age groups are to be included? What ethnic groups? What educational levels? Secondly, what kinds of programs are to be supported? Is the library to be concerned with research, instruction, reference, general information, or recreation? Finally, what limits are to be set for the collection? These are multifarious. What subjects, and in what depth, are to be collected? (The depth of coverage will probably vary with the subject, particularly in academic libraries.) What forms of materials are to be collected—books, periodicals, microprint, audio-visual materials, etc.? What languages are to be used? (Again it is most likely that various subjects will have an influence on the language.) What levels of materials are to be considered—scholarly materials, popular materials, materials of interest to adults but at an easy reading level? How much duplication is to be allowed, of what types of materials, and for what reasons? What local, regional, or even national commitments are there for cooperation? These will definitely have an effect on the collection policy of the institution.

Each subject must be examined in light of (1) the existing strengths of the collection, (2) the actual current level of collecting, and (3) the desirable level of collecting to meet adequately the program needs of the institution. How far subjects will need to be broken down into separate entities for consideration will undoubtedly depend on the size of the library. In large institutions, subjects will probably need to be examined in considerable detail, often being broken down by geographic area and chronological period. In smaller libraries, particularly public libraries, more general treatment will usually prove adequate—one entire subject area, for example, without further breakdown. Topics of special interest, such as local history, may require special consideration, however, being exceptions to the general pattern of collecting. Just as each subject area will need attention, so, in most cases, will each form of library material. Each has its own characteristics and needs individual consideration.

FORMULATION

How is a collection development policy written? This is not an easy task, and often much time is needed to gather the information. First of all, the community of users must be examined. Who is served or should be served? Information may already be available from sources within the city or institution, particularly from planning offices. If it is not, then the library must consider ways of obtaining it. Surveys may have to be undertaken. In any case, considerable research will be necessary. The next task is usually the examination of current practice. How are things done now, and for what reasons? Only then can librarians determine if procedures are adequate or whether changes should be made. The existing collection must be studied in some detail to ascertain its strengths and weaknesses. After these have been determined, then the reasons behind the strengths and weaknesses should be sought. Most of these will be historical, and staff members responsible for selection in the past should be questioned. Knowing why something was done in the past often aids in determining present actions or future policy.

Constraints on what can be done need to be recognized early in the process of writing a policy statement. Constraints can be purely financial, but often they also involve space limitations; these may affect the types of materials to be selected—microprint over hard copy, for example. Commitments to networks, to the sharing of materials, and to cooperation with other libraries also impose constraints. If they prove to be too restrictive they may have to be renegotiated, but they cannot be ignored.

At this point, or perhaps even before embarking on any of the tasks outlined here, collection development policies of other libraries should be examined to determine exactly what is involved in creating such a document. Fortunately two compilations of sample collection development policies have been published.[1] They give examples of policies for different types and sizes of libraries and samples of individual parts of policies. From these, much guidance can be

[1]Calvin J. Boyer and Nancy L. Eaton (eds.), *Book Selection Policies in American Libraries: An Anthology of Policies from College, Public and School Libraries* (Austin, Tex.: Armadillo Press, 1971); *Library Acquisition Policies and Procedures*, ed. by Elizabeth Futas (Phoenix, Ariz.: Oryx Press, 1977.)

derived. The Collection Development Committee of the Resources Section of ALA's Resources and Technical Services Division also published in 1977 "Guidelines for the Formulation of Collection Development Policies" (see Appendix 1). While these guidelines were intended for large academic libraries, they can be followed in general by all types of libraries.

Collection development policies usually consist of the following sections and are organized in the following order:

1. Introduction. This explains why the policy has been written and by whom. It also describes (sometimes in considerable depth) the community that is to be served.
2. Philosophy and goals. The objectives of the library and its parent institution (if any) are set forth here. Both the theoretical and the practical need to be considered.
3. Selection statement. This is the heart of the collection development policy and usually takes up the largest amount of space. The following items need to be considered: Who does the selection? How is it to be done? What is done? Often the policy will indicate what criteria are to be used in selecting materials (similar to the criteria outlined in Chapter Eight) and what selection aids are to be used (such as those listed in Chapters Six and Seven). Where the responsibility lies for the selection of materials should be carefully spelled out. At this point, various subject fields must be considered. What levels of selection should exist for each subject? The RTSD *Guidelines* suggest five levels: comprehensive, research, study, basic, and minimal. Some libraries reduce this to four levels. Age levels, languages, and special formats all have to be dealt with, and it may be preferable to have a separate section for each format. Finally budgetary limitations have to be considered.
4. Problem areas. These usually include the following: duplication of materials and number of copies to be purchased, replacement of worn-out or lost items, binding, and handling of desiderata. At this point, it may be necessary to consider paperbacks: under what conditions they will be added to the collection, in place of or in addition to hardback items. Some other types of books also present problems, particularly textbooks. Many academic libraries, for example, have a policy of not adding textbooks that have been assigned for a course to the library collection. Students are expected to buy these textbooks, or they are purchased for student use out of textbook funds. Dissertations may be another type of material requiring special decisions. Materials in other than book formats are usually dealt with in the fifth part, although there is no reason why parts 4 and 5 cannot be combined in one section.

5. Special formats. This section usually deals with nonbook formats such as periodicals, newspapers, pamphlets, manuscripts, micro-print, and the myriad types of audio-visual materials. Computer-based materials (data bases) would also fall into this category, as would local information files compiled to support a public library's information and referral services.

6. Gifts. What to do with materials given to the library requires a separate statement. It is hoped that the library will decide to apply the same standards for selection of gift materials that it applies to purchased materials. There is always the danger of lowering the standards, even though processing and storage costs are just as high for gifts as they are for purchases.

7. Weeding. As with selection, the responsibility for weeding must be assigned. What is to be weeded and how are other questions. Finally, it must be decided how material is to be disposed of.

8. Intellectual freedom. Although this issue no longer dominates collection development policies, as it did in the McCarthy era, it is still a very important area. It probably requires more detailed consideration by the governing board than any of the other issues, since they will undoubtedly be drawn quickly into any disputes. Most collection development policies reproduce in their entirety the American Library Association's Library Bill of Rights and the joint statement of the ALA and the American Book Publishers' Council, entitled "The Freedom to Read" (see Appendix 3). Other ALA statements on labeling and on the handling of materials for children or young adults may also be incorporated. The National Council of Teachers of English has also issued helpful materials that may be quoted. The most important part of this section is a detailed plan on how complaints are to be handled and what is to be done when the library is the subject of a campaign by an individual or a group to have materials removed from its shelves. Forms for complainants to fill out are useful tools to append here. (More will be said about how problems of censorship should be handled in Chapter Fourteen.)

9. Revision. Decisions need to be made on how the collection development policy is to be kept up to date and how and by whom it is to be revised. Many hours of work go into the creation of a collection development policy, and it should not be allowed to become outdated. Periodic revision and updating are much simpler than rewriting the policy after a long period of inattention. Furthermore the staff, governing board, and public will soon lose faith in a document that is out of touch with the current situation. This is not to say that a collection development policy should be

revised in order to take care of every decision. Policies should be flexible and general enough to take care of some changes in emphasis, but they should be reexamined at least annually to see if the library is indeed living up to them. If not, then reasons should be sought and the necessary revisions incorporated in the policy. Perhaps the financial position of the library has changed radically. Perhaps there has been a change in the governing board and its thinking. Perhaps a new administration wishes to stress different aspects of service. Perhaps the school or university curriculum has changed and the library must react accordingly. In all these cases, the collection development policy needs to be reexamined and revised where necessary.

WRITING AND ADOPTING THE POLICY

Now that we have discussed what should be in a collection development policy, we need to consider the problems of getting one written and adopted. The library staff is probably the only group that has the necessary knowledge and expertise to write a policy statement. This does not mean that they should not seek help and information from other groups, particularly library users, but in the final analysis, it is they who must write the policy statement. Once it has been written, it should be presented to the library's governing body and/or administration for approval.[2] Revision may be necessary if this body does not agree with all the attitudes or decisions adopted by the staff. The library staff may need to educate the governing authority on certain points. Full and open discussion—and the acceptance by the staff of necessary revisions in order to satisfy the governing body—are infinitely preferable to having this group or individual disown the policy in a moment of crisis. The governing body and administration need to be fully informed as to the implications of all parts of the policy. This is particularly important concerning financial commitments and all aspects of censorship and intellectual freedom. What one should try to avoid is having the governing body or administration actually take part in writing the document. After discussions take place, the staff should go back to the drawing board with all the suggestions that have been made. A revised document should then

[2]The governing body will vary from one library to another. Most public libraries have an elected or appointed board of trustees, but others may be run as a city department. Policy in school media centers may be set by the school board or by an administrator. Academic libraries may or may not have library committees; usually the librarian is responsible to an academic administrator and ultimately to a board of trustees. Whatever the case, the library needs to gain the approval of the governing body or top administration.

be presented to the authorities for further discussion and (ideally) approval. If the differences between staff and governing body are so wide that they cannot be bridged in a collection development policy statement, then there will undoubtedly have to be a parting of the ways. The governing body may well decide that different administrators are needed for the library.

It should be emphasized that a collection development policy, since it deals with controversial and touchy issues, needs to be formulated in calm and quiet, not in a moment of crisis. A policy statement adopted hastily in the midst of a crisis will never stand the test of time. It will remain an ad hoc solution to one particular issue. Furthermore complaints can be dealt with much more effectively when an agreed-upon policy exists than they can when decisions have to be made in the heat of battle.

Another point to be emphasized is that a collection development policy must be written in coordination with other libraries in the area. No library today, as I have stressed before, exists in isolation. No library can hope to be self-sufficient in all areas of its collection. Therefore its commitment to cooperation, either in a hierarchical system or through a division of responsibility among equals, needs to be considered. Any good, detailed collection development policy should assist neighboring libraries in their collection development plans as well, since it will inform them of the goals of their neighbor. Greater coordination of collection building should therefore be possible.

RESISTANCE TO COLLECTION DEVELOPMENT POLICIES

When all is said and done, the fact remains that many libraries, particularly large ones, have never adopted a collection development policy. Why is this so? First of all, they may not realize the importance of such a document. There are still library administrators in positions of authority today who came into the library profession before such a document was thought important. Since some librarians also think of collection development policies as public relations gimmicks rather than as day-to-day working tools, they do not see the necessity of writing such a document. Often the impetus for getting a collection development policy on paper comes from the lower ranks of a library staff, from individuals frustrated at attempts to carry out their jobs when no written guidelines are available. When no written policy exists—concerning personnel, collection development, or whatever—decisions often seem to be made on the whim of the administrator and to change from day to day. Policies that exist only in the head of one person can hardly be effectively carried out by a large staff.

In recent years, the main reason given in most institutions for not having a collection development policy—a written rationale for actions to be taken—is the difficulty in creating one. A great deal of data are needed as input for such a policy. These data are often not readily available, at least not in a usable form, and therefore they must be sought out, even created, at considerable expense of time and money. It may be difficult to get agreement among different factions within a library, but that is all the more reason for arriving at some kind of common policy; otherwise the library will be in a constant state of turmoil and conflicting actions. Large academic libraries have had the most difficulty in developing collection policies, but, as the RTSD *Guidelines* point out, it is in just this area that coordination is needed. It is hoped that the *Guidelines* will stimulate university libraries to make the effort. Certainly they now have some guidelines which should ease their way. The *Guidelines* stress the necessity for uniformity in detailing levels of collecting so that other institutions will have some idea of what is being done in a particular library. Large university libraries have often found that one way to initiate a collection development policy is to have various units within the library system develop one for their particular area. This may mean developing a collection development policy for one subject area or one type of material. An overall campuswide policy is then developed from these partial ones. It is my guess that financial exigencies will force most libraries to state in writing what their collecting goals are and how they expect to carry them out. Collection development policies are essential tools. Sound management practices demand that such tools be used. The days of relying upon personal whims in developing library collections are past.

SUGGESTED READINGS

No one collection development policy can be cited here as a model for all to follow. Readers are referred to the following for a wide range of examples for all types and sizes of libraries:

Boyer, Calvin J., and Nancy L. Eaton, eds. *Book Selection Policies in American Libraries: An Anthology of Policies from College, Public and School Libraries.* Austin, Tex.: Armadillo Press, 1971.

Library Acquisition Policies and Procedures, ed. by Elizabeth Futas. Phoenix, Ariz.: Oryx Press, 1977.

Further examples can be found in:

Association of Research Libraries Systems and Procedures Exchange Center. *Collection Development Policies* (SPEC Kit 38). Washington, D.C.: The Association, 1977.

This SPEC Kit also includes documents on the pros and cons of collection development policies as well as aids on planning.

Buzzard, Marion L. "Writing a Collection Development Policy for an Academic Library." *Collection Management*, 2 (Winter 1978), 217–228.

A succinct review of the steps necessary in writing a collection development policy.

"Development of a Materials Selection Program." In American Library Association. Office for Intellectual Freedom. *Intellectual Freedom Manual*. Chicago: American Library Association, 1974. Part 4, 5–10.

CHAPTER TWELVE
Collection Evaluation and Standards

Every library collection needs to be evaluated from time to time to see how well the selection policies are working out. If the library is acquiring a lot of material that is not being used or if it is not acquiring material that is needed by users, the persons involved in collection development need to know this so that they may take corrective action. This is just one of the reasons why it is necessary to examine the quality of a library collection, although it is probably the most important one. Other reasons may include the need to justify budget demands—added sums to fill gaps in the collection, to satisfy users—or the need to show an accreditation body that the institution possesses the necessary materials to support instruction in a certain subject field or at a certain academic level. As we have seen in the preceding chapter, it is often necessary to evaluate a collection as part of the process of writing a collection development policy. Finally many librarians simply like to compare their institution with others—to be able to boast that their library is better than or as good as their neighbor's. For whatever reason evaluation may be undertaken, it is a healthy and necessary task. It can only result in improved knowledge of the collection and, it is hoped, improved library service.

EVALUATION METHODS

There are numerous methods of evaluating library collections. The most common, all of which will be examined in some detail, are the compilation of statistics (on holdings, use, and expenditures), checking lists, obtaining user opinions, direct observation (examining the shelves), and applying standards. In addition, librarians are becoming increasingly convinced that collections should be judged on their use and their document delivery capability. If a collection has a lot of unused material or, in contrast, is unable to produce the necessary information when users need it, should that collection not be judged inadequate? Some of the evaluation methods used are quantitative; others are qualitative. The latter are necessarily harder to use and are subject to much greater variation in applicability and interpretation. At the present time, combination of the two methods is most commonly used.

Use of Statistics

Let us examine what kinds of statistics are useful for evaluating the collection. The most widely used statistics deal with the size of the collection—library holdings. Almost every library maintains some such statistics. If the collection has been in existence for some time, it will probably be necessary to check the accuracy of these statistics either through an actual count or through various sampling methods. Statistics can easily be inflated over the years for prestige purposes or to influence accrediting bodies. Other types of useful statistics concern the annual growth of the collection. In newer institutions, this may be a more important figure than the present total size of the collection. Statistics need to be obtained on parts of the collection as well as on the whole so that individual subject fields can be assessed. One of the most important aspects of collection evaluation is comparing how well the job of selection is being done in various subject areas. Only statistics broken down by Library of Congress or Dewey Decimal Classification class can provide the basis for such detailed evaluation. Another type of useful statistic is concerned with unfulfilled requests or requests that have to be filled through interlibrary loan. Formulas also exist against which collections can be measured. Some of these formulas have been developed by independent researchers but may later have been adopted as evaluation criteria by professional associations or accrediting bodies. These will be covered in greater detail when we discuss standards.

A favorite occupation of librarians is taking the statistics they have gathered and comparing them with those of neighboring or rival institutions. For such comparisons to be valid, the institutions compared must be of the same size and type. Since these factors are rarely identical in two different institutions, great care must be taken in interpreting the results. Where does one obtain the statistics of other libraries necessary for such comparisons? The U.S. Department of Education, through its various agencies, publishes such statistics from time to time, as do almost all state libraries or agencies. In addition, some professional library associations make attempts to assemble statistical data on collection size.

Such agencies and associations also attempt to collect statistics concerning library expenditures for materials. This is another type of statistic which is useful in collection evaluation. The total monetary value of a collection is rarely judged (in fact, that type of assessment is rarely if ever attempted). Instead the amount of money spent currently forms a basis for comparison. Usually more than one year's expenditures should be studied in order to see trends and to discount abnormal spending in a particular year. In evaluating a collection, expenditures for salaries are also sometimes evaluated in the belief that no collection can be developed successfully without adequate support staff. As with collection size, formulas have been developed by various agencies to judge the adequacy of financial support for collection development.

Finally, statistics on use of the collection are often employed for evaluation purposes. Care must be taken to measure all types of use, not just circulation of materials outside the library. Attempts should be made to measure in-house use as well, both of the reference collection and of materials in the stacks. This is not easy to do. For example, what is to be considered use—simply browsing through a book or the use of one paragraph or one page or a whole chapter? Many evaluators are not convinced that in-house use can be adequately measured, at least not as one measures outside circulation. Nevertheless new methods are tried all the time, as this is an important indicator of the value of a library.

Checking Lists

Verner Clapp and Robert Jordan were convinced that "the best yardsticks of adequacy are . . . the book-selection list and the specialized subject bibliography, frequently reviewed and brought up to date by experts and in the light of use." But they went on to say that "to apply these yardsticks is, at the present time, something else again: manual checking and searching procedures are involved— slow, tiresome and costly."[1] In spite of these difficulties, the checking of lists, along with the compilation and comparison of statistics, is probably the most common way of evaluating the quality of collections. This method, of course, works best with small or specialized collections where the amount of labor involved is minimized, but by using sampling techniques, the method is also applied in large libraries. In any large library, it is quite possible and sometimes desirable to limit evaluation to one subject area, just as statistics are compiled for this purpose.

All types of lists can be used for evaluation purposes. In fact, the same types of lists that were recommended for building collections in Chapter Seven are also suitable for evaluative purposes. These include standard catalogs and basic lists; catalogs of important libraries in specific subject fields; subject bibliographies developed for the use of scholars and researchers in the field; current selection tools; lists of reference works; lists of periodicals; and lists of the most commonly cited works in a field. Some accreditation bodies also draw up their own lists to be checked by the libraries of the institutions being examined. This helps to avoid the common problem of using a list for evaluative purposes that has previously been used for selection, with a resulting abnormally high rate of availability of the materials listed. A library may also prepare its own lists from various sources for checking purposes, usually soliciting the aid of leading scholars in the field. Ad hoc or tailormade lists are probably the best, but most libraries, particularly smaller or nonacademic ones, probably do not have the time or the resources to prepare them and must therefore rely on existing lists. One of the great problems with all types of lists is that the library may own books which are just as good or appropriate as the ones on the list, but in the checking procedure, these books will not get credit. A few lists (such as those of the Mathematical Association of America) do take this into account and offer alternative possibilities. No one has ever set a standard as to how many books on a list should be held by a library in order for it to be considered an "A" or a "B" library. It has just been assumed that the more, the better. In assessing an entire library collection, differences in the holding rates for various subject fields can easily be seen. Thus a library can readily note that it is weak in some areas and strong in others. It is hoped that this will be related to the needs of the library's users.

Standard lists or subject bibliographies become outdated very

[1]Verner W. Clapp and Robert T. Jordan, "Quantitative Criteria for Adequacy of Academic Library Collections," *College & Research Libraries*, 26 (Sept. 1965), 380.

quickly and are thus best used for checking retrospective holdings. For current materials, they should always be supplemented by the checking of current bibliographical and reviewing tools. Finally available lists seldom take into account the needs of a particular community of users. Their use for evaluative purposes presupposes a core of material that belongs in all libraries of a certain type. While I believe that such a core exists for almost every type of library, not everyone shares this belief.

Obtaining User Opinions

The third method of evaluating collections is to obtain opinions regarding the quality of the collection from its users. After all, they should be in the best position to know what can be found there and what cannot, and whether a collection is really satisfying their needs. In considering users, library staff members should be consulted as well as patrons. Often staff members, particularly those in reference positions, have an even greater knowledge of a collection's strengths and weaknesses than the average user. Researchers or scholars are also in an advantageous position to comment on the quality of a collection. They are familiar with the entire literature of a field, not only what is available in a particular library but what is available elsewhere and might be acquired. Consulting patrons as to the materials that should be purchased is a daily routine in many libraries, particularly in public and special libraries, where it is thought essential to satisfy users' needs quickly. It is a short step from this type of consultation to asking users what they think of the collection as a whole. The only problem with this method is that users may have higher expectations for the collection than what an institution is willing to spend, or they may have become so accustomed to a poor collection that they are loath to suggest radical improvements. How are users polled for their opinions? The usual ways are to interview them individually, which naturally takes time, and to use questionnaires. Finally, as all interviewers will soon discover, no two experts agree on what needs to be acquired. The best one can hope for is a general consensus among a majority of those consulted.

Direct Observation

A fourth method which is often used, although often not admitted to because of its unscientific and impressionistic nature, is direct observation: going to the shelves and examining the materials there. For this method to be effective, the person doing the examining must be an expert in the subject area. Only then will he or she be able to ascertain quickly the depth and scope of the collection. But even the uninitiated can learn some things from examining library shelves. It is very easy to spot duplicate copies of superseded editions. It is easy to see whether journal runs are complete. It is also easy to see whether the collection is in good physical condition and whether adequate sums have been expended for binding or microfilming. The absence of materials in an area may mean that the library does not own much material on that subject, but it may also mean that the materials are all in use. In either case, some remedy is called for.

Applying Standards

A fifth way of evaluating a collection is to apply the standards set up by various professional associations or accrediting bodies. Such standards often call for the gathering of statistics or for the checking of lists. In addition, however, they usually apply specific formulas to judge the adequacy of a collection. Standards may also be qualitative rather than quantitative. Library standards are rarely enforceable codes, other than those used by accrediting bodies that have the power to rate institutions; most are models to be followed or aimed at. Library standards that are concerned with collections can be either of a benchmark nature (measuring existing conditions against some desired model condition that is deemed "good") or of a prescriptive nature (setting goals for the future and providing guidelines for development). Library standards that exist at the present time have all been criticized for being primarily descriptive, which makes comparisons between institutions difficult. Furthermore those that are quantitative are based on arbitrary figures, usually an average of what is found in the so-called best institutions. Sometimes quantitative standards are actually feared or opposed by the better libraries, which view them as the lowest common denominator and a hindrance to excellence rather than a help. Their fear is that minimum standards will be seen as maximum standards by public or academic authorities, who may then feel that they do not have to provide for their own libraries as generously as they have in the past, since a professional body has indicated that they already come up to "standard." In fact, very few libraries in the past have met even the minimum standards set by the various divisions of the ALA; thus this fear of debasement has not occurred in most institutions. Another criticism of library standards is that they are usually concerned only with the measurement of input (collections) rather than output (service or use). Gradually, however, some methods are being developed to measure such use, so that future standards should be more broadly based.

The recently published "Mission Statement for Public Libraries" is an effort to develop a program whereby a library can measure its performance in reference to the needs of its own community rather than by some arbitrary national standard. Furthermore the "Mission Statement" starts from the premise of measuring the needs of the community and individuals first rather than the needs of the library.

To be effective, standards must meet certain criteria. First, they must be based on research and on the compilation of statistics in the areas being standardized. While statistics have long been used as a basis for standards in the library profession, research to back up standards is still needed in most cases. Second, the activity must be measurable. Third, the standard must be definable in terms that will convey the same meaning to all users; otherwise the standard will be applied in such differing ways as to become meaningless. Fourth, the standard must be appropriate to the type of institution being measured. Because of this need, no one standard for all types of libraries has ever been attempted; instead each division of the ALA has developed its own. Fifth, standards must be authoritative (backed by a respected body) and based on actual practice and research, not on mere assumptions. Finally, standards must be realistic; otherwise they will be ignored.

Standards promulgated by the type-of-library divisions of the ALA are concerned with all aspects of library service. However, in this book we shall be concerned only with those that have to do with collections. Standards currently exist for academic and school libraries. Public libraries are in the process of reevaluating theirs. (Copies of those sections applying to collections will be found in Appendix 2.)

The Association of College and Research Libraries has been among the most active in recent years in developing standards. Those for the four-year liberal arts college were developed first, then those for the two-year community college, and most recently, those for university libraries. It was long considered impossible for agreement to be reached on standards for university libraries, which varied so widely in size and purpose. However, the necessity for such a document has finally resulted in success. The standards for two-year learning resource centers have been criticized for lack of quantitative measurements. This has recently been remedied with an additional set of quantitative standards.

The standards for school media collections (adopted in 1975) are probably the most detailed ones currently in use. They set specific numerical goals for a "base collection" and for future additions for all types of materials: books, periodicals, pamphlets, microforms, film-strips, slides and videotapes, recordings, and tactile formats. They also set numerical standards for the equipment necessary to use these various formats. A further document was adopted in 1976 on "Policies and Procedures for Selection of Instructional Materials" (as was mentioned in Chapter Nine). No other type of library is currently served by so comprehensive a set of guidelines.

All standards for collections deal with the quality and size of the collection in relationship to the population served. They also deal with the maintenance of the collection, with assurances that it is being kept up to date and that weeding is being carried out. The formulas used for academic libraries take into consideration not only the population served (number of students and faculty) but other factors as well. These include the number of subjects in which a major or minor is offered and the levels (undergraduate, master's, and doctoral) at which instruction is offered. In measuring the size of collections, definitions are provided in most standards as to how to count books, periodicals, microforms, and A-V and other materials. This is necessary since various libraries have different ways of maintaining statistics and an attempt must be made to make the statistics as comparable as possible.

Many standards provide formulas for measuring the quality of the collection. Some have developed formulas of their own; others may rely upon such independently developed tools as the Clapp-Jordan formula. Since the Clapp-Jordan formula is cited so often in the literature about collection evaluation, a word should be said about it here. It was developed by Verner W. Clapp and Robert T. Jordan of the Council on Library Resources in 1965.[2] It has since been refined by R. M. McInnis.[3] Students should study the formula in detail since it was the first to introduce multiple factors concerning levels of instruction offered and because its influence can be seen in almost every formula constructed since. The Clapp-Jordan formula presupposes a basic number of volumes in an academic library collection below which no adequate service can be given, no matter how small the student body served. To that basic figure it adds additional volumes according to the number of faculty members, students (FTE), and honors students or those in independent study programs. It then adds further volumes for each major subject field in which instruction

[2]Verner W. Clapp and Robert T. Jordan, "Quantitative Criteria for Adequacy of Academic Library Collections," *College & Research Libraries*, 26 (Sept. 1965), 371–380.

[3]R. M. McInnis, "The Formula Approach to Library Size: An Empirical Study of Its Efficiency in Evaluating Research Libraries," *College & Research Libraries*, 35 (May 1972), 190–198.

is given at each of three levels (undergraduate, master's, and doctoral). It distinguishes between number of titles and number of volumes. It also does the same for periodicals. The formula was further refined by McInnis, who found that the weight for doctoral fields was so high as to present the danger of distortion, at least in its application in large research libraries. It still remains a useful measurement tool, as it is not based on one set of statistics but rather on several different elements weighted differently.

RESEARCH AND COLLECTION USE: SOME FINDINGS

Research on the use of collections (largely those of academic libraries) has increased substantially in recent years. This research has interesting ramifications for collection development in all types of libraries. For a long time, many librarians have been concerned about the materials in their collections that never seemed to be used. In undergraduate libraries, in particular, there has also been a concern for providing enough copies of some heavily used materials so that the library could promptly satisfy all the demands that were being placed upon it. In scientific libraries, in particular, there seemed to be evidence that books and journals were subject to rapid obsolescence and decreased use. Thomas J. Galvin and Allen Kent state bluntly in a 1977 article that "The hard facts are that research libraries invest very substantial funds to purchase books and journals that are rarely, or never, called for, as well as equally large sums to construct and maintain buildings designed to make accessible quickly titles that are no longer either useful to or sought by their clienteles."[4] They go on to say that "Responsible library management would seem to demand major revision of library acquisitions policies in response to findings such as these by the legion of investigators who have provided corroborating evidence to support and strengthen the original conclusions of Fussler and Simon in 1961 regarding patterns of use of research library collections. Yet such major shifts in philosophies of collection development have not occurred."[5] In reality, until very recently, it was probably not feasible to give up collecting this little-used material, as there was no other source for it when it was needed, however infrequently. That picture is changing radically with the wider adoption of networks and resource sharing (see Chapter Thirteen). No longer are most libraries pretending that they

---

[4]Thomas J. Galvin and Allen Kent, "Use of a University Library Collection: A Progress Report on a Pittsburgh Study," *Library Journal*, 102 (Nov. 15, 1977), 2317.
[5]Ibid.

can collect everything that any faculty member or student might want for study or research. Therefore the studies of Fussler and Simon, as well as those of Kilgour at Yale and Trueswell at Northwestern, are being looked at carefully for what they tell those responsible for building collections.

This research provides methods that can be used to evaluate the use of a collection or parts of it. In turn, the information obtained from this research can provide valuable input into decisions on which materials to duplicate and which ones to eliminate or relegate to less costly storage. If whole subject areas or various types of materials show little or no use, then those responsible for building the collection need to ask whether any such materials should be bought or whether library funds would not be more wisely expended elsewhere. The methods that have been tried vary in detail, but most are based upon circulation statistics. It has been proven that past use of a book or journal is a pretty good indicator of future use. What is needed, if possible, is a good data base of circulation statistics. If such a data base is not available, there are other ways of obtaining such statistics, as was mentioned in Chapter Ten in connection with weeding and storage. Those interested in undertaking such evaluation are referred to Chapter Five in F. Wilfrid Lancaster's *The Measurement and Evaluation of Library Services* (1977), which provides an extremely good summary of the research carried out prior to 1977 as well as a guide, through its bibliographies, to the original research literature. This is an area with which librarians need to concern themselves to a much greater extent than they have to date. Funds for library purchases are no longer unlimited, and what is available must be expended as effectively as possible. Studying how a collection is used is one of the best ways of ascertaining how to develop that collection for the future.

In this chapter we have examined a number of ways of evaluating a collection. We have also talked about how essential it is for rational collection development that a collection be evaluated from time to time. In conclusion, it should be stated that there is no one best way to evaluate a collection. No method is better than another; all complement each other. If a thorough examination is to be attempted, then it will be necessary to use as many of the suggested methods as possible. Only then can the evaluator be reasonably sure that valid results have been obtained. Nor is collection evaluation an easy task; it is not. It requires a good deal of time and effort (if the checking of lists is undertaken, which it certainly should be), but it should be considered part of the daily task of collection development. Nothing less than the most knowledgeable selection based on the best information available can be countenanced in this day and age.

SUGGESTED READINGS

Evaluation

Bonn, George S. "Evaluation of the Collection." *Library Trends*, 22 (Jan. 1974), 265–304.

A basic survey of evaluation methods as applied to library collections. More readily understandable than Lancaster (see below). Extensive bibliography.

Galvin, Thomas J., and Allen Kent. "Use of a University Library Collection: A Progress Report on a Pittsburgh Study." *Library Journal*, 102 (Nov. 15, 1977), 2317–2320.

A summary of the findings of the most recent research on use of a library collection.

Lancaster, F. Wilfrid. "Evaluation of the Collection." In *The Measurement and Evaluation of Library Services*. Washington, D.C.: Information Resources Press, 1977. Chapter 5.

A detailed summary of all the research on evaluation of library collections. A large portion of the chapter is devoted to the evaluation of the use of a collection.

Standards

Lancaster, F. Wilfrid. "The Relevance of Standards to the Evaluation of Library Services." In *The Measurement and Evaluation of Library Services*. Washington, D.C.: Information Resources Press, 1977. Chapter 10.

A critique of library standards: their character and possible value.

"Standards for Libraries." Issue edited by Felix E. Hirsch. *Library Trends*, 21 (Oct. 1972).

A series of articles discussing library standards for all types of libraries in the United States, as well as comparisons with Canada and Great Britain.

CHAPTER THIRTEEN
Resource Sharing

At several points in this book, we have mentioned that libraries today need to cooperate and share their resources in order to serve their patrons better. In this chapter, we shall explore this problem in much greater detail. Until very recently, the goal of every library was to provide all the materials its clientele needed. Even if that goal was not realizable, it still was actively pursued. Douglas Bryant, former Director of the Harvard University Library, put it very well when he said:

> Through all the centuries since the Alexandrian Library, the aim of librarians and the hope of scholars has been to amass in a single library all the resources for research in any branch of knowledge. Though this aim was always a chimeric notion, nonetheless, it has persistently seduced collectors and readers into nursing unrealistic objectives and into making false assumptions as to the completeness of collections. This doctrine of self-sufficiency is finally coming to be realized for what it is: a will-o'-the wisp. We are seeing at last the gradual abandonment of this creed, even for the very largest of libraries. That any library could provide all the resources for research required by its readers is now generally recognized by scholars and librarians, albeit reluctantly, as an unattainable aspiration.

Accordingly, a sharing of holdings among libraries is increasingly accepted as an ineluctable necessity and as the only realistic means of providing the full range of resources needed for scholarly research.[1]

Thus a shift in emphasis has occurred in many libraries from attempted self-sufficiency to finding a truly effective means of gaining access to needed materials wherever they may be. There are still many critics of resource sharing who want everything immediately and who do not realize that rising publishing costs in the last decade, coupled with the rising volume of publication, make this impossible. It must be admitted that resource sharing is not as convenient as the self-sufficient library, but no one has ever been able to point to a *completely* self-sufficient library anyway. Scholars in the humanities and social sciences have always had to turn to more than one source for their primary research materials—not everything has been duplicated on microfilm or fiche—and for the true scholar, travel was always a necessity. Thus the idea is not so new, even though admitting it probably is.

FORMS OF RESOURCE SHARING

Resource sharing entails three things: having resources to share, a willingness to share them, and a plan for sharing them. Resource sharing has existed for a very long time, although under different names. Its oldest and most commonly known form is that of interlibrary loan. Interlibrary loan (ILL) has become an integral part of U.S. library practice and has been formalized by the American Library Association into a code. There are also local and regional variations of the national code, and interlibrary loan exists at the international level as well. In recent years interlibrary loan has had serious problems, caused mainly by too great a burden being placed on a small group of large research libraries, which were expected to loan materials far in excess of those they themselves borrowed and without adequate compensation. An essential element in any resource-sharing program is that everyone involved should receive some benefit. Since the largest research libraries began to feel that they were receiving no benefits from the traditional free interlibrary loan system, many of them began to impose fees in order to recover some of the costs involved. This defeated the purposes of the system. Nevertheless the system still works among other types of libraries and is indeed a form of resource sharing.

In order to facilitate interlibrary loans, union catalogs and union

[1]Douglas W. Bryant, "The Changing Research Library," *Library Scene*, 4 (Sept. 1975), 2.

lists of serials have been developed in many areas of the country. The aim of these catalogs and lists was to make known who owned certain materials and therefore who might be in a position to lend them to other libraries. The National Union Catalog, which publishes the locations reported to it by certain cooperating libraries, is the apex of a network of local and regional union catalogs, as is the *Union List of Serials* and *New Serial Titles*. From a sharing of materials through interlibrary loan and through the compilation of union lists and catalogs, it was but a short step to the common storage and ownership of certain materials. Two well-known examples of this type of cooperation between libraries are, on the local or regional level, the Hampshire Inter-Library Center in Massachusetts and, on the national scene, the Center for Research Libraries in Chicago.

If one stops to think about it, another movement toward resource sharing has occurred throughout the twentieth century, particularly since World War II: the trend toward consolidation and unification of small independent community libraries into larger county-wide or multicounty systems. Within the academic world, there has also been a movement toward groupings of public academic institutions into regional or statewide systems. Within such systems, materials are often moved from one location to another as the need for them shifts. All materials owned by the component members are considered available to anyone using the system. Thus resource sharing has increased dramatically in many areas of the country, at least on a local basis. Within such systems it consists of the sharing of materials between similar kinds of libraries. In the past ten or fifteen years, a further step has occurred in many areas as various independent libraries and systems have joined together to form networks. Networks can be formed by the same types of libraries, but they are often formed among many different types, even crossing the boundaries between public and private institutions if some way can be found to compensate the private institutions for the service they provide to the public. Networks can be formed for many purposes, but the ultimate purpose of all of them is to work together toward a common goal. All networks are based on some kind of formal agreement. In this book, we are concerned with networks only from the point of view of resource sharing. While resource sharing can include the sharing of objects, persons, or expertise, our discussions here are limited to the objects—the library resources.

Resource sharing, at least on the large scale that is now being proposed, has been made possible only by recent developments in technology, particularly in computers, which have made possible the creation of indexes and catalogs that are needed to gain access to materials in different locations. Union catalogs and union lists have always been extremely time-consuming and expensive to construct. They have proved even more expensive to maintain. The result was that much of the nation's wealth of books and other materials was hidden away in unknown depositories. Libraries often sought materials halfway across the country simply because they did not know that one of their near neighbors possessed the document needed. Computer data bases are increasingly changing that picture. It is often forgotten that the Ohio College Library Center (OCLC) was originally conceived of by a group of Ohio academic librarians who were eager to gain access to each others' holdings, rather than as a cooperative cataloging venture. It happened that the cataloging records had to be created first, but increasingly in recent years the OCLC data base has become a source for information on which library owns which book. Another element increasingly introduced into libraries in order to facilitate communication is the teletype, linking many libraries within an area or even on a national basis.

ELEMENTS OF SUCCESSFUL RESOURCE SHARING

What is involved in making a resource-sharing plan work? There are several necessary elements, but the first is the availability of materials to be shared. While theoretically there are no limits to sharing materials, practically a library can share only those materials that are not needed locally. There are, of course, gradations in local needs. Some materials are used every day, almost every hour, others only occasionally; some, as we have seen in the last chapter, are never used. Many of the problems in resource sharing have come from attempts to juggle the needs of local patrons with those outside. The ideal situation is to develop a central source that has no local clientele but only serves as a library's library. At the present time, few such institutions exist in the United States, the prime example—and a most successful one—being the Center for Research Libraries. Another necessary element, closely linked to the availability of resources, is a precise understanding of how the materials are to be shared, what the priorities for use are, and other factors. Only then can harmonious working relationships be developed.

Adequate bibliographic access must be provided if resource sharing is to succeed. As was indicated earlier, computer technology is now making this much more feasible. A rapid delivery system must also be organized. Either the materials must be delivered to the readers or the readers must be provided with transportation to take them to the materials. Some systems provide both, although the more heavily used method is undoubtedly the former. A courier service is probably the best way to provide good service, since the U.S. mail service has become slow and unreliable in recent years. UPS and other parcel services are also frequently used. While courier service would seem to be feasible only within a limited metropolitan area, it has been instituted successfully over much wider ranges. In Canada, for example, a courier service links the two vast provinces of Quebec and Ontario, all the way from Quebec City to Windsor, providing twenty-four-hour service within each province and forty-eight-hour service between the two via a link-up at the National Library in Ottawa. Distances should not prove a barrier if the need really exists.

The last element needed for an effective resource-sharing plan is a delegation to the network of power to purchase materials in a coordinated fashion and to administer the system in such a way as to provide consistent and reliable service. Since there will undoubtedly be resistance to a resource-sharing plan, if only as resistance to any change, it is necessary for the network to offer good service from the beginning; otherwise the plan will have a difficult time succeeding.

REPRESENTATIVE RESOURCE-SHARING PLANS

We have spoken of the need for materials to be available for use in a resource-sharing plan. We have also mentioned the desirability of developing a central source of supply that has no local clientele and serves only as a resource center for other libraries. Let us now examine a few resource-sharing programs—two that failed and two that have succeeded—so that we may determine the elements that have brought about success or failure. One of those that failed was the Farmington Plan. It was begun in 1942 as an attempt by a group of major university and research libraries to make sure that at least one copy of every valuable publication from every country would be available in some library in the United States. The responsibility for collecting was divided by subject and by geographic area. Division by subject was used for the countries of Western Europe, Australia, Mexico, and South Africa. The rest of the world was divided by country, with one library taking responsibility for all publications issued in that country. The plan continued until the end of 1972, when it was formally dissolved. At the same time another program, LACAP (Latin American Cooperative Acquisitions Program), which was the work of a commercial organization, Stechert-Hafner, also terminated. While the reasons for terminating LACAP were financial and business-related, there were other reasons for the failure of the Farmington Plan. Foremost among them was the fact that there was no central coordinating body to monitor the program. How each member carried out its responsibilities was left to that member to determine. Increasingly local needs took precedence over shared needs. This was particularly true of the subject assignments. Some libraries were not very enthusiastic over the assignments they received and could perceive little local use for the materials. When funds became scarce, these acquisition programs were the first to be cut. It was only when local interests coincided with the assignments—as with some of the country assignments—that the plan worked well. But the basic lesson for us is that this was a shared responsibility with no coordinating force at the center.

Two very successful examples of resource sharing can be cited for others to emulate. First is the British Library Lending Division (BLLD) at Boston Spa, part of Great Britain's national library. Originally set up as a lending library for materials in the sciences and technology, it has expanded in the last few years to take in the humanities and social sciences as well. It is a library's library. Its main purpose is to provide copies (now mostly in the form of photocopies rather than originals) of materials needed by other libraries that are unavailable in their own collections or inaccessible for use. Instead of collecting little-used materials, as the Center for Research Libraries does, the BLLD from the beginning sought to acquire the most frequently used materials, largely periodicals, believing that those were the most needed materials. In fact, if one looks at what is most commonly requested by interlibrary loan, one will discover that these are not esoteric materials but recent English-language materials. The BLLD has proved that this is the case, and by providing photocopies of articles rather than the periodicals themselves, it assures its library users of always having the material they seek available. Furthermore, by instituting an exceedingly efficient method of handling all orders, the BLLD has been able to institute an Overseas Photocopying Service, which many U.S. libraries have found to be as quick as and often more efficient in supplying needed periodical articles than any U.S. source. Financing for the BLLD comes from national funds, as this is seen as a needed national service that no other established library could provide.

The Center for Research Libraries in Chicago was set up on a completely different basis. Originally the Mid-West Inter-Library Center, it was the creation of a dozen or so Midwestern university libraries. It was meant to house their little-used materials and to acquire jointly other infrequently used materials for sharing by all members, thus relieving members from the responsibility of acquiring these items individually and often in multiple copies within the area. Such materials include foreign dissertations, foreign government documents, newspapers, state documents, and foreign scientific and technical reports. They are indeed so seldom used that there is rarely a conflict with more than one person trying to use them at the same time. The success of the venture is shown by its change of name and its decision to operate on a national basis. It now has 110 full members, which may deposit material as well as use it, and 68 associate members, which only have access to the collections. Originally limited to university libraries, membership now includes all types. Financing of the center comes from membership dues. Duplicates are also sold in order to obtain other materials. The active acquisitions program is administered by representatives from member libraries, and the program attempts to fill the gaps in the collections deposited by member libraries and to obtain materials that no member libraries own. For example, over the years, member libraries have been polled to see which journals abstracted in *Chemical Abstracts* they held. It was discovered that a considerable number of journals were not subscribed to by any member; the center instituted a subscription to them. Similar projects have been undertaken in other subject areas.

PROBLEMS WITH RESOURCE SHARING

Increasingly other countries are seeing the need to establish libraries like the BLLD and CRL. France has recently created a lending library modeled on the BLLD, and in the United States there is increasing call for a national periodicals center that would collect the most used material rather than little-used items. At the regional and local levels, there is also increasing interest in resource sharing. Unfortunately numerous problems must be solved before plans can become actuality. There are legal and administrative barriers to be overcome. Most can, but it is not always easy and may take time. There are the barriers of geography, but again, successful delivery systems have been created where needed, even over long distances. There is often the lack of space. A building must be erected or leased or space found in a member institution (not often possible). And finally there is the barrier of tradition, often the hardest to break down. It is difficult to get both librarians and users to think in terms of access to materials rather than ownership. Use patterns must change, and any delays in obtaining materials, even if these are unique materials obtainable nowhere else, bring complaints. The desire of libraries to cooperate and to share resources is not helped by the fact that institutions themselves, of which the libraries are a part, do not often cooperate on educational or other programs. Thus librarians usually find themselves as pioneers in such ventures.

One of the most common complaints about resource sharing is that browsing among the materials in a subject area is impossible. Of course, it is possible to browse in union lists and bibliographies, but many scholars claim this is not the same. How much information is ever obtained this way has yet to be proven, so the question remains open. There is, of course, the danger that if everyone relies on resource sharing, no one will have anything to lend. The answer to this problem seems to be that every library should have enough materials to provide for its own daily needs. Care should be taken not to slacken up on essential areas of collection building at the local level. Resource sharing should be looked upon as providing wider access to additional materials, not as a substitute for basic needs. Finally, if libraries are to commit themselves to resource sharing on a large scale, then there needs to be a reexamination of how a library is judged. A library should no longer be judged on its size but rather on the adequacy of its service.

There are several financial aspects to resource sharing. One of the defects in most of our interlibrary loan transactions today is that the predominantly lending libraries are not compensated for the loans they make. (In some states, this has been remedied—at least for loans within the state—by the use of state-appropriated funds, usually administered by the state library. For example, in Connecticut *Connecticard* permits a person with a public library card to borrow materials from any public library within the state. Libraries keep a record of loans to outsiders and are compensated by the State Library at the end of the year if they have loaned more materials to outsiders than their residents have borrowed from other libraries.) Cooperation today cannot be based on altruism; some system of remuneration must be devised. Funds must come either from pooled resources or from state or federal grants. Secondly, most resource sharing does not bring about reduced costs to member libraries; it brings about better service. Some of the problems of cost effectiveness have not been solved yet, simply because the shared system runs parallel with one working toward self-sufficiency. This is one argument for establishing a nonrival superlibrary serving other libraries, rather than attempting to work out cooperation among existing collections.

NETWORKS

Formalized networks, based on written agreements, seem to be the best answer to the problem of resource sharing. Agreements are needed on what is to be shared, on what is to be acquired jointly, on bibliographic control, and on conditions of use. Networks can be of several types. Resources can be equally distributed among the members and so used, or resources can be in the hands of one member, which serves all others, or concentrated in a group of libraries, having similar and overlapping collections, all of which are expected to serve the members. There are also hierarchical networks in which requests are passed up the line from smaller to larger libraries until the materials are located and supplied. We have spoken of networks limited to one type of library. Increasingly networks are being opened to all types. Who owns what type of material varies so widely from region to region in the United States and Canada that it is foolish to think of resource sharing except as sharing all of the resources in an area in whatever type of institution may own them. Within certain subject fields, such as law and medicine, there is also probably a need for specialized networks to care for the information needs of these professions, although access to these networks from the more general information systems should be possible.

One of the most successful networks to include all types of libraries has been the 3R's program in New York State. This is a statewide program launched in 1966 which attempts to provide improved access to advanced reference and research materials for serious library users such as university and college faculty, students, researchers, writers, scholars, doctors, lawyers, and other professional persons no matter where they live throughout the state. The idea behind it was that a doctor practicing in the smallest town in upstate New York should have just as ready access to any medical information needed as the physician in New York City. The 3R's program operates at two levels—state and regional. The regional programs are voluntary associations of all types of libraries—public, academic, and special—within an area to facilitate the sharing of resources. Funds are provided from the state to compensate participating libraries for the services they render. The state has established certain regulations in order to assure that each regional association is viable, with the necessary materials to provide adequate service. For example, the membership must include at least one academic institution offering graduate programs at the master's level or higher or a public library which holds at least 400,000 adult volumes and currently receives at least 1,500 periodicals annually. In addition, at least four four-year colleges and all the public library systems within the region must be members. There are further criteria based on population and geography. Each regional resource agency is to have a coordinating board of trustees.

The statewide program is intended to undertake projects of such magnitude that a statewide approach is necessary. To date, these have included the testing of certain experimental programs, such as communications networks, and the provision of research and resource materials in special subject areas, such as law and medicine. In the latter area, Cornell and Columbia universities make their medical libraries available on a contract basis to the entire state as a final backup for this type of information. The State Library itself serves as a bibliographic information center and as a referral center for materials that cannot be found within one region and must be sought elsewhere. Needless to say, this program has been successful only because of the added state funds that have been invested in it. It is a model that merits study by other states and regions.

In the long run, what is undoubtedly needed is a national network that will provide for the needs of all citizens. If this is not to become a reality within the near future, then statewide and regional networks should be attempted. The 3R's program in New York State, described above, which includes all types of libraries, provides a good example to be followed. National and state funds are needed to get some of these programs off the ground. The problem in the next decade will be to persuade Congress and the state legislatures that these programs are essential. Before librarians can persuade state legislators and representatives of this, some of them must be persuaded themselves. We began by stating that self-sufficiency is no longer a viable policy. We must admit that this is true and get on with our planning. We shall probably never again see the affluent days of the 1960s. There has been a taxpayer's revolt in this country, and demographic projections see no expanded enrollments in schools and colleges in the next two decades. Therefore we must rethink our priorities and see how we can best meet the collection needs of our library clienteles. Resource sharing seems to be the only sure answer.

SUGGESTED READINGS

The literature on resource sharing has reached enormous proportions in recent years. Only a few titles are cited here.

Boylan, Ray. "Scholarly Citadel in Chicago: The Center for Research Libraries." *Wilson Library Bulletin*, 53 (Mar. 1979), 503–506.

A brief overview of the history and current role of the CRL.

Casey, Genevieve M. "Cooperation, Networking, and the Larger Unit in the Public Library." *Library Quarterly*, 48 (Oct. 1978), 447–462.

An excellent review of the past, present, and possible future state of cooperation among public libraries and between them and other types of libraries. Of major importance in understanding current trends.

de Gennaro, Richard. "Austerity, Technology, and Resource Sharing: Research Libraries Face the Future." *Library Journal*, 100 (May 15, 1975), 917–923.

Examines various strategies for resource sharing using the British Lending Library as an example of what might be copied by U.S. libraries.

Edelman, Hendrik. "The Death of the Farmington Plan." *Library Journal*, 98 (Apr. 15, 1973), 1251–1253.

Discusses reasons for the failure of the Farmington Plan and raises questions regarding cooperative acquisitions and programs.

"Library Cooperation." Issue ed. by Pearce S. Grove. *Library Trends*, 24 (Oct. 1975).

The seventeen articles here discuss the political and technological issues of cooperation, some of the legal questions, and planning cooperative arrangements. Several articles survey regional and state-level developments. The last three articles discuss cooperative developments in Latin America, Canada, and England.

Resource Sharing in Libraries: Why, How, When, Next Action Steps. Edited by Allen Kent. New York: Marcel Dekker, Inc., 1974.

The most extensive study of resource sharing. Based on papers presented at a 1973 conference in Pittsburgh.

CHAPTER FOURTEEN
Censorship

As careful as a librarian may be in selecting materials for the library collection, there will always be someone who will disagree with that selection. In recent years, such persons have no longer remained quiet; they are increasingly vocal in their demand that the book or periodical or other offending item be removed from the collection. They may also feel the opposite—that the collection fails to include material on all sides of a question—and they may insist that something be added to the collection even though it may not meet the library's selection standards. While a great deal of this action consists of pressure brought to bear on librarians, school administrators, or library and school boards, increasingly legal action is also threatened, particularly if obscenity is involved. Public and school libraries are the biggest targets for attempts at censorship. Rarely are academic libraries involved, except in colleges supported by certain conservative religious bodies. Also, one almost never hears of a special library having such a problem, probably because of the specialized and limited nature of its collections.

Librarians—and their professional associations, such as the American Library Association—have been in the forefront of the battles against censorship and the suppression of library materials for the past forty or fifty years. Prior to the 1930s, libraries were usually perceived as being on the side of the censors, representing the "better" things of life, the status quo and middle-class values. The actions of totalitarian regimes, such as Nazi Germany in the 1930s, in burning books and suppressing all criticism undoubtedly led librarians to rethink their role in society as the defenders of the right to read, or intellectual freedom; in 1939 the first Library Bill of Rights was adopted by the ALA. During the McCarthy era of the 1950s, libraries were heavily attacked for what was on their shelves. This resulted in an amended version of the Library Bill of Rights, as well as a "Statement on Labeling" adopted by the ALA. Also, in 1953, an important statement on the "Freedom to Read" was issued jointly by the ALA and the American Book Publishers Council (the predecessor of the current Association of American Publishers). This "Freedom to Read" statement has subsequently been endorsed by a wide range of organizations, such as the American Booksellers Association, the American Civil Liberties Union, the Magazine Publishers Association, the Motion Picture Association of America, and the National Council of Teachers of English. (All these documents will be found in Appendix 3 and should be studied carefully in conjunction with this chapter.) The ALA has created an Office for Intellectual Freedom and increasingly over the years has become involved in court cases, usually as an *amicus curiae* (friend of the court), submitting briefs to present the librarian's side of obscenity or other censorship issues.

THE LEGAL QUESTION

Early Obscenity Laws

What have these court battles been about? For the most part, librarians, publishers, and booksellers have been involved in obscenity cases. While the censorship of unpopular ideas, or writings against the state or organized religion, have occurred in other countries—particularly in dictatorships—the United States has seen few legal actions in this area. The First Amendment to the U.S. Constitution states clearly: "Congress shall make no law . . . abridging the freedom of speech, or of the press." This has protected most expressions of unpopular ideas, whether political or religious. The Supreme Court, however, has ruled that obscenity is not entitled to protection under the First Amendment. Therefore there has been extensive litigation in the courts over this matter, with one court ruling supplanting another over the years as society's (and the courts') ideas of what constitutes obscenity have changed. Actually obscenity did not become an important issue in this country until the mid-nineteenth century. While a few states, such as Vermont (1821), Connecticut (1834), and Massachusetts (1835), had passed statutes prohibiting the publication and sale of obscene materials, the first federal action did not occur until 1842, when the Customs Law prohibited the importation of obscene works from abroad. The real crusade against obscenity in the nineteenth century was led by Anthony Comstock. His campaigns resulted in the passage of the federal Comstock Act in 1873, which prohibited the importation, carriage by mail, or interstate commerce of "every obscene, lewd, lascivious, indecent, filthy or vile article, matter, thing, device or substance." Many states also adopted Comstock acts at the same time. Over the years, the courts (in most cases the Supreme Court) began to limit the grounds on which a work could be declared obscene. Among these were decisions which declared that a work had to be judged in its entirety, not on isolated passages; that a work had to be judged by its effect on the average normal member of the community, not the most susceptible; that defendants were entitled to introduce expert testimony as to the merits and probable effects of a book. One of the most famous cases was the 1933 litigation involving James Joyce's *Ulysses*, in which Judge John M. Woolsey, in a beautifully written decision, declared that the work was not obscene and could be imported into the United States.

The Roth and Miller Decisions

These earlier cases culminated in 1957 in the *Roth v. United States* decision of the U.S. Supreme Court, later expanded and clarified by other cases, which established a three-part test for obscenity. "Three elements must coalesce: it must be established that (a) the dominant theme of the material taken as a whole appeals to a prurient interest in sex; (b) the material is patently offensive because it affronts contemporary community standards relating to the description or representation of sexual matters; and (c) the material is utterly without redeeming social value."[1] The difficulties with this definition lie in the interpretation of the terms "dominant theme," "prurient interest," and "community standards." It is clear from subsequent litigation that not even the justices themselves are able to define clearly the terms that they used. The Supreme Court did declare that "sex and obscenity are not synonymous" and further held that "obscenity is not within the area of constitutionally protected speech

[1]Justice William J. Brennan in *A Book Named 'John Cleland's Memoirs of a Woman of Pleasure' v. Attorney General of the Commonwealth of Massachusetts*, 383 U.S. 413.

or press." Most librarians were confident that the Roth decision would remain the law of the land for some time, but unfortunately a change in the membership of the court through several appointments by President Richard Nixon changed the basic philosophy of a majority of the court. The Warren Court became the Burger Court and in 1973 handed down a different three-part test in *Miller v. California*.[2] The new guidelines were: "(a) whether 'the average person, applying contemporary community standards' would find that the work, taken as a whole, appeals to the prurient interest, (b) whether the work depicts or describes, in a patently offensive way, sexual conduct specifically defined by the applicable state law, and (c) whether the work, taken as a whole lacks serious literary, artistic, political, or scientific value." Furthermore the court ruled that "community standards" were no longer to be construed as national standards but as local ones. Thus material acceptable in New York City or Las Vegas might be declared obscene in Iowa City or Little Rock.

The initial reaction of the publishing, bookselling, and library communities to the Miller decision was one of panic. All sorts of deleterious effects were imagined, with books and magazines being banned in one community but offered for sale in a neighboring one. Publishers feared being dragged into innumerable lawsuits throughout the country. Fortunately this has not happened to any great extent. Publishers still publish for the entire nation, and their works are sold everywhere. A few publicity seekers, such as the prosecutors in Shelby County (Memphis), Tennessee, have sought to prosecute the makers (and even the actors) of pornographic films, but little widespread action has taken place in regard to books and periodicals. In some states, one of the problems has been resolved by making the state the community and not allowing individual towns or cities to legislate in these matters. Another problem has been that judges and juries have found it very difficult to agree on "community standards." If thousands of people pay $5 to see *Deep Throat*, does that not mean that the film is accepted by the average citizen of the community? With the proliferation of "adult" bookstores into the smallest American communities, it now seems that anything printed can be sold. Many district attorneys and prosecutors are now seeking to stop only the sale of visual material (photographs or films), and then only when it involves minors or exposure to an unwilling public.

As a result of the *Miller* decision, states have been forced to rewrite their obscenity legislation to make it more specific. In so doing, some of them (California, for example) have added statutes that forbid the distribution or sale of "harmful matter" (i.e., without

[2]413 U.S. 15 (1973).

redeeming social value) to minors. Librarians often feel threatened by such laws, as most library collections contain much material acquired for adults which may be deemed harmful to children by some parents or other members of the community. How is a library to keep this material out of the hands of minors without putting all the books under lock and key? So far, no librarian has been prosecuted in California under this law, but many have been intimidated. Librarians are also bothered by the test in *Miller* that a work must have "serious literary, artistic, political, or scientific value" rather than be "utterly without redeeming social value." Many works are purchased by a library for their mere entertainment value; these often have no other reason for existing. Are they to be denied constitutional protection? Many legal authorities grant libraries enough prestige to say that the mere fact of selection by a library endows a work with the necessary redeeming qualities to put it beyond the reach of obscenity prosecution. The fact remains, however, that obscenity laws are troublesome to librarians, to publishers, and to booksellers because they may be badly interpreted. Standards are so vague that there is opportunity for all kinds of abuse in law enforcement. Any law enforcement officer seeking a little publicity can cause untold harm to a librarian or a bookseller, even though the case may later be thrown out of court. Persons who attack obscenity legislation and court decisions feel strongly that the persons who actually engage in obscene acts should be punished—not the distributors, most of whom cannot hope to know in detail the contents of all the books or periodicals they sell or distribute (as in a library).

How long the *Miller* decision will stand as the law of the land remains in question. The decisions in all recent obscenity cases have been 5 to 4, so that the replacement of one conservative judge on the Supreme Court would probably bring about a return to the *Roth* decision or to even more liberal interpretations. However, two elements of recent court decisions are not likely to be overturned for some time to come. These involve (1) respecting the rights of individuals not to have obscene materials forced upon them and (2) some form of protection for minors. In fact, in many legal jurisdictions these are the only types of prosecution now being attempted. It has proven too difficult and too expensive to get convictions in ordinary types of obscenity cases.

THE CENSOR

Censorship was clearly on the rise throughout the 1970s. Furthermore many more organized groups became involved. Schools and libraries are easy targets for the frustrations of the blue-collar, lower middle classes, from which most of these organizations draw their membership. Many conservative religious groups have also gotten involved. It is clear that censorship may occur anywhere—in big cities, in small rural communities, in sophisticated Westchester County, New York, in impoverished Appalachia. It is harder and harder to know what will offend. Most of what is attacked is not legally obscene; it is merely offensive to someone. Any book or periodical may be a target. In fact, a 1977 survey by the National Council of Teachers of English found that *Time*, *Newsweek*, and the *U.S. News & World Report* were among the most frequently censored periodicals. To librarians, much censorship appears to be capricious and irrational.

Many of the problems in schools may occur because there has been such a great change in the teaching of literature. Parents think of schools as presenting the best in literature, the classics. They think of the school's role as one of setting standards, of improving tastes and cultural values. When English teachers or librarians choose books that are "relevant" to today's teen-ager or books to stimulate discussion (and therefore likely to contain controversial material), parents are bewildered and angered. Most parents do not like what is being written today as literature. They object to substandard English, to profanity, to many types of plot situations; they may even find these objectionable elements in the classics. Most groups wishing to censor library materials will not attack works for their ideological content, but it is clear that the real goal of some censors is not the language used but the ideas behind it.

What do censors believe? They work on the following premises: (1) books can harm people; (2) the government has a responsibility to protect people from themselves (from their baser instincts); (3) the protection of youth, the weak, is more important than adult freedom; (4) there is a consensus that exists about what is obscene; and (5) there is a consensus about what good literature is and should be. The first premise—that books can harm people—is the opposite of the corollary accepted by many librarians: that books have good effects on people, that they enrich their lives, that they can change a person's outlook. This question has been studied extensively only in the last twenty years, and the results are far from conclusive. The research findings will probably not bring much comfort to either censors or librarians. One belief of the censors is that works affect people in the same way, that obscene literature has the same deleterious effect on all people. Research shows that one's personality is far more pervasive than literature and strongly influences one's response to reading. In other words, individuals impose themselves far more on what they read than the reverse. Readers clearly respond very differently to the same work. They bring all types of backgrounds, reading ability, and interests to their reading, and the results are unique in each case.

Censors usually believe that exposure to obscene literature will bring about a breakdown in the moral character of the individual. Research indicates that persons who have frequent contact with ← sexually explicit works tend to view them as providing information and entertainment; they fail to associate them with a breakdown in moral values. Their moral values are formed elsewhere, not in connection with sexually explicit works. This is another way of stating that a person's moral values are the result of things other than reading. They are more likely to be shaped by the home environment, the personality of the individual, and other factors. Additional research, particularly in Denmark, tends to prove that increased availability of sexually explicit materials results in a decrease in sex crimes. Pornography proves to be a harmless outlet for certain individuals, who might otherwise be driven to commit sexual crimes. Finally research shows that once a book has been banned it becomes more desirable, and thus censors often defeat themselves in attempting to make something unavailable.

To those of us who have lived through the 1940s and 1950s, it is very evident that time is a great determining factor in the area of censorship. The books that were censored thirty and forty years ago now look positively innocent compared with the average novel or film today. Thus if a library is required by law to withdraw a book or magazine from its collection, it would do well to preserve that item somewhere, as it is quite probable that at a later date the work will become permissible. Before leaving this issue of obscenity and censorship, another question must be raised. That is the issue of whether the rights of the majority to read a work are to be infringed for the sake of a minority. In the past the courts ruled that a community's literature cannot be reduced to the level of adolescents or children just to protect them. Children and adolescents must be protected in other ways, largely by controlling access to certain works. Most individuals agree that some control is necessary as long as the material remains available to those adults who want it. The rights of children and young people to read what they wish are also defended by some. This is a controversial issue and involves parental control over the lives of their offspring. An interesting statement in this area was issued by the Association of American Publishers in 1976 (see Appendix 3), which pleads the case against those who would deny everyone access to materials just because they themselves disapprove. The publishers argue for diversity and against conformity; for the availability of information on all sides of a question rather than just one point of view.

THE LIBRARIAN AND CENSORSHIP

So far, we have talked largely about legal and moral questions, about how censors think, and about the areas which cause controversy and differences of opinion. Now let us examine censorship from the point of view of the individual librarian. When it comes to legal censorship, the librarian must obey the law. Most librarians have little day-to-day contact with such legal decisions. They are made at a higher level and are beyond the reach of most librarians. Librarians do feel the influence of censorship, however, on a local and intimate level. It usually comes in the form of pressure rather than legal action. The librarian is approached and asked to remove an objectionable item from the collection either by an individual or by a group. Sometimes these pressures are open and blatant; sometimes they are subtle. Librarians can react in many ways. Many, fearing for their jobs or fearing adverse publicity for the library, quietly acquiesce. Some librarians try to avoid any possible confrontation by simply not buying anything for their collections that could possibly be challenged. As we have seen, this is rather naive, as today the most innocuous-looking materials are being challenged. It is impossible to predict what will offend some individual.

The best way of handling objections to materials in a library collection is to ask for a formal complaint. The library should, of course, have a written collection development policy. It should also have, as part of that policy or as a supplement to it, a system of handling complaints, a procedure that is clear to all, both staff and complainant. Many times trouble starts at the circulation desk, where only a clerk is on duty. It is essential that all staff members know what to do the moment a situation like this arises. By asking for a formal complaint, the librarian is trying to move the situation away from an emotional to a factual context. Complainants should be asked to fill out a form such as the one shown on page 265.

A form such as this makes the situation more impersonal and provides a cooling-off period. It also signifies to the complainant that the complaint is being taken seriously and is not being brushed off. It should be pointed out, however, that some complainants may feel threatened by the form. They may feel that they do not have the expertise to fill it out adequately. As a result, many may give up their

Request for Reconsideration of Library Materials

Title _____ ☐Book ☐Periodical ☐Other _____

Author _____

Publisher _____

Request initiated by _____

Address _____

City _____ State _____ Zip _____ Telephone _____

Do you represent:

☐Yourself

☐An organization (name) _____

☐Other group (name) _____

1. To what in the work do you object? (Please be specific. Cite pages.)
   _____

2. Did you read the entire work? _____ What parts? _____
   _____

3. What do you feel might be the result of reading this work? _____
   _____

4. For what age group would you recommend this work? _____
   _____

5. What do you believe is the theme of this work? _____
   _____

6. Are you aware of judgments of this work by literary critics? _____
   _____

7. What would you like your library/school to do about this work?
   ☐Do not assign/lend it to my child.
   ☐Return it to the staff selection committee/department for reevaluation.
   ☐Other. Explain: _____
   _____

8. In its place, what work would you recommend that would convey as valuable a picture and perspective of the subject treated?
   _____

Signature _____

Date _____

attempts at this point. Organized groups, of course, will not. After the form has been filled out, there should be a definite procedure for handling the complaint. The complainant should be informed as to what steps will be taken and how long they will take. If the matter becomes serious, the complaint may have to be resolved at the policymaking level. It is hoped that the governing body or administration, having previously adopted a collection development policy, will be prepared to deal with the matter in a calm and collected manner.[3]

Would-be censors should never be treated lightly. In this day of mass media, the censor has many opportunities to make a lot of noise and cause a lot of grief. Of course, many censors will not come first to the library but will go to the local newspapers, radio and TV stations instead. It is therefore essential that the library maintain lines of communication with these important media. If librarians have friends among newspaper, radio, or TV reporters or editors, they may alert them to impending trouble or even be kind enough to get the librarian's side of the story before broadcasting or publishing it. The library should also maintain a vigorous public relations program on behalf of intellectual freedom at all times—before crises occur—so that public officials and the community will understand the problems involved when a specific case arises. It is also essential to inform board members, school administrators, and public officials as soon as trouble arises. They should not be left to learn about it from the public media, which may present a distorted version of the case, at least from the library's point of view. It may also be wise to seek the help and support of local civic organizations, such as the ACLU, trade unions, or teachers' organizations. In most cases, it is wise to defend the principle of intellectual freedom and the professional responsibility of librarians and teachers to select materials rather than the individual item. Persons can be reminded that legal steps must be taken in obscenity cases and that such judgments should be left up to the courts. Responsibility for removal of material from the shelves should rest with this established process. It is, of course, often difficult to get people to realize that there is a difference between what is obscene (and therefore subject to legal challenge) and what is merely offensive to some people. Complainants often insist that their views prevail for everyone, even if there are no legal grounds for such action.

Finally librarians should realize that help in censorship matters can be had from outside the community. The ALA Office for Intellectual Freedom (OIF) stands ready to help at all times. It is

---

[3]The American Association of School Librarians has adopted a recommended procedure for handling complaints. This is included in "Policies and Procedures for Selection of Instructional Materials," which is reproduced in Appendix 1.

particularly important for the librarian who is facing a censorship challenge for the first time and who may be uncertain of the best way to handle it to call the OIF. Its staff has been through these situations many times and can be very helpful. The OIF issues the bimonthly *Newsletter on Intellectual Freedom*, to which all libraries should subscribe. With increasing attacks from organizations that are planned and run on a national basis, it is the better part of wisdom to be aware of what is going on in other communities. The *Newsletter* provides information on what groups are challenging libraries and what materials they are attacking. It also discusses how other libraries are successfully defending intellectual freedom. The OIF, through its Freedom to Read Foundation, also provides legal help at both the local and national levels when issues of great import to libraries arise in the courts. The ALA consistently retains expert legal counsel in the area of censorship and intellectual freedom. Finally the ALA maintains the LeRoy C. Merritt Humanitarian Fund to provide direct financial aid for the support, maintenance, medical care, and welfare of librarians who are threatened with loss of employment or are discharged because of their support for intellectual freedom. The American Library Association is not alone in these battles for intellectual freedom, as the list of organizations that have endorsed the "Freedom to Read" statement shows. Foremost among them are the National Council of Teachers of English, the National Education Association, and the American Civil Liberties Union. All offer support and counsel to the beleaguered librarian and teacher.

Censorship is an issue that many librarians would like not to think about. It would be so nice if it would just go away; unfortunately it will not. If anything, librarians are likely to be faced with more of it in the future than they have in the past, and they should be prepared to handle it in a reasoned manner. The great difficulty in this area is that so much is subjective and open to differing views. Little can be proved beyond the shadow of a doubt. Communities vary enormously, and what material is considered acceptable may be very different in neighboring communities. Librarians cannot get too far ahead of their communities in what they select; on the other hand, they have the responsibility to see that the will of a vocal minority is not imposed upon everyone. The individual citizen has the right to information on all sides of a question. This is one of the cornerstones of our democratic society. It differentiates us from the dictatorships that rule in so many areas of the world, preventing any but approved materials from reaching the people. Would-be censors need to be reminded that in defending democracy they often resort to totalitarian methods. These cannot be countenanced in our nation.

SUGGESTED READINGS

American Library Association. Office for Intellectual Freedom. *Intellectual Freedom Manual*. Chicago: American Library Association, 1974.

The basic manual for librarians on the problems of censorship and intellectual freedom. All students should be familiar with this and with the OIF's bimonthly *Newsletter for Intellectual Freedom*.

Dealing with Censorship. Edited by James E. Davis. Urbana, Ill.: National Council of Teachers of English, 1979.

How to deal with censorship as seen from the school teacher's point of view. While almost all the articles are of interest, librarians should take particular note of an excellent summary of current research on the effects of reading.

"Intellectual Freedom." Issue edited by Everett T. Moore. *Library Trends*, 19 (July 1970).

Seventeen articles discuss various aspects of intellectual freedom and censorship, including legal issues, the concerns of librarians (in all types of libraries), publishers, and politicians. Several articles survey developments in Western Europe and in parts of the English-speaking world (Australia, New Zealand, and South Africa).

Serebnick, Judith. "The 1973 Court Rulings on Obscenity: Have They Made a Difference?" *Wilson Library Bulletin*, 50 (Dec. 1975), 304–310.

The results of a study undertaken in ten medium-sized cities on the effects of the 1973 Supreme Court decision on obscenity. This report also considers library selection policies in general.

Swan, John C. "Librarianship Is Censorship." *Library Journal*, 104 (Oct 1, 1979), 2040–2043.

A thought-provoking argument that in selecting materials, librarians are constantly practicing censorship.

AFTERWORD

After the great influx of federal funds to libraries in the 1960s came the cutbacks of the 1970s. Reduced federal funding was coupled with reduced enrollment in the schools (upon which the level of funding is often based) and a general tax revolt. All these factors were aggravated by inflation, with the result that even those libraries that had more money to spend were buying less. Fewer books could be purchased with the same amount of money. Furthermore the prices of periodicals climbed much faster than the general cost of living, so that libraries were forced to allocate a larger percentage of their budget to this one type of material, cutting back on the funds that had once been spent for books. With a shift also to greater purchase of nonprint materials and a greater number of foreign books being offered for sale on the U.S. market (particularly by English publishers, which have established U.S. offices in increasing numbers in the last few years), U.S. trade publishers found themselves getting a smaller and smaller share of the library dollar.

The outlook for the 1980s, as predicted in the study of John Dessauer for the Book Industry Study Group,[1] is one of further shrinkage. School libraries are being hit the hardest due to their decreasing enrollments and the refusal of many communities to pass

---

[1] "Publishers, Librarians Ponder BISG Study of Expected Lower Library Acquisitions," *Publishers Weekly*, 211 (Mar. 28, 1977), 32–33.

any bond issues to increase funding for education (or for any other need). But public and academic libraries are also feeling the crunch. Academic libraries are no longer purchasing large quantities of retrospective materials, as they were in the 1960s. They have all they can do to keep up with current publications. Public libraries have had to cut back on multiple copies and on many of the frills they had enjoyed for a number of years. Only special libraries, financed largely by the private industrial and business sector, have escaped the money crunch.

What does this all mean for selection in libraries, for library collection development? It means that careful selection is even more important than in the immediate past. The expenditure of every dollar must be justified. Librarians will be held more and more accountable for how they spend public monies. It means, too, that with the continued increase in the volume of information available, coupled with a decrease in available funds, librarians will be forced to think much more in terms of resource sharing and networks.

Furthermore a knowledge of the content of materials, as well as subject expertise, will increasingly be looked for as a basic qualification of the selector and collection builder. Thus this book ends with an appeal to the would-be selector to read, read, read, to view, to listen—anything to gain that expertise, that knowledge. Nothing less will do if one truly wishes to be an outstanding collection builder.

APPENDIX ONE

Collection Development Policies

Guidelines for the Formulation of Collection Development Policies (RTSD)

Policies and Procedures for Selection of Instructional Materials (AASL)

GUIDELINES FOR THE FORMULATION OF COLLECTION DEVELOPMENT POLICIES

**American Library Association
Resources and Technical Services Division
Collection Development Committee**

1. INTRODUCTION

1.1 Purpose.

The Committee offers these *Guidelines for the Formulation of Collection Development Policies* in the belief that collection development policy statements must be comprehensible and comparable if they are to prove useful in the implementation of long-range goals for sharing of resources. To promote comprehensibility and comparability, policy statements must employ language which is clearly defined, and measures whose values are commonly understood.

Reprinted by permission of the American Library Association from *Guidelines for Collection Development*, copyright © 1979 by the American Library Association.

1.2 Objectives.

The immediate aims of the designers of these *Guidelines* are to identify the essential elements of a written statement of collection development policy, and to establish a standard terminology and structure for use in the preparation of such policies.

1.3 Need.

Widespread budgetary constraints and the growth of interlibrary cooperation for shared resources and service networks have given impetus to the pressure to analyze collection activity in universally comprehensible terms.

1.4 Scope.

The Committee has attempted to provide an instrument that will be of use to libraries of all kinds and sizes in formulating statements of their collection development policies. All elements of the *Guidelines,* however, will not be equally applicable to all libraries.

1.5 Audience.

The *Guidelines* are intended to help library administrators and collection development librarians to produce a document that can serve as both a planning tool and a communications device. The resulting policy statements should clarify collection development objectives to staff, users, and cooperating institutions, enabling them to identify areas of strength in library collections; and by this means should facilitate the coordination of collection development and cooperative services within an area or region. The policy statement can itself serve as a communication to some audiences. For other selected audiences, among them library users, funding authorities, and governing boards, the statement should be reviewed as the data file from which interpretative statements can be formulated.

1.6 Methodology.

The *Guidelines* have been submitted to the Committee in open meeting at several Midwinter and Annual Conferences. The group discussions, in which numerous visitors have participated, have resulted in extensive revisions of the initial drafts.

1.7 Assumptions.

1.7.1 A written collection development policy statement is for any library a desirable tool, which: (a) enables selectors to work with greater consistency toward defined goals, thus shaping stronger collections and using funds more wisely; (b) informs library staff, users, administrators, trustees, and others as to the scope and nature of existing collections, and the plans for continuing development of resources; (c) provides information which will assist in the budgetary allocation process.

1.7.2 A library's policy for deselection (that is, identification of works which may be removed to remote storage locations or discarded) should be coordinated with its collection development policy. (See below, *Guidelines for the Review of Library Collections.*)

1.7.3 It is desirable that form and terminology of collection development policy statements be sufficiently standardized to permit comparison between institutions.

1.7.4 Libraries have acknowledged the impossibility of building totally comprehensive collections, and will increasingly need to rely on cooperative activities. Collection development policy statements will assist cooperative building, and will also be of value to users and user-service units in locating materials.

1.8 Definitions.

1.8.1 Levels of collection density and collecting intensity.

1.8.1.1 Assumptions.

Definitions of collecting levels are not to be applied in a relative or *ad hoc* manner (that is, relative to a given library or group of libraries), but in a very objective manner. Consequently, it is quite likely that a large number of libraries will not hold comprehensive collections in any area. Similarly, academic libraries that do not support doctoral programs, or other types of libraries that are not oriented toward special research, may not have any collections that would fall within the research level as defined herein. The definitions are proposed to describe a range and diversity of titles and forms of materials; they do not address the question of availability of multiple copies of the same title.

1.8.1.2 Codes.

The codes defined below are designed for use in identifying both the extent of existing collections in given subject fields (collection density) and the extent of current collecting activity in the field (collecting intensity).

A. Comprehensive level. A collection in which a library endeavors, so far as is reasonably possible, to include all significant works of recorded knowledge (publications, manuscripts, other forms) for a necessarily defined field. This level of collecting intensity is that which maintains a "special collection"; the aim, if not the achievement, is exhaustiveness.

B. Research level. A collection which includes the major published source materials required for dissertations and independent research, including materials containing research reporting, new findings, scientific experimental results, and other information useful to researchers. It also includes all important reference works and a wide selection of specialized monographs, as well as an extensive collection of journals and major indexing and abstracting services in the field.

C. Study level. A collection which supports undergraduate or graduate course work, or sustained independent study; that is, which is adequate to maintain knowledge of a subject required for limited or generalized purposes, of less than research intensity. It includes a wide range of basic monographs, complete collections of the works of important writers, selections from the works of secondary writers, a selection of representative journals, and the reference tools and fundamental bibliographical apparatus pertaining to the subject.

Note: Some college librarians have expressed a need for further refinement of the "Study level" code for use by libraries without comprehensive or research level collections, to enable them to define their collecting policies explicitly enough to meet the needs of network resources planning. We include the following optional subcodes for such institutions.

(1) Advanced study level. A collection which is adequate to support the course work of advanced undergraduate and master's degree programs, or sustained independent study; that is, which is adequate to maintain knowledge of a subject required for limited or generalized purposes, of less than research intensity. It includes a wide range of basic monographs both current and retrospective, complete collections of the works of more important writers, selections from the works of secondary writers, a selection of representative journals, and the reference tools and fundamental bibliographical apparatus pertaining to the subject.

(2) Initial study level. A collection which is adequate to support undergraduate courses. It includes a judicious selection from currently published basic monographs (as are represented by *Choice* selections) supported by seminal retrospective monographs (as are represented by *Books for College Libraries*); a broad selection of works of more important writers; a selection of the most significant works of secondary writers; a selection of the major review journals; and current editions of the most significant reference tools and bibliographies pertaining to the subject.

D. Basic level. A highly selective collection which serves to introduce and define the subject and to indicate the varieties of information available elsewhere. It includes major dictionaries and encyclopedias, selected editions of important works, historical surveys, important bibliographies, and a few major periodicals in the field.

E. Minimal level. A subject area in which few selections are made beyond very basic works.

Note: Some subject fields may be completely out of scope for a library's collections. These class numbers can be lined out in the analysis, or "0" can be used to indicate "not collected."

1.8.2 Language codes.

The following codes should be used to indicate languages in which material is collected. Libraries wishing a greater refinement of this data may subcode with the MARC language codes.

F. All applicable language (i.e., no exclusions)

G. English

H. Romance languages

J. Germanic languages

K. Slavic languages

L. Middle Eastern languages

M. Asian languages

N. African languages

P. Other languages

2. GUIDELINES

2.1 Principles governing formulation and application of collection development policies.

2.1.1 Libraries should identify the long- and short-range needs of their clientele, and establish priorities for the allocation of resources to meet those needs. A collection development policy statement is an orderly expression of those priorities as they relate to the development of library resources.

2.1.2 Collection development policy statements should be reviewed at regular intervals to insure that changes in defined goals, user needs, and priorities are recognized, and that changing budgetary situations are confronted.

2.1.3 A library's collection development policy should be coordinated with those of appropriate other libraries, whether in a hierarchy of dependence, or in a division of responsibility among equals. A collection development policy statement should assist librarians to select and deselect in conformity with regional needs and resources.

2.2 Elements of a collection development policy statement.

2.2.1 Analysis of general institutional objectives.

This selection should include:

A. Clientele to be served

B. General subject boundaries of the collection

C. Kinds of programs or user needs supported (research, instructional, recreational, general information, reference, etc.)

D. General priorities and limitations governing selection, including:

(1) Degree of continuing support for strong collections

(2) Forms of material collected or excluded

(3) Languages, geographical areas collected or excluded

(4) Chronological periods collected or excluded

(5) Other exclusions

(6) Duplication of materials (generally treated)

Note: The collection development policy statement addresses the question of breadth and depth of subject coverage. Libraries will need to formulate separate statements of policy relating to duplication of materials; and such additional policy statements must be given consideration in fund allocation.

E. Regional, national, or local cooperative collection agreements which complement or otherwise affect the institutions policy

F. Legal, regulatory, or policy requirements of the institution

2.2.2 Detailed analysis of collection development policy for subject fields.

It is recommended that this analysis be organized by classification scheme, with a parenthetical subject following the class number for ease of interpretation. The organization by class assures that the library's practice and policy with regard to the entire range of knowledge will be examined; and that the language used in the subject analysis will be as much as possible in a *lingua franca* for internal and interinstitutional discussions. Many libraries have chosen to design their collection development policy statements with an organization by academic program or broad subject descriptor. In such instances an index by class will facilitate cooperative resources planning with other libraries.

Libraries will differ in the degree of detail they will require for the analysis of their collection development policy by class. A suggested minimum refinement of the Library of Congress classification on which to structure the analysis is the breakdown into approximately five hundred subdivisions used in *Titles Classified by the Library of Congress Classification: National Shelflist Count, 1977*, Berkeley, General Library, Univ. of California, 1977 (see Appendix A). For Dewey or other classification schemes a comparably refined breakdown should be attempted. It must be stressed that this recommendation indicates a minimal refinement of classification analysis needed for interinstitutional comparisons. Many libraries will prefer to analyze their collections in greater detail.

For each subject category (i.e., classification number or group of numbers), indicate the following:

A. Level of collecting intensity codes to indicate
  (1) Existing strength of collection
  (2) Actual current level of collection activity
  (3) Desirable level of collecting to meet program needs
B. Languages
C. Chronological periods collected
D. Geographic areas collected
E. Forms of material collection
F. Library unit or selector with primary selection responsibility for the field.

2.2.3 Detailed analysis of collection development policy for form collections.

In some libraries special collection development policy statements are required for certain forms of materials, where policy governing the collection of those materials differs from the library's general policy for subject collections. Some examples of forms for which special policy statements may be needed include:

A. Newspapers
B. Microform collections
C. Manuscripts
D. Government publications
E. Maps
F. Audiovisual materials
G. Data tapes.

Where possible, it is desirable that the basic structure of the policy statement for a form collection follow subject classification; but with some form collections it will be necessary to use another primary arrangement (kind of material, area, etc.). For example, the policy statement for a map collection might be divided first into "general maps," "topographic maps," "raised relief maps," etc., with subdivision by area classification; that for a newspaper collection might be primarily by political division.

Whatever the basic structure chosen, the detailed analysis of collection development for a form collection should include the elements identified in 2.2.3.A-F above.

2.2.4 Indexes.

The information in the policy statement should be made accessible for a wide variety of purposes. To this end an index should be appended which correlates subject terms to class numbers. Individual libraries may also wish to index by academic programs, library units, or other key words or concepts.

POLICIES AND PROCEDURES FOR SELECTION OF INSTRUCTIONAL MATERIALS (1976)

American Association of School Librarians

I. INTRODUCTION

The human worth that democratic societies seek to protect and develop rests upon commitment to educational programs which meet the individual purposes and developmental needs of students and prepare them to resolve the problems that continually confront them. Social, economic, and political issues, national and international as well as the changing expectations of individuals and groups, represent the human concerns to which education must respond if it is to perpetuate and improve the society that supports it.

Those who would create better educational opportunities must strive to develop comprehensive systems that meet the needs of students of differing abilities, backgrounds, and interests, enabling them both to adjust to and influence the changing society in which they live. Media programs which reflect applications of educational technology, communication theory, and library and information science contribute at every level, offering essential processes, functions, and resources to accomplish the purposes of the school.[1]

Committed to the philosophy of school media programs as expressed in *Media Programs: District and School* and the selection of quality media collections which ensure that "learners will have the opportunity to grow in their ability to find, generate, evaluate, and apply information that helps them to function effectively as individuals and to participate fully in society," the American Association of School Librarians has prepared this material as a guide for the formulation of selection policies and procedures for the school media program.

The selection of quality instructional materials is one of the most important and controversial tasks performed by school personnel. Often school districts are subject to challenge by individuals or groups who are concerned about what the collection does or does not include. Such action may be based on considerations involving political, social, or personal values, religion, profanity, treatment of matters relating to sex, or other controversial issues.

A selection policy, therefore, should provide a procedure for maintaining a consistent quality of excellence in the materials for use

[1]Reprinted by permission of the American Library Association.

in the teaching-learning process including continuing evaluation of the media collection. The American Association of School Librarians *believes* that such a policy and procedures statement should be adopted formally and approved officially by each school district as a basis for selecting instructional materials, and used as a document to help students, parents and other citizens better understand the purposes and standards used to select instructional materials.

II. GUIDELINES

A. Statement of Policy

The governing body of a school district should declare that it is the policy of the school district to provide a wide range of instructional materials on all levels of difficulty, with diversity of appeal, and the presentation of different points of view for all students. Further, the governing body should declare it is their policy to allow the systematic review of existing media collections and to permit the reconsideration of allegedly inappropriate instructional materials through established procedures.

B. Statement of Selection Procedures

Responsibility for Selection of Instructional Materials

The governing body of a school district is legally responsible for all matters relating to the operation of the school district. The responsibility for the selection of instructional materials, however, should be delegated to the certificated library/media personnel employed by the school district.

While selection of instructional materials involves many people (library/media specialists, teachers, students, supervisors, administrators, and community persons), the responsibility for coordinating the selection of most instructional materials and making recommendations for acquisition rests with certificated library/media personnel.

The selection of textbooks* may rest with department chairpersons or with textbook evaluation committees.

*Textbook definition: "any manual of instruction; a book dealing with a definite subject of study systematically arranged, intended for use at a specified level of instruction, and used as a principal source of study material for a given course" (Carter V. Good, ed., *Dictionary of Education* [3d ed.; McGraw-Hill, 1973]).

Acquisition Procedure

A selection procedure should include provisions for the acquisition of all forms of instructional materials. Consistent criteria for selection should be applied to all acquisitions, including gifts, leased materials, and loans.

Criteria for Selection

The school media program is an integral part of the educational program of the school or district. Criteria for the selection of instructional materials should implement this basic purpose.

Instructional materials should be selected on the basis of the: appropriateness of the medium, varying levels of difficulty, student interests, curriculum needs, and representation of varying points of view.

The selection process should provide for the consideration of requests from students, teachers, administrators and the community. Selection of instructional materials should be based upon preview or evaluation reviews in professionally prepared selection aids or other appropriate sources.

Recommendations for acquisition will be solicited from faculty and students.

Gift materials should be judged by the criteria listed in the preceding section and should be accepted or rejected on the basis of those criteria.

It should be understood that selection is an ongoing process which should include the removal of instructional materials no longer appropriate and the replacement of lost and worn materials which are still of educational value.

A media advisory committee following local policy for such appointments may be appointed to assist in the selection and evaluation process.

Procedures for Reconsideration of Challenged Materials

Occasional objections to instructional materials will be made despite the quality of the selection process; therefore, the procedure for handling reconsideration of challenged materials in response to questions concerning their appropriateness should be stated. This procedure should establish the framework for registering a complaint that provides for a hearing with appropriate action while defending the principles of freedom of information, the student's right to access of materials, and the professional responsibility and integrity of the certificated library/media personnel. The principles of intellectual freedom are inherent in the First Amendment of the Constitution of the United States and are expressed in the *Library Bill of Rights*[2] adopted by the Council of the American Library Association in 1948 and amended in 1961 and 1967 and in the *Students' Right to Read*,[3] a publication of the National Council of Teachers of English. In the event instructional materials are questioned, the principles of intellectual freedom should be defended rather than the materials.

III. POLICY AND PROCEDURES MODEL

Policy for Selection of Instructional Materials

The _____ School Board hereby declares it is the policy of the _____ District to provide a wide range of instructional materials on all levels of difficulty, with diversity of appeal, and the presentation of different points of view and to allow the review of allegedly inappropriate instructional materials through established procedures.

Objectives of Selection

In order to assure that the school media program is an integral part of the educational program of the school, the following selection objectives are adopted:

To provide materials that will enrich and support the curriculum and personal needs of the users, taking into consideration their varied interests, abilities, and learning styles;

To provide materials that will stimulate growth in factual knowledge, literary appreciation, aesthetic values, and ethical standards;

To provide a background of information which will enable pupils to make intelligent judgments in their daily lives;

To provide materials on opposing sides of controversial issues so that users may develop under guidance the practice of critical analysis;

To provide materials which realistically represent our pluralistic society and reflect the contributions made by these groups and individuals to our American heritage;

To place principle above personal opinion and reason above prejudice in the selection of materials of the highest quality in order to assure a comprehensive media collection appropriate for the users.

Responsibility for Selection

Although the _____ School Board is legally responsible for the operation of the school, the responsibility for the selection of instructional materials is delegated to the certificated library/media personnel.

While selection of materials involves many people, including library/media specialists, teachers, students, supervisors, administrators, and community persons, the responsibility for coordinating and recommending the selection and purchase of instructional materials rests with the certificated library/media personnel. Responsibility for coordinating the selection and purchase of textbooks may rest with appropriate department chairpersons or with textbook evaluation committees.

Criteria for Selection

Educational goals of the local school district, individual student learning modes, teaching styles, curricula needs, faculty and student needs, existing materials and networking arrangements should be considered in developing the media collection. Guidelines for the evaluation and selection of curricula resources are listed.

Curricula materials should:

Be relevant to today's world;
Represent artistic, historic, and literary qualities;
Reflect problems, aspirations, attitudes and ideals of a society;
Contribute to the objectives of the instructional program;
Be appropriate to the level of the user;
Represent differing viewpoints on controversial subjects;
Provide a stimulus to creativity.

Technical materials should:

Be of acceptable technical quality; clear narration and sound, synchronized pictures and sound;
Be readable; typographically well-balanced.

For specific criteria for various forms of materials and equipment, refer to *Media Programs: District and School*, pp. 70–86.

Procedures for Selection

In selecting materials for school media programs, the certificated library/media personnel in consultation with the selection committee will: evaluate the existing collection; assess curricula needs; examine materials and consult reputable, professionally prepared selection aids. Recommendations for acquisition will be solicited from faculty and students.

Gift materials should be judged by the criteria listed in the preceding section and should be accepted or rejected on the basis of those criteria.

It should be understood that selection is an ongoing process which should include the removal of materials no longer appropriate and the replacement of lost and worn materials still of educational value.

Procedures for Reconsideration of Materials

Occasional objections to instructional materials will be made, despite the quality of the selection process. The _____ School Board supports principles of intellectual freedom inherent in the First Amendment of the Constitution of the United States and expressed in the *Library Bill of Rights* of the American Library Association and *Students' Right to Read* of the National Council of Teachers of English. In the event that materials are questioned, the principles of intellectual freedom, the right to access of materials and the integrity of the certificated library/media personnel must be defended rather than the materials.

If a complaint is made, the following procedures should be followed:

1. Inform the complainant of the selection procedures and make no commitments.
2. Request the complainant to submit a formal "Request for Reconsideration of Instructional Materials" (see Appendix A).
3. Inform the superintendent and other appropriate personnel.
4. Keep challenged materials on the shelves during the reconsideration process.
5. Upon receipt of the completed form, the principal requests review of the challenged material by an ad hoc materials review committee within fifteen working days, and notifies the district media director and superintendent that such review is being done. The review committee is appointed by the principal, with the concurrence and assistance of the certificated library/media personnel, and includes media professionals, representatives from the classroom teachers, one or more parents, and one or more students.
6. The review committee takes the following steps after receiving the challenged materials:

a. reads, views, or listens to the material in its entirety;
b. checks general acceptance of the material by reading reviews and consulting recommended lists;
c. determines the extent to which the material supports the curriculum;
d. completes the appropriate "Checklist for School Media Advisory Committee's Reconsideration of Instructional Material" (see Appendixes B and C), judging the material for its strength and value as a whole and not in part.
7. Present written recommendation of review committee to the superintendent and the school board.
8. Retain or withdraw challenged materials as mandated by the decision of the school board.

   (Appointment of committee members and specific procedures to follow should be made in accordance with local policy. The steps listed above are given as a model to be used in development of local policies and are not suggested as the only procedures which are effective. A procedures policy should include these steps.)

REFERENCES

1. American Association of School Librarians, ALA, and Association for Educational Communications and Technology, *Media Programs: District and School* (Chicago: American Library Assn., 1975), p.1.

2. Council of the American Library Association, *The Library Bill of Rights* (Chicago: American Library Assn., 1967).

3. National Council of Teachers of English, *The Students' Right to Read* (Urbana, Ill.: National Council of Teachers of English, 1972).

IV. APPENDIX A

Request for Reconsideration of Instructional Materials *(Sample)*

School _____

Please check type of material:
( ) Book	( ) Film	( ) Record
( ) Periodical	( ) Filmstrip	( ) Kit
( ) Pamphlet	( ) Cassette	( ) Other

Title _____

Author _____

Publisher or Producer _____

Request initiated by _____

Telephone _____ Address _____

City _____ State _____ Zip _____

The following questions are to be answered after the complainant has read, viewed, or listened to the school library material in its entirety. If sufficient space is not provided, attach additional sheets. (Please sign your name to each additional attachment.)

1. To what in the material do you object? (Please be specific, cite pages, frames in a filmstrip, film sequence, et cetera.)

    _____

    _____

    _____

2. What do you believe is the theme or purpose of this material?

    _____

    _____

    _____

3. What do you feel might be the result of a student using this material?

    _____

    _____

    _____

4. For what age group would you recommend this material?

    _____

5. Is there anything good in this material? Please comment.

    _____

    _____

6. Would you care to recommend other school library material of the same subject and format?

_____

_____   _____
Signature of Complainant   Date

Please return _completed_ form to the school principal.

V. APPENDIX B

Checklist for School Media Advisory Committee's Reconsideration of Instructional Material—Nonfiction _(Sample)_

Title _____

Author _____

A. Purpose
   1. What is the overall purpose of the material? _____

_____

   2. Is the purpose accomplished? _____ Yes _____ No.

B. Authenticity
   1. Is the author competent and qualified in the field? _____ Yes _____ No.
   2. What is the reputation and significance of the author and publisher/producer in the field?

_____

_____

   3. Is the material up-to-date? _____ Yes _____ No.
   4. Are information sources well documented? _____ Yes _____ No.
   5. Are translations and retellings faithful to the original? _____ Yes _____ No.

C. Appropriateness
   1. Does the material promote the educational goals and objectives of the curriculum of District Schools? _____ Yes _____ No.
   2. Is it appropriate to the level of instruction intended? _____ Yes _____ No.
   3. Are the illustrations appropriate to the subject and age levels? _____ Yes _____ No.

D. Content
   1. Is the content of this material well presented by providing adequate scope, range, depth and continuity? _____ Yes _____ No.
   2. Does this material present information not otherwise available? _____ Yes _____ No.
   3. Does this material give a new dimension or direction to its subject? _____ Yes _____ No.

E. Reviews
   1. Source of review _____
      Favorably reviewed _____   Unfavorably reviewed _____
   2. Does this title appear in one or more reputable selection aids? _____ Yes
      _____ No. If answer is yes, please list titles of selection aids.

_____

_____

Additional Comments

_____

_____

_____

Recommendation by School Media Advisory Committee for Treatment of Challenged Materials

_____

_____

_____

_____

                                        Date _____

Signature of Media Advisory Review Committee

_____   _____

_____   _____

_____   _____

VI. APPENDIX C

Checklist for School Media Advisory Committee's Reconsideration of Instructional Material—Fiction and Other Literary Forms *(Sample)*

Title _____

Author _____

A. Purpose
   1. What is the purpose, theme or message of the material? How well does the author/producer/composer accomplish this purpose?

_____

_____

_____

   2. If the story is fantasy, is it the type that has imaginative appeal and is suitable for children? _____ Yes _____ No; for young adults? _____ Yes _____ No. If both are marked no, for what age group would you recommend?
   3. Will the reading and/or viewing and/or listening to material result in more compassionate understanding of human beings? _____ Yes _____ No.

4. Does it offer an opportunity to better understand and appreciate the aspirations, achievements, and problems of various minority groups? ___ Yes ___ No.
5. Are any questionable elements of the story an integral part of a worthwhile theme or message? _____ Yes _____ No.

B. Content
1. Does a story about modern times give a realistic picture of life as it is now? _____ Yes _____ No.
2. Does the story avoid an oversimplified view of life, one which leaves the reader with the general feeling that life is sweet and rosy or ugly and meaningless? _____ Yes _____ No.
3. When factual information is part of the story, is it presented accurately? _____ Yes _____ No.
4. Is prejudicial appeal readily identifiable by the potential reader? _____ Yes _____ No.
5. Are concepts presented appropriate to the ability and maturity of the potential readers? _____ Yes _____ No.
6. Do characters speak in a language true to the period and section of the country in which they live? _____ Yes _____ No.
7. Does the material offend in some special way the sensibilities of women or a minority group by the way it presents either the chief character or any of the minor characters? _____ Yes _____ No.
8. Is there preoccupation with sex, violence, cruelty, brutality, and aberrant behavior that would make this material inappropriate for children? _____ Yes _____ No; young adults? _____ Yes _____ No.
9. If there is use of offensive language, is it appropriate to the purpose of the text for children? _____ Yes _____ No; for young adults? _____ Yes _____ No.
10. Is the material free from derisive names and epithets that would offend minority groups? _____ Yes _____ No.
11. Is the material well written or produced? _____ Yes _____ No.
12. Does the story give a broader understanding of human behavior without stressing differences of class, race, color, sex, education, religion or philosophy in any adverse way? _____ Yes _____ No.
13. Does the material make a significant contribution to the history of literature or ideas? _____ Yes _____ No.
14. Are the illustrations appropriate and in good taste? _____ Yes _____ No.
15. Are the illustrations realistic in relation to the story? _____ Yes _____ No.

Additional Comments

_____

_____

_____

_____

Recommendation by School Media Advisory Committee for Treatment of Challenged Materials

_____

_____

_____

_____

_____
                                    Date _____
Signature of Media Advisory Review Committee

_____   _____

_____   _____

_____   _____

VII. APPENDIX D

American Association of School Librarians Statement on *Library Bill of Rights*

The American Association of School Librarians endorses the *Library Bill of Rights* of the American Library Association. (See Appendix Three.)

APPENDIX TWO
Standards for Library Collections

Guidelines for Two-Year
College Learning Resources
Programs (1972)

Statement on Quantitative
Standards for Two-Year
Learning Resources
Programs (1979)

Standards for College
Libraries (1975)

Standards for University
Libraries (1979)

Media Programs: District
and School (1975, 1977)

GUIDELINES FOR TWO-YEAR COLLEGE LEARNING RESOURCES PROGRAMS (1972)

Association of College and Research Libraries

D. Materials

1. *Materials are selected, acquired, designed, or produced on the basis of institutional and instructional objectives, developed by the faculty, students, and administration in cooperation with Learning Resources.*

A written statement regarding acquisition and production of learning materials has such an important and pervasive effect upon

Reprinted by permission of the American Library Association.

the instructional program and the services of the Learning Resources Program that all segments of the academic community should be involved in its development. The statement should be readily available in an official publication.

Learning Resources Programs provide materials presenting all sides of controversial issues. The position of the American Library Association, and comparable associations, on the subject of censorship is firmly adhered to.

2. *Materials may be acquired and made available from a variety of sources.*

In an effort to meet the needs of the instructional process and cultural enrichment, it will be necessary to acquire materials through:

    a. purchase of commercially available materials;
    b. lease or rental of materials where purchase is neither possible nor practical in terms of cost, utilization, or type;
    c. loan through free loan agencies;
    d. acquisition of materials as gifts;
    e. design and production of materials not readily available.

3. *Materials must be accessible to authorized individuals.*

Although there is no uniformly accepted system to make all resources available, the materials must be properly organized and the necessary staff, facilities, and hardware provided. Highly sophisticated systems for computer, video, and audio access for retrieving, manipulating, and displaying information might be necessary.

4. *Final management decision as to the order in which materials are to be purchased or produced is the responsibility of the chief administrator or his delegated subordinate.*

Within the established framework of the written statement on acquisition and production, and the budgetary restraints, the final management decision and priority judgment must be the responsibility of the chief administrator and his duly designated subordinates.

5. *Representative works of high caliber which might arouse intellectual curiosity, counteract parochialism, help to develop critical thinking and cultural appreciation, or stimulate use of the resources for continuing education and personal development are included in the collection even though they do not presently meet direct curricular needs.*

One function of higher education is to develop adult citizens intellectually capable of taking their places in a changing society. Provision of materials beyond curricular needs is essential for this goal.

6. *Materials reflect ages, cultural backgrounds, intellectual levels, developmental needs, and vocational goals represented in the student body.*

Two-year college students represent all strata of community and national life. To meet their needs, the collection must contain materials of all kinds and at all levels. Those students who require basic remedial materials, those who seek vocational and technical training or retraining, those who seek an understanding of their culture, and those who are utilizing their retirement years for personal stimulation should each find the materials which can serve their interests and solve their problems. Special care is taken to include representative materials related to the needs of cultural or racial minorities as well as materials reflecting divergent social, religious, or political viewpoints.

7. *A board policy is developed concerning gifts to a Learning Resources Program.*

Generally, gifts are accepted only when they add strength to the collection and impose no significant limitations on housing, handling, or disposition of duplicate, damaged, or undesirable items. It is recognized that gifts frequently require more time to screen, organize, catalog, and process than new materials. Storage space and staff time requirements must be considered in accepting gift materials. In acknowledgment of gifts, attention should be called to government recognition of such contributions for tax purposes, as well as to the impropriety of any appraisal by the recipient of a donation.

8. *In local reproduction of materials for instructional use, care is taken to comply with copyright regulations.*

Laws restrict the copying of many items without permission. Procedures and guidelines must be established regarding reproduction of copyrighted materials and made easily accessible.

9. *The reference collection includes a wide selection of significant subject and general bibliographies, authoritative lists, periodical indexes, and standard reference works in all fields of knowledge.*

Every two-year college requires extensive bibliographical materials for use in locating and verifying items for purchase, rental, or borrowing, for providing for subject needs of users, and for evaluating the collection.

10. *Newspapers with various geographical, political, and social points of view on national and state issues are represented in the collection.*

Newspapers should reflect community, national, and worldwide points of view. Back files of several newspapers are retained in print or microform.

11. *Government documents are required as significant sources of information.*

Some two-year colleges which are document depositories receive government publications as a matter of course. All Learning Resources Programs should acquire regularly such publications.

12. *Files of pamphlets and other ephemeral materials are maintained.*

An effective and up-to-date pamphlet file is a strong resource in any college. Included are vocational and ephemeral materials developed through systematic acquisition of new materials, including subscriptions to pamphlet services and requests for free materials. References in the catalog to subjects contained in pamphlet files are desirable in providing the fullest access to the materials. Periodic weeding of the collection is essential.

Manufacturers' and publishers' catalogs and brochures which describe new materials and equipment are needed to supplement published lists and to provide up-to-date information.

13. *A collection of recorded and other materials should be available for individual use as well as for meeting instructional needs.*

14. *The conservation of materials, as well as the elimination of those which are obsolete, should be developed as part of on-going procedures.*

The materials in the collection should be examined regularly to eliminate obsolete items, unnecessary duplicates, and worn-out materials. Prompt attention must be given to damaged materials so that repairs and replacement (including rebinding of printed materials or replacement of portions of projected or recorded materials) are handled systematically, along with prompt action to replace important items, including those discovered to be missing.

15. *The Learning Resources Unit functions as an archive for historical information and documents concerning the college itself.*

An effort should be made to locate, organize, and house institutional archives to the extent defined by the administration.

STATEMENT ON QUANTITATIVE STANDARDS FOR TWO-YEAR LEARNING RESOURCES PROGRAM (1979)

Collection Size

Size of the collection available on any two-year college campus is best expressed as "bibliographical unit equivalents." Where a multi-campus district maintains some materials centrally, these holdings should be distributed for statistical purposes proportional to use by the various campuses.

Bibliographical unit equivalents (BUE) consist of written, recorded, or other materials. Each item in the following three groups is one BUE.

Written Materials

1. One cataloged bound volume.
2. One periodical volume.
3. One cataloged document.
4. One reel of microfilm.
5. One cataloged microfiche.
6. Five uncataloged microfiche.
7. Five microcards.
8. One cataloged musical work.
9. One periodical currently received.

Recorded Materials

10. One videocassette or videotape reel.
11. One reel of 16mm motion picture film.
12. One cataloged 8mm loop film.
13. One cataloged 35mm slide program.
14. One cataloged set of transparencies.
15. One cataloged slide set or filmstrip.
16. Fifty cataloged 2 x 2 slides, not in sets.
17. One cataloged sound recording (disc, reel, or cassette).
18. Five films rented or borrowed during an academic year.

Other Materials

19. One cataloged map, chart, art print, or photograph.
20. One cataloged kit.

TABLE 2   Collection Size

| FTE Enrollment | Level | Written Materials | | Recorded Materials | | Other Materials | BUE Collection Size Totals |
		Periodical Subscriptions	Other Written Materials	Motion Pictures & Videotapes	Other Recorded Materials		
Under 1,000	M	200	20,000	15	350	50	20,615
	G	300	30,000	125	1,350	350	32,125
1,000–3,000	M	300	30,000	125	1,350	350	32,125
	G	500	50,000	350	3,200	1,200	55,250
3,000–5,000	M	500	50,000	350	3,200	1,200	55,250
	G	700	70,000	700	5,350	2,350	79,100
5,000–7,000	M	700	70,000	700	5,350	2,350	79,100
	G	800	85,000	1,250	8,500	4,500	100,100
Additional each 1,000 FTE over 7,000	M	5	6,000	13	10	5	6,133
	G	30	12,000	150	405	305	12,890

21. One cataloged item of realia, model, or art object.
22. Any other comparable cataloged item(s).

Table 2 shows the total number of BUEs used to measure the collection. Normally, written materials should constitute at least 70 percent of the BUEs. All other proportions of the totals may be adapted to the Learning Resources Program of the institution. Flexibility in determining the informational needs of the program then makes it possible to choose to purchase either a book or an audiovisual item, a periodical subscription, or any other materials. No two-year college should be without some BUEs in each of the five categories used in Table 2. Technical institutes with extremely specialized programs may reduce the total BUE requirements as much as 40 percent.

Annual Accessions

If the materials are to meet the instructional needs of the institution served, continued acquisitions accompanied by continued weeding are needed even where holdings exceed recommendations. New materials are needed for presentation of new information and new interpretations or the collection becomes dated and decreases in educational value. New courses added to the curriculum and new instructional programs require new materials to meet classroom and individual needs of students. As enrollment increases there is need for more duplication and for broader approaches to topics already represented in the collection.

Five percent of the collection size should be the minimum annual acquisition for each Learning Resources Program. This percentage does not include replacements of lost or stolen items or materials to support new courses or curricula, which should be additional.

· · · · · ·

Equipment for Distribution

There is need for sufficient equipment for distribution to classrooms beyond equipment necessary for individual utilization of audiovisuals in the learning centers. Recommendations are limited to major types of equipment. Opaque projectors should be available even in minimal programs; quantity will depend upon utilization. Overhead projectors should be available in all classrooms. Recommendations in Table 4 are for classroom equipment distribution only and assume a replacement schedule not longer than five years.

Quantitative formulas for some equipment are inherent in use. In a laboratory situation, type and quantity of equipment will depend upon what the course or program is. Permanent sound and projection equipment will be installed in large lecture halls. All classrooms will have permanently installed projection screens and room-darkening drapes or shades and will have connections and outlets for closed-circuit television where it exists.

In determining the number of pieces of equipment, a reasonable distribution of demand is assumed, i.e., that all use will not be concentrated on a peak period of either the days or the academic year. Random access or broadcast delivery systems will also affect the needs for equipment.

TABLE 4   Equipment for Distribution

Uses per year	16mm Projector	Super 8mm Projector	Video-cassette Player	Slide Projector	Audio-cassette Player	Record Player
1–100	2–9	2–9	2–9	2–24	2–49	2–9
101–1,000	10–24	10–14	10–24	25–49	50–99	10–24
1,001–3,000	25–44	15–19	25–32	50–64	100–174	25–35
3,001–5,000	45–49	20–24	33–49	65–99	175–249	36–49
5,000+	50+	25+	50+	100+	250+	50+

Production

All Learning Resources Programs should provide some production capability according to the needs and requirements of the curricula, the availability of commercial materials, and the capability of the delivery system. Production, except where part of an instructional program or meeting a specific institutional need, is not an end in itself. Neither is it related to institutional size.

Basic production capability for all campuses consists of minimal equipment items for:

Still photography (1 35mm camera and arrangements for developing film elsewhere).
Ability to make and duplicate sound recordings.

Sign production.
Graphics layout and lettering.
Laminating and dry-mounting.
Ability to make overhead transparencies.
Simple illustrations.
Videoplaying and duplication.
One-camera videotaping and videodubbing.

Intermediate production capability consists of all elements above and in addition equipment items for:

Photographic black-and-white and processing.
Ability to edit sound recordings.
Two-camera video production.

Advanced production when justified consists of all above and in addition equipment items for:

Simple studio videoproduction in color.
Simple studio for sound recording and editing.

Optional production (justifiable only when needed for programs for cooperative distribution or highly sophisticated institutional needs) in addition consists of:

Color television directing, production, and editing.
16mm motion picture directing, production, and editing.
Color photographic developing and processing.

STANDARDS FOR COLLEGE LIBRARIES (1975)

Association of College and Research Libraries

Standard 2: The Collections

2 *The library's collections shall comprise all corpuses of recorded information owned by the college for educational, inspirational, and recreational purposes, including multi-dimensional, aural, pictorial, and print materials.*

2.1 *The library shall provide quickly a high percentage of such materials needed by its patrons.*

2.1.1 *The amount of print materials to be thus provided shall be determined by a formula* (see Formula A) *which takes into account the nature and extent of the academic program of the institution, its enrollment, and the size of its teaching faculty.*

Commentary on Standard 2

The records of intellectual endeavor appear in a wide range of formats. Books represent extended reports of scholarly investigation, compilations of findings, creative works, and summaries prepared for educational purposes. The journal has become the common medium for scientific communication and usually represents more recent information. Scientific reports in near-print form are becoming an even faster means of research communication. Documents represent compilations of information prepared by governmental agencies, and newspapers contain the systematic recording of daily activities throughout the world.

Many kinds of communication can be better and sometimes faster accomplished through such non-print media as films, slides, tapes, radio and television recordings, and realia. Microphotography is an accepted means of compacting many kinds of records for preservation and storage. Recorded information may also come in the form of manuscripts, archives, and machine-readable data bases. Each medium of communication provides unique dimensions for the transmission of information and each tends to complement the others.

This inherent unity of recorded information, and the fundamental commonality of its social utility, require that regardless of format, all kinds of recorded information needed for academic purposes by an institution be selected, acquired, organized, stored, and delivered for use within the library. In this way the institution's information resources can best be articulated and balanced for the greatest benefit of the entire community.

It is less important that a college hold legal title to the quantity of library materials called for in Formula A than it be able to supply the amount quickly—say within fifteen minutes—as by contract with an adjacent institution or by some other means. An institution which arranges to meet all or part of its library responsibilities in this way, however, must take care that in doing so it not create supernumerary or unreimbursed costs for another institution and that the materials so made available are relevant to its own students' needs.

Since a library book collection once developed, and then allowed to languish, loses its utility very rapidly, continuity of collection development is essential. Experience has shown that even after collections have attained sizes required by this Standard, they can seldom retain their requisite utility without sustaining annual gross growth rates, before withdrawals, of at least five percent.

Higher education has thus far had too little experience with non-print library materials to permit tenable generalizations to be made about their quantitative requirements. Since consensus has not yet been attained among educators as to the range, extent, and configuration of non-print services which it is appropriate for college libraries to offer, no generally applicable formulas are possible here. It is assumed, however, that every college library should have non-print resources appropriate to institutional needs.

The goal of college library collection development should be quality rather than quantity. A collection may be said to have quality for its purpose only to the degree that it possesses a portion of the bibliography of each discipline taught, appropriate in quantity both to the level at which each is taught and to the number of students and faculty members who use it. Quality and quantity are separable only in theory: it is possible to have quantity without quality; it is not possible to have quality without quantity defined in relation to the purposes of the institution. No easily applicable criteria have been developed, however, for measuring quality in library collections.

The best way to assure quality in a college library collection is to gain it at point of input. Thus rigorous discimination in the selection of materials to be added to the library's holdings, whether as purchases or gifts, is of considerable importance. Care should be exerted to select a substantial portion of the titles listed in the standard, scholarly bibliographies reflecting the curriculum areas of the college and supporting general fields of knowledge. A number of such subject lists for college libraries have been prepared by learned associations. Among general bibliographies *Books for College Libraries* is useful especially for purposes of identifying important retrospective titles. For current additions, provision should be made to acquire a majority of the significant new publications reviewed in *Choice*. Generous attention should be given also to standard works of reference and to bibliographical tools which provide access to the broad range of scholarly sources as listed in [Sheehy's] *Guide to Reference Books*. Institutional needs vary so widely for periodical holdings that quantitative standards cannot be written for them at this time, but in general it is good practice for a library to own any title that is needed more than six times per year. Several good handlists have been prepared of periodical titles appropriate for college collections.

College library collections should be evaluated continuously against standard bibliographies and against records of their use, for purposes both of adding to the collections and identifying titles for prompt withdrawal once they have outlived their usefulness to the college program. No book should be retained in a college library for which a clear purpose is not evident in terms of the institution's current or anticipated academic program; when such clear purpose is lacking, a book should be retired from the collections.

Although in the last analysis the library staff must be responsible for the scope and content of the collections, it can best fulfill this responsibility with substantial help and consultation from the teaching faculty and from students. Of greatest benefit to the library is continuing faculty assistance in defining the literature requirements of the courses in the curriculum, definitions which should take the form of written selection policies. In addition, members of the teaching faculty may participate in the selection of individual titles to be obtained. If this latter activity, however, is carried out largely by the library, then the teaching faculty should review the books acquired both for their appropriateness and the quality of their contents.

FORMULA A—
The formula for calculating the number of relevant print volumes (or microform volume-equivalents) to which the library should provide prompt access is as follows (to be calculated cumulatively):

1. Basic Collection	85,000 vols.
2. Allowance per FTE Faculty Member	100 vols.
3. Allowance per FTE Student	15 vols.
4. Allowance per Undergraduate Major or Minor Field	350 vols.
5. Allowance per Masters Field, When No Higher Degree is Offered in the Field	6,000 vols.
6. Allowance per Masters Field, When a Higher Degree is Offered in the Field	3,000 vols.

7. Allowance per 6th-year Specialist Degree Field . . . .   6,000 vols.
8. Allowance per Doctoral Field . . . .   25,000 vols.

A "volume" is defined as a physical unit of any printed, typewritten, handwritten, mimeographed, or processed work contained in one binding or portfolio, hardbound or paperbound, which has been cataloged, classified, and/or otherwise prepared for use. For purposes of this calculation microform holdings should be included by converting them to volume-equivalents. The number of volume-equivalents held in microform should be determined by actual count or by an averaging formula which considers each reel of microform as one, and five pieces of any other microformat as one volume-equivalent.

Libraries which can provide promptly 100 percent as many volumes or volume-equivalents as are called for in this formula shall, in the matter of quantity, be graded A. From 80–99 percent shall be grade B; from 65–79 percent shall be graded C; and from 50–64 percent shall be graded D.

STANDARDS FOR UNIVERSITY LIBRARIES (1979)

Association of College and Research Libraries

Section B: Collections

Standard B.1

A university library's collections shall be of sufficient size and scope to support the university's total instructional needs and to facilitate the university's research programs.

Commentary on Standard B.1

A university library should provide all of the resources that are necessary for direct support of the university's full instructional programs at both the undergraduate and the graduate levels. If these resources are not readily available in the library, the instructional programs cannot be carried out successfully. These resources include required and assigned readings, reference and bibliographical materials, basic journals and serials, as well as any other library materials that undergraduate or graduate students are expected to be able to consult readily in their courses of study, or in the preparation of theses and dissertations.

Weak collections can hamper research. The accumulation and preservation of substantial collections and the implementation of comprehensive acquisition programs must be recognized as providing a resource whose presence within a university is essential to the conditions under which knowledge is effectively increased and transmitted. It is clear that no university library can be expected to possess in its collection all of the recorded information which faculty or doctoral students may need to consult as they pursue their research. Nevertheless, it is essential that collections be of such size, scope, and quality that they promote rather than restrict research. While every library should take care to develop collections whose areas of concentration reflect and support the academic priorities and strengths within the university, interlibrary arrangements, which have long been established for the mutual support of exceptional research needs, must continue to be relied upon to supplement even the most comprehensive research collections.

The continued rapid growth of scholarly literature and the costs of providing access to this literature for those in the university community have necessitated formal and informal arrangements among libraries to ensure maximum access to this literature. Common methods of sharing resources and improving access have been loans between libraries, provision of visiting privileges for scholars, agreements on the acquisitions of materials, and sharing of bibliographic information.

While interlibrary cooperation, as presently practiced, may not promise large cost savings in the immediate future, significant improved methods of supplementing local resources are in the active planning stages. University libraries must participate in the development of these new access mechanisms to ensure that local, regional, national, and international interests are effectively served.

Attempts have been made to identify precise quantitative measures of adequate collection size and growth rates for a university library. No such formula has yet been developed which can be generally applied. At present, such formulas as exist can only yield approximations which indicate a general level of need. If they are applied arbitrarily and mechanically, they can distort the realities of a given situation. Nevertheless, quantitative measures are increasingly important in guiding the qualitative judgment that must ultimately be applied to university libraries and their collections. One technique is the use of regression analysis to facilitate the comparison of similar libraries to one another; another of some general applicability is the "index of quality" developed by the American Council on Education for relating library collection size to graduate program quality.

Standard B.2

A university library's collections shall be developed systematically and consistently within the terms of explicit and detailed policies.

Commentary on Standard B.2

Given the great breadth of university library collections and the wide variations in depth of collections among subjects held, it is essential that there be a collections development policy to guide the selection and acquisition of materials.

By establishing such a policy, librarians seek to ensure that the library's collections are planned and developed in relation to the university's academic, research, and service goals and priorities and within the limits of resources available.

Working in close consultation with faculty and administration, librarians, particularly subject specialists, should assume the responsibility for drafting and implementing this policy.

Recognizing the inherent difficulties in collection development, it is imperative that the library have full and continuous access to information about all developments, actual and planned, in the academic, research, and service programs of the university and its components which affect the library.

Once codified, the library's collection development policy should be made known to and endorsed by the university faculty and administration. To ensure that this policy reflects changes within the university, the policy should be regularly and carefully reviewed.

Standard B.3

A university library's collections shall contain all of the varied forms of recorded information.

Commentary on Standard B.3

The university library has traditionally been recognized as the repository within the university for the printed information needed to support the university's instructional and research programs. As recorded information becomes increasingly available in a variety of nonprint formats, such as films, sound recordings, and video tapes, it is appropriate that this material, except where needed exclusively for classroom use, also be acquired, organized, and made available through the university library.

MEDIA PROGRAMS: DISTRICT AND SCHOOL (1975, 1977)

Prepared by the American Association of School Librarians, ALA and Association for Educational Communications and Technology

6. Collections

Strong media collections provide the primary means for teaching, learning, and interest fulfillment. A school's media collection represents the essential informational base of the instructional program. Media professionals contribute expertise in evaluating and selecting materials and equipment to the process of building and maintaining adequate collections.

Guiding Principles

1. Every school, regardless of size, has its own collection of materials and equipment. This collection, which is organized and ready for use when the school opens, is developed and expanded on a planned basis.
2. The district provides collections of materials and equipment, such as 16mm films, professional materials, and examination collections of new materials, to supplement collections in the individual schools.
3. Selection of collections is guided by a selection policy formulated by media staff, administrators, consultants, teachers, students, and representative citizens, and adopted by the board of education. The district policy is supplemented by selection and acquisitions guidelines formulated by individual schools within the district.
4. Selection of materials is a cooperative process involving the media staff, curriculum consultants, teachers, students, and community representatives and is coordinated by the director of the district media program and the head of the school media program respectively.
5. Materials and equipment are evaluated prior to purchase by use of reliable evaluative selection tools and by firsthand examination, wherever possible.
6. Collections are reevaluated continuously to insure that they remain current and responsive to user needs.

7. Organization and arrangement make the collection easily accessible to users.
8. Materials in print, visual, auditory, and tactile formats, with associated equipment, constitute the collection.
9. Collections include textbooks and related instructional materials and systems.
10. Current professional materials for faculty and staff use are a part of the collection.

School media personnel assume responsibility for insuring that users have ready access to the materials and equipment they need or want. Ready and convenient access is the essence of media program development, matching interests or desires with one or more of a broad range of media, with confidence in the power generated by the union of user and material. The special training and skills of media personnel provide leadership in building a relevant, diverse collection, in making it accessible, and in supplying services that enhance the quality of participants' experiences as they relate their involvement in media to their own fulfillment.

The user's first point of convenient access to materials is the media center in his own school. No substitute can replace the individual school collection in guaranteeing a high degree of user satisfaction, but it is unrealistic to claim that any school can provide within its own walls all of the materials and equipment that users need. The media staff takes the initiative in obtaining needed information and material from other sources, using interlibrary loans from other schools, school district media collections, local public libraries, college and university libraries, and regional, state, and national networks.

Sharing of materials between schools is a cooperative venture. Leadership emanates from the district media program, but cooperative approaches in collections development rest upon joint planning in which each participating school assumes responsibility for building strong collections in specific subject areas and/or for developing specified holdings of periodicals and pamphlets in microform editions, with accompanying provisions for sharing these materials with other schools.

Identification and organization of information on available community resources, both human and material, is another approach by which users' needs are staisfied.

Selection Policies and Procedures

Formulation of a district media selection policy which guides the selection of materials and equipment is coordinated by the director of the district media program. This policy, developed cooperatively with representation of media staff, administrators, consultants, teachers, students, and other community members, is adopted by the board of education as official district policy.

The media selection policy reflects basic factors influencing the nature and scope of collections, such as curriculum trends, innovations in instruction, research in learning, availability of materials and equipment, the increased sophistication of youth, and the rising expectations of teachers and students. It establishes the objectives of media selection; identifies personnel participating in selection and their roles; enumerates types of materials and equipment to be considered with criteria for their evaluation, as well as criteria for evaluating materials in specific subject areas; and defines procedures followed in selecting materials, including initial selection, reexamination of titles in existing collections, and handling challenged titles.

The selection policy reflects and supports principles of intellectual freedom described in the *Library Bill of Rights*,[1] the *School Library Bill of Rights for School Library Media Center Programs*,[2] *The Students' Right to Read*,[3] and other professional statements on intellectual freedom. Procedures for handling questioned materials follow established guidelines and are clearly defined.[4]

The district selection policy is supplemented by selection and acquisitions guidelines formulated by each school which provide more detailed and specific guidance for building and maintaining the school's collections.

Basic to effective selection is the establishment of cooperatively developed priorities that consider the existing collection and identify its strengths, gaps, and pertinency. Selection of materials involves the media staff, administrators, curriculum consultants, teachers, and students, with the process coordinated by the head of the school media program.

Building a collection calls for careful planning; understanding of the school program and the interests, abilities, and problems of the population; broad current knowledge of materials available and the related equipment; and an understanding of the district selection policy and budgeting procedures. It also requires objective judgments, discriminating taste, and a sensitivity to the needs and

---

[1]The *Library Bill of Rights* was adopted by the Council of American Library Association in 1948 and amended in 1961 and 1967.

[2]The *School Library Bill of Rights for School Library Media Center Programs* was approved by the American Association of School Librarians in 1969.

[3]National Council of Teachers of English, *The Student's Right to Read* (Urbana, Ill.: National Council of Teachers of English, 1972.)

[4]"Intellectual Freedom and School Libraries; An In-Depth Case Study." *School Media Quarterly*, 1:111–35 (Winter 1973).

concerns of learners and teachers. Continuous reassessment, both of the program priorities and the appropriateness of the collection, insures an adequate response to changing programs, populations, and opportunities.

Examination and Evaluation of Media

The process of examining and evaluating materials and equipment being considered for purchase is continuous and systematic. The district media program supports the selection process by providing examination collections of materials and equipment, arranging for released time for preview and examination of materials, and conducting an active evaluation program involving media personnel, teachers, other staff, and students. Published evaluations, including those in reviews, recommended lists, and standard bibliographic tools are used in selection. Materials and equipment within existing collections are monitored and examined continuously in order to replace worn items and to withdraw out-of-date and inappropriate items.

District Collections

The school district through the district media program provides for individual schools additional materials or equipment which meet one or more of the following criteria:

> Too expensive for each school to afford in sufficient quantity, i.e., 16mm films
> Infrequently used
> Rare, e.g., certain specimens and museum objects not available in duplicate
> Needed on a temporary basis, e.g., equipment to replace school-owned equipment being repaired
> Provided for examination and consideration for purchase, e.g., new materials and equipment included in a district educational media selection center.

Films, Videotapes, and Related Collections

Through its own collection or through participation in a multidistrict film library program, the district media program provides access for individual schools to at least 3,000 titles, with sufficient duplicate prints to satisfy 90 percent of all requests. This is a minimal figure and access to additional titles up to a total of 5,000 titles may be needed. In addition, sufficient funds are provided for purchase and/or rental of new and specialized titles as needed throughout the year. Selection of materials in 16mm or video format is based on quality of image, utilization mode, size of intended viewing audience, availability of materials and equipment, and cost of changeover from one format to the other.

Professional Materials

The district professional library gives administrators, curriculum consultants, teachers, media professionals, and other district and school staff convenient access to professional materials by which to keep informed of trends, developments, techniques, research, and experimentation in general and specialized areas of education. It includes works in such related subjects as communications, sociology, anthropology, behavioral psychology, the humanities, linguistics, and philosophy. Information sources may include books and pamphlets, government documents, journals, films, filmstrips, videotapes, and audiotapes. The collection of professional materials provided at the district level is complemented by smaller, working collections in individual schools.

The professional library also includes the following types of resources:

Curriculum materials, including courses of study, curriculum guides, resource units, and teacher's manuals

Selection tools that index, evaluate, and review instructional materials

Television and radio program guides and manuals

Indexes of community resources including catalogs and brochures of sites of educational value and field trip evaluations

Information on teachers' organizations and associations, forthcoming meetings, and programs for continuing education.

Media Selection and Evaluation Center

The district media program supports the selection of materials and equipment by individual school media programs by providing examination collections of materials and equipment, arranging for released time for school personnel to preview and examine materials, and conducting an active evaluation program that involves media personnel, teachers, curriculum consultants, and other users.

The media selection center staff facilitates the evaluation process through these activities:

Collection and organization of materials for examination

Capture and dissemination of published evaluations of media

Development and provision of improved criteria and data forms to gather responses from users

Arranging for user evaluations (assignment of persons and media, assistance and guidance)

Collecting and organizing the resulting date and dissemination of the findings on a timely basis.[5]

School Collections

The collection in each school is rich in breadth and depth of content and represents varied types of materials, points of view, and forms of expression. It provides a broad range of media formats and meets the requirements of all curriculum areas, accommodating diverse learning skills and styles of users at varying maturity and ability levels.

Funds provided for media center collections are sufficient to enable the school media program to meet accepted standards for the collection, secure additional materials and equipment needed for changing curricula and student populations, and maintain the collection in satisfactory condition.

Capital outlay funds provided for new schools establish initial collections ready for use when the school opens. Allocations in addition to the usual operating funds are essential to expand collections in new and reorganized schools. Higher than average per pupil allocations are required for schools with small enrollments, changing needs, or special programs that require extensive materials and resources.

The primary factors in building a school media collection are the requirements of the instructional program and the needs and interests of users. Budgeting practices provide for flexibility in the choice of media formats, with proper relationships between collections, staff requirements, and physical facilities, particularly space required for the use and storage of materials and equipment, rationally derived. Other considerations include the packaging or repackaging of items to increase durability, the assembling of kits of materials that complement or enhance each other, and the transferring of content from one format to another.

A single model for the collection of materials and equipment is not presented here, since decisions concerning amounts of materials, their formats, and quantities of supporting equipment are made on the basis of program and user needs. However, these guidelines do

[5]Cora Paul Bomar, M. Ann Heidbreder, and Carol A. Nemeyer, *Guide to the Development of Educational Media Selection Centers* (ALA Studies in Librarianship, no. 4 [Chicago: American Library Assn., 1973]), p. 30.

identify base quantities of materials and associated equipment needed to insure adequate provisions for content coverage, range in levels, and choice of media formats, responding to general information needs and personal interests and preferences.

It is recommended that a school with 500 or fewer students have a minimum collection of 20,000 items or 40 per student. An item is defined as a book (casebound or paperback), film, videotape, filmstrip, transparency, slide, periodical subscription, kit, any other form of material, or associated equipment. It is possible that the collection in larger schools may provide the needed range in content, levels, forms of expression, and formats at a ratio of less than 40 items per student.

Recommendations recognize the need to obtain materials and equipment that supplement items provided within the individual school. Access to additional collections is recommended and can be achieved only through arrangements designed to guarantee availability of a broader choice of media, as, for example, planning for the school population to use a public library which offers breadth and depth in collections. Cooperative relationships that prescribe both the means by which to implement interlibrary loans and the measure of the adequacy of such provisions are essential. Similarly, planning for the use of any community, school district, or multidistrict resource should include adequate guarantees for a high degree of satisfaction of users' needs.

The recommended base collection for the media program in the individual school, with accompanying suggestions for achieving excellence in meeting user needs, follows. The total number of items in the lower range is less than the recommended minimum of 20,000 items, while the total number in the higher range is greater. Final decisions about the mix of materials, including actual quantities in each category, are made in the individual school. The development of the media collection is based on program goals and characteristics of the school and reflects needs, prior action, and resources. The recommendations which follow provide a continuum leading to excellence in meeting student needs.

Collections: Recommendations for Meeting User Needs

Base Collection in the School	*Extended Provisions*
Note: Base recommendations are presented for a school with 500 or fewer users, and represent items located within the school.	*Note:* Recommendations for access to collections beyond the school call for planned arrangements that guarantee a high degree of user satisfaction.

TOTAL COLLECTION
At least 20,000 items located in the
  school
  or
40 items per user

     There is no limit to potential user need and therefore no justifiable quantitative limit to the size of a collection. Beyond the recommended base, the budget permits expansion of the collection when needs arise.

     The media staff obtains for users additional items available from local, regional, state, and federal agencies.

PRINT MATERIALS: *Books, Periodicals and Newspapers, Pamphlets, Microforms*

Books

8,000 to 12,000 volumes
  or
16 to 24 per user

     Access to 60,000 titles to insure satisfaction of 90 percent of initial requests

Considerations in making choices:

1. The collection provides for subject, interest, and reference coverage, multiple reading and maturity levels in each subject area, and representation of varying points of view.
2. Titles are selected on the basis of such established elements of evaluation as appeal and value for users, accuracy, currency, style, and quality of format.
3. Sufficient duplication of titles is provided to satisfy user demands.
4. Paperback books are purchased to satisfy heavy demands for particular titles, to provide less-used titles in an inexpensive format, and to respond to user preferences.

Periodicals and Newspapers

50 to 175 titles

     Access to research capability in periodical/newspaper literature, by purchasing microform collections, by photocopying, and/or interlibrary loan

Considerations in making choices:

Base Collection in the School	*Extended Provisions*

1. The collection supports the curriculum, caters to the interests of users, represents different points of view, provides intellectual and aesthetic stimulation, and responds to the professional needs of teachers.
2. Appropriate indexes are provided for magazine and newspaper holdings.
3. Magazines and newspapers that contribute to satisfaction of user needs are considered for acquisition although they may not be indexed.
4. Back issues of selected periodicals are readily available in the media center. Holdings that extend back more than five years are retained, discarded, or replaced by microform editions, according to needs.
5. Local, state, national, and international newspapers are represented in the collection.
6. Duplicate titles are provided for periodicals in heavy demand.

Pamphlets

The type and quantity vary according to program needs

Use of depository libraries provides access to extensive holdings of government documents

Considerations in making choices:
1. The collection includes state, national, and international government documents, which represent important sources of information.
2. Items in the collection are useful, current, and varied in points of view.
3. Persons or organizations responsible for the publication are clearly identified on items included in the collection.
4. Free and inexpensive materials, selected with care, are included as appropriate. Simplified order procedures permit rapid acquisition of free and inexpensive materials.
5. Much time and effort are required to maintain and index a clipping file; preferred alternatives include increasing periodical subscriptions and/or indexes and use of commercial clipping services, if needed.

Microforms: Microfilm, Microcard, and Microfiche

Types and quantity vary with program needs.

User access to extensive microform data bases, e.g., Educational Resources Information Center (ERIC), Human Relations Area Files (HRAF), etc.

Cooperative approaches among schools in collection-building, with accompanying arrangements for inter-library loans and/or photocopying

Base Collection in the School	Extended Provisions

Microform Equipment: Readers and Printers

2 readers, 1 of which is portable, plus 1 reader-printer	Sufficient number of readers (portable and stationary) and reader-printers to satisfy user needs

Considerations in making choices:
1. Microforms are important sources for primary source materials, back issues of periodicals, and government documents.
2. Factors of use, need for subject matter, technical quality, and availability of equipment are considered in purchasing microforms.
3. Provisions for appropriate indexing, storage, and equipment are made to insure easy and dependable retrieval of items in microform formats.
4. Equipment selection is based on quality of image reproduction, ease of operation, and durability.
5. Both portable and stationary equipment is provided.

VISUAL MATERIALS: *Still Images*

Filmstrips: Sound and Silent

500 to 2,000 items or 1 to 4 items per user	Access to sufficient items to insure satisfaction of 90 percent of initial requests In individualized programs in which students work with this format, a collection of 5,000 items is recommended.

Filmstrip Equipment: Silent and Sound Projectors and Viewers

10 projectors and 30 viewers	One projector per teacher and one viewer per three users

Considerations in making choices:
1. Filmstrips meet accepted criteria for accuracy and scope of content, organization, and technical qualities. In addition they have user appeal and are appropriate in treatment for the intended use, i.e., self-directed use or teacher presentation.
2. Sound filmstrips selected for the collection have appropriate relationships between visual and auditory content.
3. Packaging of the filmstrip(s) and related materials is convenient for effective use and storage. Choices between alternative formats for audio reproduction are based on the same considerations.
4. The relative emphasis given to sound versus silent projectors and viewers is based on the nature of the collection and predominant patterns of use.

Base Collection in the School	Extended Provisions

5. Remote control attachments are provided to promote effective use and interaction in group settings.

Slides and Transparencies

2,000 to 6,000 items	Access to 15,000 items, including
or	specialized subject collections, as
4 to 12 items per user	needed in relation to instructional
	and user interests

Slide and Transparency Equipment

Slide projectors: 6, or	Sufficient slide projectors to
1 for every 100 users.	satisfy user demands plus
Slide viewers: 10, or	additional dissolve units and
1 for every 50 users.	synchronizers for displays
Overhead projectors: 10,* or	Additional overhead projectors
1 for every 50 users.	available on demand from the
	district media program

*Varies with type of instructional program (see no. 6 in the following list of considerations).

Considerations in making choices:
1. Slides and transparencies are evaluated carefully for accuracy and technical qualities, including color, mounting, and (in the case of art slides) fidelity to the original. Legibility for the viewer is essential.
2. High selectivity is exercised in the purchase of sets of transparency masters.
3. Locally produced slides and transparencies are added to the collection when they meet criteria for quality and need.
4. Appropriate storage for single slides and sets of slides is provided.
5. Overhead projectors selected for the collection provide a standard 10" × 10" aperture and provide a sharp and clearly focused projected image appropriate in size for the intended use.
6. The proportion of overhead projectors needed is higher in schools with instructional patterns that emphasize teacher lecture and lower in schools that emphasize individualized and independent study approaches.
7. In the selection of slide projection equipment, care is taken to choose appropriate automatic slide projectors together with the most compatible and standardized dissolve units, synchronizers, and programming units. Choices made insure both design capability to do the job needed and ease in accomplishing it.
8. Remote control devices, as well as lenses of appropriate focal length, are acquired for slide projectors.
9. Selected slide viewers use slide trays compatible with those used with slide projectors.

Base Collection in the School	Extended Provisions

Graphics: Posters, Art and Study Prints,
Maps and Globes

800 to 1,200 items

Additional items to respond to program needs, with provision for original art, children's art, and loans of circulating collections from museums

Considerations in making choices:
1. Fidelity of reproduction to original artwork, including sharp focus and accurate color, is essential in collections of posters and art prints.
2. The collection includes examples of varied reproduction processes.
3. Items within a set of posters or prints are evaluated individually in order to determine the contribution and impact of the set as a whole.
4. Selection of maps and globes takes into account such factors as the following:
   True sizes and relationships of hemispheres are represented only through globes
   The larger the globe size, the greater the detail that can be shown
   Illumination of globes is minimally preferable
   Topographic and road maps of local areas are included in the collection
   Some maps may be provided in alternative formats, e.g., transparencies and microforms.
5. Criteria applied in evaluation of maps and globes include currency of features; appropriateness of scale; quality of drafting, engraving, and printing; clearly executed design that avoids confused appearance; clear typefaces.
6. Consideration is given to appropriate processing and storage of materials in fragile formats by such means as laminating, mounting, or framing items.

VISUAL MATERIALS: *Moving Images*

16mm and Super 8mm Sound Films,
Videotapes, and Television Reception

Access to a minimum of 3,000 titles, with sufficient duplicate prints to satisfy 90 percent of all requests

In addition, sufficient funds for rental of specialized films, including feature-length films, when needed

Availability of sufficient funds throughout the year to provide for purchase and/or rental of new and specialized titles, on demand

Access to additional titles up to a total of 5,000 titles, from district film library, may be desirable

Base Collection in the School	*Extended Provisions*

*16mm and Super 8mm Sound Projection
and Video Playback and Reception Equipment*

6 units, with 2 assigned to the media center
 plus
1 additional unit for each 100 users
 The mix of 16mm and Super 8mm sound projectors and video playback and reception units depends upon the availability of materials in each format

Additional units to satisfy use by students, individually and in small groups, and for home use
 Ratio of 1 unit per 50 users

Considerations in making choices:

1. Selection of 16mm or Super 8mm sound film or video (open-reel, cassette, and cartridge) format is based on consideration of quality of image, utilization mode, size of viewing audience, availability of materials and equipment, and cost of changeover from one format to the other.
2. Centralized collections of materials provided at the district (or multidistrict) level supply materials in sufficient depth to satisfy 90 percent of users' requests.
3. To serve the needs of film study programs, collections include frequently used feature films acquired on a long-term loan or purchase basis and/or make provisions for obtaining such films through a cooperative rental program.
4. 16mm film prints used six or more times a year in an individual school merit consideration for purchase.
5. Collections include materials produced by students and staff that meet criteria for quality and need.
6. Acquisition of Super 8mm sound films and projectors is based on careful evaluation of capability to reproduce sound and availability of appropriate materials and equipment.
7. Satisfactory condition of materials is assured by a maintenance and distribution system that checks, rewinds, cleans, and repairs each item after use.
8. Collections are evaluated continuously to identify materials requiring replacement and to withdraw obsolete items.
9. Equipment selection emphasizes adequacy and reliability of equipment and availability of servicing and repair, as well as availability of spare parts.
10. Selection of video playback and reception equipment provides for standardization of formats, to facilitate development of collections of video materials.

Base Collection in the School	*Extended Provisions*

11. Video playback equipment is selected to provide for maximum simplicity and error-free operation with a minimum of controls.
12. Selection of 16mm projectors is based on specific criteria related to the intended use of the equipment. Choice between self-threading and manual-threading projectors takes into account convenience of use and ease of operation.
13. Each school acquires at least one 16mm projector with stop-motion (still frame) mechanism.
14. It is desirable, especially for the use of feature films, to provide for location of the projector's speaker close to the projection screen. Such provision can be made by use of an extension speaker or by installation of specialized wiring systems for remote sound.
15. For auditorium projection, a projector with a high intensity light source is desirable.

Super 8mm Films, Silent

Base Collection	Extended Provisions
500 to 1,000 items or 1 to 2 per user	Access to 4,000 titles from the individual school's collection, other schools, and a supplementary collection at the district level Development of specialized subject collections to be shared by individual schools is recommended

Super 8mm Equipment

Base Collection	Extended Provisions
20 cartridge-loaded projectors and sufficient open-reel projectors to accommodate use of available films plus 1 additional projector for every 75 users	Additional projectors, the number based on program needs and availability of materials

Considerations in making choices:
1. Materials selected meet appropriate standards in projected-image quality in relation to size of intended audience.
2. Selection takes into consideration content areas—such as the sciences, physical education, and industrial education—in which this format offers potential strengths, e.g., short lengths, repeatability, and ease of use of cartridge-loaded films.
3. 8mm films produced by students and staff are incorporated in the collection on the basis of quality and need.
4. Both cartridge-loaded and open-reel films are considered for acquisition.
5. Consideration is given to standardization of Super 8mm formats used within a school and among schools sharing materials.

Base Collection in the School	*Extended Provisions*

6. Selection of Super 8mm projectors reflects attention to the durability of the equipment which is subject to heavy use, including home circulation.
7. Both cartridge-loaded and open-reel projectors are considered for purchase.
8. The stop-motion (still frame) feature is a desirable option on Super 8mm projectors.
9. Provisions are made for rear screen projection of Super 8mm films, especially for use by small groups in media centers, laboratories, and shops.

AUDITORY FORMATS

Audio Recordings: Tapes, Cassettes, Discs, and Audio Cards

1,500 to 2,000 items or 3 to 4 per user	Access to 5,000 items from the individual school's collection and loans from other sources

Audio Equipment: Tape Recorders and Record Players

30 audio reproduction units (open-reel and cassette tape recorders, stereo and monaural record players) Listening units: 1 set of earphones for each audio reproduction unit and 1 portable listening unit per 25 users	Highly individualized programs will require additional audio reproduction units, in the ratio of 1 per 5 users Access to specialized headsets to meet specific user needs may be provided from a district collection
Audio card units: available in sufficient quantity for use on a shared basis	Sufficient audio card units for permanent assignment to specific user locations

Considerations in making choices:
1. Auditory formats, offering content ranging from music to documentaries to drill materials, promote individualized development of listening skills and aural literacy.
2. Materials selected meet high standards in quality of audio reproduction, insuring intelligibility to the user.
3. Materials selected are evaluated for adequacy in fidelity, full frequency, and non-distortion of the original sound.
4. In choice of format(s), consideration is given to ease of use, availability of materials, and ability to produce recordings locally.
5. Blank tapes are provided for production of recordings by users and staff.
6. Equipment is selected carefully to insure accurate, high quality reproduction of the original sound.

Base Collection in the School	*Extended Provisions*

7. Ease of equipment operation relative to intended use is considered in selection.
8. Equipment selection insures the provision of compatible units for use in synchronized audio productions.
9. Access to editing and mixing equipment is provided for users.
10. Open-reel and cassette tape duplicating equipment, needed for extensive collections of auditory materials, is provided at the district level and may be needed also in individual schools which make extensive use of auditory materials.

Educational Broadcast Radio

5 AM and FM receivers, plus a central distribution system	Access to specialized programs through public-service broadcasting and through special sources, e.g., university and state agencies

Considerations in making choices:
1. The media program identifies, obtains, and makes available to users program information, including guides and manuals when available from producers of educational broadcasting programs.
2. In districts that provide a broadcasting station access to sub-channel carriers for instructional purposes is considered.

TACTILE FORMATS

Games and Toys

400 to 750 items	Access to a sizable district-level collection Computer access from the district level may be provided for use with simulation games

Considerations in making choices:
1. Collections include materials chosen to augment the curriculum and to stimulate user interest.
2. Both commercially produced and locally developed games and toys are considered for inclusion in the collection.
3. Selection criteria emphasize a high degree of aesthetic appeal that invites handling of the objects in the process of use.
4. The collection includes materials for individual as well as group use.
5. Games and toys are repackaged as necessary to promote convenience, durability, and appeal in intended use.

Models and Sculpture

200 to 500 items	Access to sizable collections available from the school district

Base Collection in the School	*Extended Provisions*
	and other agencies, including community resources

Considerations in making choices:
1. Models and sculpture reproductions exhibit a high degree of verisimilitude.
2. Items selected are sufficiently sturdy to withstand handling and examination by users.

Specimens

200 to 400 items	Access to larger collections available from the school district and other agencies, including loan collections from zoos and museums

Considerations in making choices:
1. The collection makes adequate provision for specimens of long-term use, short-term use, and those which may be expendable.
2. Preserved specimens are selected with consideration for exactitude of representation and motivational appeal to the user.
3. Use of live specimens, where permitted, conforms with care to the rules and recommendations of humane societies.

INSTRUCTIONAL SYSTEMS, INCLUDING TEXTBOOKS

Types and quantities vary with
program needs

Considerations in making choices:
1. Choices in instructional systems range from series of textbooks to multimedia packages of instructional materials to complex systems that combine materials and equipment in a program designed to meet precisely defined instructional objectives.
2. Emphasis is placed on the provision of a variety of instructional materials, including basic and supplementary texts and other instructional programs.
3. The organization, housing, distribution, and inventory of instructional systems, including textbooks, is recommended as a function of the school media program. This function requires the provision of one or more media aides, as needed, working with media professionals and teachers. In cases where instructional systems that include extensive hardware components are employed, a media technician may be needed to keep instructional equipment operating on a continuous basis. In addition, media center facilities will require adequate space for housing instructional systems.
4. Textbooks and other instructional programs may be assigned to individual classrooms or other locations within the school for extend-

Base Collection in the School	*Extended Provisions*

ed periods of time. Instructional packages that include a variety of materials used by students, individually, as well as in classrooms, are housed in media centers for maximum accessibility (except as they may be assigned to classrooms for periods of time).

5. Media professionals participate with classroom teachers, curriculum consultants, and other staff in the selection of appropriate instructional systems.

MISCELLANEOUS EQUIPMENT

Opaque Projectors

1 per media center
and
1 per 500 users (or 1 per floor in
  multistory building)

Microprojectors

1 per media center
and
1 or more additional per school

Quantity sufficient to meet the needs of students and teachers in courses making extensive use of microprojectors

Auditorium and Large-Group Projection Equipment

Auditorium-type 10″ x 10″
  overhead projector
Screen with antikeystone device,
  and width equal to one-sixth the
  distance between the farthest
  viewer and the screen
16mm projector(s), auditorium-
  type, with high intensity light
  source
2″ x 2″ automatic slide projector,
  with high intensity light source
All projectors equipped with lenses
  matched to projection distance
  and screen size

Projection Carts

Ratio of projection carts to items of
  equipment is based on portability
  and distribution requirements, as
  well as storage space
Cart height is appropriate to type
  of equipment and age of
  students

1 per motion picture, overhead, and opaque projector; video tape recorder; and classroom model tape recorder

Projection Screens

1 permanently mounted screen per
  teaching station, usually 70″ x 70″

Base Collection in the School	*Extended Provisions*

in size (a width of one-sixth the
distance between the farthest
viewer and the screen), with
antikeystone provisions
Additional screens of suitable size,
   as needed, for individual and
   small group use; white matte
   walls can be used as projection
   surfaces
Multi-image projection requires
   larger or multiple screening
   surfaces

Closed-Circuit Television

All new construction includes
provisions for reception of
closed-circuit television in the
media center and in each teaching
station

   Older buildings are wired for
closed-circuit television reception
when television programming is
initiated

A complete distribution system
of at least six channels is available
in a school so that broadcast TV
2500 MHZ, CATV, UHF, or VHF
can be received; signals can be
distributed to each teaching station
from the central television
reception area and/or a central
studio; signals can be fed into the
system from any teaching station;
and signals are available
simultaneously

Local Production Equipment: Additional Considerations

Note: Basic requirements include
the following items of equipment
(in addition to other items listed in
the foregoing categories).

Note: Other types of equipment
needed vary with the school and
district production programs.
Types include (but may not be
limited to) the following items.

Copying machines
   1 per media center
     and
   1 per 500 users

Duplication machines   Press(es)
   1 per media center
     and
   1 per 500 users

Dry mount press   Rotary laminator
   1 per building, with platen-size
   approximately 18″ x 23″ and
   tacking iron

Base Collection in the School	*Extended Provisions*
Paper cutters 1 cutter (30″ or 36″) in media center and Additional cutters to meet user demands	
Transparency makers 1 thermal unit (unless included in copying machines, above) 1 photocopier	Diazo printer and developer Copy camera, 8″ x 10″ Equipped darkroom
Typewriters for graphics production 1 typewriter with large (10–12 point) size type and carbon ribbon. Variable spacing is optional.	Mechanical lettering devices
Cameras and related equipment Cartridge-load slide-format camera with copy stand Super 8mm camera Light box	35mm single-lens reflex camera 35mm half-frame camera with appropriate accessories Large-format roll- or sheet-film camera, 2¼″ x 2¼″ or larger 16mm camera Programmer Dissolve unit
Videotape equipment Videotape recorder, ½″ or ¾″ Video camera(s)	Switcher, video and audio Film chain
Film and video production equipment Film splicers, 16mm and Super 8mm	Film rewind Film editors Storyboard Simple animation stand Portable chalkboard
Audiotape production equipment Tape splicers	Audiotape recorder with synchronizer Audiomixer, with monaural and stereo capacity

Base Collection in the School	*Extended Provisions*

Considerations in making choices:

1. Types and amounts of local production equipment needed in the school reflect the scope and amount of media production performed within the school and the availability of production services at the district level.
2. Specialized equipment is selected on the basis of program needs and use requirements.
3. Selection of equipment takes into consideration the alternatives currently available, reflecting changes in technology.
4. School programs that emphasize filmmaking and photography require substantial increases in the collection of school-owned cameras and related equipment.

APPENDIX THREE
Censorship

**Library Bill of Rights
Statement on Labeling
The Freedom to Read
Books and the Young Reader**

LIBRARY BILL OF RIGHTS

The American Library Association affirms that all libraries are forums for information and ideas, and that the following basic policies should guide their services.

1. Books and other library resources should be provided for the interest, information, and enlightenment of all people of the community the library serves. Materials should not be excluded because of the origin, background, or views of those contributing to their creation.
2. Libraries should provide materials and information presenting all points of view on current and historical issues. Materials should not be proscribed or removed because of partisan or doctrinal disapproval.
3. Libraries should challenge censorship in the fulfillment of their responsibility to provide information and enlightenment.
4. Libraries should cooperate with all persons and groups concerned with resisting abridgment of free expression and free access to ideas.
5. A person's right to use a library should not be denied or abridged because of origin, age, background, or views.
6. Libraries which make exhibit spaces and meeting rooms available to the public they serve should make such facilities available on an equitable basis, regardless of the beliefs or affiliations of individuals or groups requesting their use.

Adopted June 18, 1948; Amended February 2, 1961; June 27, 1967; and January 23, 1980 by the ALA Council.

Reprinted by permission of the American Library Association.

STATEMENT ON LABELING

AN INTERPRETATION OF THE "LIBRARY BILL OF RIGHTS"

Because labeling violates the spirit of the "Library Bill of Rights," the American Library Association opposes the technique of labeling as a means of predisposing readers against library materials for the following reasons:

1. Labeling* is an attempt to prejudice the reader, and as such it is a censor's tool.
2. Although some find it easy and even proper, according to their ethics, to establish criteria for judging publications as objectionable, injustice and ignorance rather than justice and enlightenment result from such practices, and the American Library Association must oppose the establishment of such criteria.
3. Libraries do not advocate the ideas found in their collections. The presence of a magazine or book in a library does not indicate an endorsement of its contents by the library.
4. No one person should take the responsibility of labeling publications. No sizable group of persons would be likely to agree either on the types of material which should be labeled or the sources of information which should be regarded with suspicion. As a practical consideration, a librarian who labels a book or magazine might be sued for libel.
5. If materials are labeled to pacify one group, there is no excuse for refusing to label any item in the library's collection. Because authoritarians tend to suppress ideas and attempt to coerce individuals to conform to a specific ideology, the American Library Association opposes such efforts which aim at closing any path to knowledge.

---

*"Labeling," as it is referred to in the "Statement on Labeling," is the practice of describing or designating certain library materials, by affixing a prejudicial label to them or segregating them by a prejudicial system, so as to predispose readers against the materials.

Adopted July 13, 1951. Amended June 25, 1971, by the ALA Council.

THE FREEDOM TO READ

The freedom to read is essential to our democracy. It is continuously under attack. Private groups and public authorities in various parts of the country are working to remove books from sale, to censor textbooks, to label "controversial" books, to distribute lists of "objectionable" books or authors, and to purge libraries. These actions apparently rise from a view that our national tradition of free expression is no longer valid; that censorship and suppression are needed to avoid the subversion of politics and the corruption of morals. We, as citizens devoted to the use of books and as librarians and publishers responsible for disseminating them, wish to assert the public interest in the preservation of the freedom to read.

We are deeply concerned about these attempts at suppression. Most such attempts rest on a denial of the fundamental premise of democracy: that the ordinary citizen, by exercising his critical judgment, will accept the good and reject the bad. The censors, public and private, assume that they should determine what is good and what is bad for their fellow-citizens.

We trust Americans to recognize propaganda, and to reject it. We do not believe they need the help of censors to assist them in this task. We do not believe they are prepared to sacrifice their heritage of a free press in order to be "protected" against what others think may be bad for them. We believe they still favor free enterprise in ideas and expression.

We are aware, of course, that books are not alone in being subjected to efforts at suppression. We are aware that these efforts are related to a larger pattern of pressures being brought against education, the press, films, radio and television. The problem is not only one of actual censorship. The shadow of fear cast by these pressures leads, we suspect, to an even larger voluntary curtailment of expression by those who seek to avoid controversy.

Such pressure toward conformity is perhaps natural to a time of uneasy change and pervading fear. Especially when so many of our apprehensions are directed against an ideology, the expression of a dissident idea becomes a thing feared in itself, and we tend to move against it as against a hostile deed, with suppression.

And yet suppression is never more dangerous than in such a time of social tension. Freedom has given the United States the elasticity to endure strain. Freedom keeps open the path of novel and creative solutions, and enables change to come by choice. Every silencing of a heresy, every enforcement of an orthodoxy, diminishes the toughness and resilience of our society and leaves it the less able to deal with stress.

Now as always in our history, books are among our greatest instruments of freedom. They are almost the only means for making generally available ideas or manners of expression that can initially command only a small audience. They are the natural medium for the new idea and the untried voice from which come the original contributions to social growth. They are essential to the extended discussion which serious thought requires, and to the accumulation of knowledge and ideas into organized collections.

We believe that free communication is essential to the preservation of a free society and a creative culture. We believe that these pressures towards conformity present the danger of limiting the range and variety of inquiry and expression on which our democracy and our culture depend. We believe that every American community must jealously guard the freedom to publish and to circulate, in order to preserve its own freedom to read. We believe that publishers and librarians have a profound responsibility to give validity to that freedom to read by making it possible for the readers to choose freely from a variety of offerings.

The freedom to read is guaranteed by the Constitution. Those with faith in free men will stand firm on these constitutional guarantees of essential rights and will exercise the responsibilities that accompany these rights.

We therefore affirm these propositions:

1. *It is in the public interest for publishers and librarians to make available the widest diversity of views and expressions, including those which are unorthodox or unpopular with the majority.*

Creative thought is by definition new, and what is new is different. The bearer of every new thought is a rebel until his idea is refined and tested. Totalitarian systems attempt to maintain themselves in power by the ruthless suppression of any concept which challenges the established orthodoxy. The power of a democratic system to adapt to change is vastly strengthened by the freedom of its citizens to choose widely from among conflicting opinions offered freely to them. To stifle every nonconformist idea at birth would mark the end of the democratic process. Furthermore, only through the constant activity of weighing and selecting can the democratic mind attain the strength demanded by times like these. We need to know not only what we believe but why we believe it.

2. *Publishers, librarians and booksellers do not need to endorse every idea or presentation contained in the books they make available. It would conflict with the public interest for them to establish their own political, moral or*

aesthetic views as the sole standard for determining what books should be published or circulated.

Publishers and librarians serve the educational process by helping to make available knowledge and ideas required for the growth of the mind and the increase of learning. They do not foster education by imposing as mentors the patterns of their own thought. The people should have the freedom to read and consider a broader range of ideas than those that may he held by any single librarian or publisher or government or church. It is wrong that what one man can read should be confined to what another thinks proper.

3. *It is contrary to the public interest for publishers or librarians to determine the acceptability of a book solely on the basis of the personal history or political affiliations of the author.*

A book should be judged as a book. No art or literature can flourish if it is to be measured by the political views or private lives of its creators. No society of free men can flourish which draws up lists of writers to whom it will not listen, whatever they may have to say.

4. *There is no place in our society for extra-legal efforts to coerce the taste of others, to confine adults to the reading matter deemed suitable for adolescents, or to inhibit the efforts of writers to achieve artistic expression.*

To some, much of modern literature is shocking. But is not much of life itself shocking? We cut off literature at the source if we prevent writers from dealing with the stuff of life. Parents and teachers have a responsibility to prepare the young to meet the diversity of experience in life to which they will be exposed, as they have a responsibility to help them learn to think critically for themselves. These are affirmative responsibilities, not to be discharged simply by preventing them from reading works for which they are not yet prepared. In these matters taste differs, and taste cannot be legislated; nor can machinery be devised which will suit the demands of one group without limiting the freedom of others.

5. *It is not in the public interest to force a reader to accept with any book the prejudgment of a label characterizing the book or author as subversive or dangerous.*

The ideal of labeling presupposes the existence of individuals or groups with wisdom to determine by authority what is good or bad for the citizen. It presupposes that each individual must be directed in making up his mind about the ideas he examines. But Americans do not need others to do their thinking for them.

6. *It is the responsibility of publishers and librarians, as guardians of the people's freedom to read, to contest encroachments upon that freedom by individuals or groups seeking to impose their own standards or tastes upon the community at large.*

It is inevitable in the give and take of the democratic process that the political, the moral, or the aesthetic concepts of an individual or group will occasionally collide with those of another individual or group. In a free society each individual is free to determine for himself what he wishes to read, and each group is free to determine what it will recommend to its freely associated members. But no group has the right to take the law into its own hands, and to impose its own concept of politics or morality upon other members of a democratic society. Freedom is no freedom if it is accorded only to the accepted and the inoffensive.

7. *It is the responsibility of publishers and librarians to give full meaning to the freedom to read by providing books that enrich the quality and diversity of thought and expression. By the exercise of this affirmative responsibility, bookmen can demonstrate that the answer to a bad book is a good one, the answer to a bad idea is a good one.*

The freedom to read is of little consequence when expended on the trivial; it is frustrated when the reader cannot obtain matter fit for his purpose. What is needed is not only the absence of restraint, but the positive provision of opportunity for the people to read the best that has been thought and said. Books are the major channel by which the intellectual inheritance is handed down, and the principal means of its testing and growth. The defense of their freedom and integrity, and the enlargement of their service to society, requires of all bookmen the utmost of their faculties, and deserves of all citizens the fullest of their support.

We state these propositions neither lightly nor as easy generalizations. We here stake out a lofty claim for the value of books. We do so because we believe that they are good, possessed of enormous variety and usefulness, worthy of cherishing and keeping free. We realize that the application of these propositions may mean the dissemination of ideas and manners of expression that are repugnant to many persons. We do not state these propositions in the comfortable belief that what people read is unimportant. We believe rather that what people read is deeply important; that ideas can be dangerous; but that the suppression of ideas is fatal to a democratic society. Freedom itself is a dangerous way of life, but it is ours.

A Joint Statement by:
American Library Association
Association of American Publishers

Subsequently Endorsed by:
American Booksellers Association
American Civil Liberties Union
American Federation of Teachers AFL-CIO
Anti-Defamation League of B'nai B'rith
Association of American University Presses
Bureau of Independent Publishers & Distributors
Children's Book Council
Freedom of Information Center
Freedom to Read Foundation
Magazine Publishers Association
Motion Picture Association of America
National Association of College Stores
National Book Committee
National Council of Negro Women
National Council of Teachers of English
National Library Week Program
National Board of the Young Women's Christian Association of
    the U.S.A.
P.E.N.—American Center
Periodical and Book Association of America
Sex Information & Education Council of the U.S.
Women's National Book Association

This statement was originally issued in May of 1953 by the Westchester Conference of the American Library Association and the American Book Publishers Council, which in 1970 consolidated with the American Educational Publishers Institute to become the Association of American Publishers.

BOOKS AND THE YOUNG READER

Publishers of textbooks and other kinds of books designed for children and young people, or recommended for their use, recognize that different standards and attitudes toward the content of books exist in different communities. Each community, or each school or library, must necessarily determine what books will be bought for use in its own area.

Publishers believe, however, that schools, libraries and communities should take certain factors into consideration when making these choices. First, they must remember that no community, no matter how small, is completely homogeneous. What one parent will approve for a child, another will not. The rights of one parent to provide a child with the materials that parent finds acceptable should not be abridged by the views of another.

Secondly, the rights of children and young people to read books that seem relevant to their own lives and to society as they see it cannot be abridged without courting the danger that books themselves will seem to them obsolete. In the books they read, children and young people have both a constitutional right and a civic duty to seek and find truth as it is seen from many vantage points. Young people are constantly surrounded by the raw materials of life as it is lived by a wide variety of people. Therefore, they need thoughtful fiction and nonfiction that will allow them to examine these materials from more than one angle. Without the opportunity to examine various kinds of life situations through books—thereby to gain strength of judgment—young people will be suddenly thrust into situations in real life without adequate preparation.

Finally, if one book from a publisher is unacceptable to a community as a whole, even taking the above considerations into account, community selection agencies should remember that the publisher of that book is preparing and publishing books by many authors on many subjects for use in many communities, some of which really want that book. A publisher's total output should not be judged on the basis of one book. Publishers recognize that no book published can suit the needs of every reader, every library, every school, every community. Therefore, they offer a wide variety of books, so there will be suitable books for everyone. The book you like and need may be wholly unacceptable somewhere else.

Publishers are opposed to book censorship of any kind. But they also recognize that the budgets of public book-buying institutions do not allow for purchase of all books published, and that choices must be made. They ask only that those choices reflect a wide variety of points of view and as objective an evaluation of the books presented as can be made.

Freedom to Read Committee
Association of American Publishers (1976)

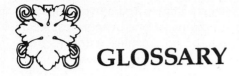 **GLOSSARY**

AA's Author's alterations. Changes made by author to matter already typeset (in proofs), apart from changes necessary to correct errors made by the compositor.

ALA American Library Association.

alternative publishers See *small presses*.

analytical index A classified index arranged alphabetically by main subject headings. Entries in each main heading may be further subdivided, and all entries are arranged alphabetically in each heading.

approval plan An arrangement between a library and a publisher or dealer in which the library receives all current books in specified subjects. The materials are selected by the publisher or dealer, and returns are generally permitted.

backlist Titles on a publisher's list which, though published in previous seasons, are still available.

base (basic) collection A list of agreed-upon standard works in a field.

blanket order An agreement between a library and a book dealer or publisher for the automatic supplying of one or more copies of all titles issued by a publisher or of all titles within certain subject categories. Items may not usually be returned.

BLLD British Library Lending Division.

CIP Cataloging-in-Publication.

collation The part of the description of an item which provides information on its physical characteristics, including number of pages, volumes, reels, discs, photographs, format, size, etc.

colophon "Logo" or trademark of the publisher (incorrect although frequent modern use of term).

COM Computer-output-on-microform.

community analysis A method that employs a range of social science techniques for investigating the information needs of the population served by a library.

compositor A person who sets type.

comprehensive bibliography A list which attempts to include everything published on a subject.

computerized data base Data files produced, maintained, and accessed with the aid of computers.

consulting editor A person outside a publishing house (frequently a professor) who serves as a consultant for a series of books, often suggesting subjects for books and getting persons to write them.

cross reference Instruction directing the user from one heading to another. It may be single (to look elsewhere for all items related to the subject), multiple (a reference to several places), or reciprocal (a reference to look elsewhere for other references).

cumulation Usually applied to periodicals to indicate the progressive gathering together of items maintaining the same ordering and arrangement.

dépôt légal See *legal deposit*.

direct mail Advertising material sent by mail to lists of prospective purchasers for the purpose of soliciting orders.

display item Item distinguished by being set in larger or different type and usually on a line by itself in order to draw attention to the matter.

duplicate exchange union An arrangement among libraries for the exchange of materials that the owning library considers surplus or no longer needs.

dust jacket A paper (or, in some cases, plastic) cover folded over a hardbound book. Originally designed to protect the book from dust, it now provides printed matter and illustrations which help sell the book.

edition binding   Hardcover binding in commercial quantities. Also known as *trade binding* or *publisher's binding*.

ERIC   Educational Resources Information Center.

Farmington Plan   A former cooperative acquisitions agreement (1948–1972) among approximately sixty U.S. academic libraries to purchase and make available, through interlibrary loan, materials published in foreign countries.

free-lance   Writers, editors, designers, or other persons who are not on the regular payroll of a company but who sell their services to any buyer.

galley proof, galley   Proof (trial print) made from type for the purpose of correction before being set in page form.

GPO   Government Printing Office.

Greenaway Plan   A form of blanket order (q.v.) used by public libraries to obtain a single copy of a work immediately upon publication so that duplicate orders for branches can be considered based on examination of the work rather than reviews.

hardbound   Bound in cloth- or paper-covered books. Hard cover.

I and R Service   Information and Referral Service.

imposition   Arrangement of pages in a press form so that they will be in proper sequence when folded for binding.

imprint   Name of a publisher, usually with place and date of publication.

independent publishers   See *small presses.*

ISBN   International Standard Book Number.

jobber   A wholesale bookseller who serves as middleman between the publisher and library or retail bookseller.

justification   Spacing out of letters and words in a line of type so that there is an even alignment on the right side.

LACAP   Latin American Cooperative Acquisition Plan.

LC Card Number   Unique number assigned by the Library of Congress to each cataloged item in the collection. The first two digits indicate the year of publication. The number appears as the last item on the last line of information on an LC card.

leading   The space between lines of type.

legal deposit   Regulation or law requiring the sending of a certain number of copies of a book or other work upon publication to a central library or libraries. May or may not operate in conjunction with deposit for copyright purposes.

machine-readable data bases   Data or information in a form which can be read or identified by a machine.

MARC   Machine-readable catalog.

microcard   Micro images printed on paper.

microfiche Micro images printed on a sheet of film normally in standardized size of 105 x 148 mm (approximately 4 x 6 inches).

microfilm Micro images arranged on cellulose film usually in 16, 35, or 70 mm widths; can consist of either negative or positive images.

microform The general term for all types of micro records.

multimedia package Information presented through a combination of communications techniques, including print, nonprint, and audio-visual materials.

networks An arrangement of interconnected elements to facilitate the transfer and exchange of information.

NTIS National Technical Information Service. Established by the U.S. Department of Commerce in 1970 to facilitate public access to federal government publications and data in business, technical, and scientific fields. Also a central source for government-produced machine data files and programs.

OCLC Ohio College Library Center. A computerized library network for academic, public, and special libraries providing cataloging, serials, control, interlibrary loan, acquisition, and circulation services.

offset printing The printing process in which the impression is transferred from a lithographic stone or printing plate to a rubber-covered cylinder, and thence offset by pressure on to the paper.

OIF Office for Intellectual Freedom, American Library Association.

OP Out-of-print. Materials no longer available from the original publisher through regular commercial channels.

"over the transom" manuscripts Unsolicited manuscripts arriving in a publisher's office.

page proof Second stage of a proof, when the corrected galley proof (q.v.) is cut and set in final page size.

perfect binding A method of binding, without stitching or sewing, in which the pages are held together by means of a layer of glue or plastic adhesive along the spine.

periodical A publication issued at regular intervals without a predetermined termination date, usually containing a variety of articles.

preview copy Copy (usually of a film) supplied by a producer or dealer for examination prior to purchase.

printout Information or data printed automatically from stored files in a computer.

public domain The condition of being free from copyright protection.

register To superimpose exactly the various color impressions in color printing.

retrospective selection The process of identifying and acquiring items that are not of recent issue.

RLIN Research Libraries Information Network. Library network formed in 1978 through an agreement between BALLOTS and the members of the Research Libraries Group.

RTSD Resources and Technical Services Division, American Library Association.

running head The book, part, or chapter title repeated at the top of each page of a book.

scholarly publisher Publisher of books for scholars. University presses are one form of scholarly publisher.

searching The process of checking an item in catalogs, bibliographies, and lists to determine whether to add a copy to a collection. In working with computerized data bases, the term has come to mean the process of retrieving information from machine-readable files.

seasonal catalog Catalog issued by a publisher at the beginning of each publishing season (fall, spring, etc.) listing its new books. Distinguished by considerable descriptive information about the books and their authors. Often lavishly illustrated.

self-publisher Person who finances and publishes his or her own work.

serial A publication issued in separate and successive parts, generally in a uniform format with a constant title, and intended to be continued indefinitely.

signature A folded, printed sheet forming one section of a book; usually sixteen or thirty-two pages but may be any multiple of four or eight.

small presses Publishers of materials not acceptable to commercial publishers because of their subject matter, format, or limited appeal. Often privately or personally financed. Also known as alternative publishers or independent publishers.

smashing Compressing folded signatures along the folds (after sewing) to make them more compact for binding.

stamping die A device for imparting a desired shape or image to a surface by pressure or a blow.

subject heading A word or words under which materials on a given subject are entered in a catalog, bibliography, or list.

subscription books Book available only from the publishing or issuing organization, usually only after joining or subscribing.

Superintendent of Documents   Head of the U.S. Government Printing Office.

technical report   A paper presenting the results of scientific research or technical development.

tracing   The record of additional headings under which added entries appear.

trade book   Book intended for the general public and marketed through retail bookstores.

trade publisher   Publisher of trade books (q.v.).

typeface   Any design of type, usually identified by a specific name given by the designer.

union catalog   A catalog which indicates the holdings (complete or partial) of all the branches of a library or numbers in a system or network.

union list   A complete record, in print or machine-readable form, of all the holdings of a group of libraries on a certain subject or field.

vanity publisher   A publisher that contracts to produce books at an author's risk and expense. Sometimes known as a subsidy or cooperative publisher.

Index